MW01601439

Brief Biography And Popular Account Of The Unparalleled Discoveries Of T.J.J. See

William Larkin Webb

BRIEF BIOGRAPHY

AND

POPULAR ACCOUNT

OF THE

UNPARALLELED DISCOVERIES

OF

T. J. J. SEE,

A. M., LT. M., SC. M. (MISSOU.); A. M., PH. D. (BEROL.);

FAMOUS ASTRONOMER, NATURAL PHILOSOPHER, AND FOUNDER OF THE
NEW SCIENCES OF COSMOGONY AND GEOGONY.

———————

"The Simple Truth — the Best Inspiration to the Youth of the Land."

———————

BY W. L. WEBB,

Amateur Astronomer, Author of "The Story of the Stars," and Inventor of the "Star Finder;"
Author of a "History of Missouri;" "History of Greater Kansas City;"
"Biography of Champ Clark;" etc.

———————

1913

THOS. P. NICHOLS & SON CO.,
PUBLISHERS,
LYNN, MASS., U. S. A.

WM. WESLEY & SON, LONDON, ENGLAND.

Copyright, 1913
by
W. L. WEBB.

T. J. J. See

DEDICATED TO THE MEMORY
OF
SIR WILLIAM HUGGINS,
"THE HERSCHEL OF THE SPECTROSCOPE,"
FOUNDER OF THE NEW SCIENCE OF ASTROPHYSICS,
EX-PRESIDENT OF THE ROYAL SOCIETY,
STEADFAST FRIEND OF PROFESSOR SEE,
AND
ONE OF THE EARLIEST TO RECOGNIZE HIS HIGH PROMISE
FOR THE DISCOVERY OF NEW TRUTH.

CONTENTS.

CHAPTER X.

CHAPTER XI.

CHAPTER XII.

CHAPTER XIII.

CHAPTER XIV.

CHAPTER XV.

CHAPTER XVI.

CHAPTER XVII.

CHAPTER XVIII.

APPENDIX.

INTRODUCTION.

THE most eminent philosophers occasionally establish new foundations for the individual physical sciences. But, so far as we are aware, history presents no previous record of *one man* revolutionizing and laying new foundations for *two great physical Sciences*. And yet this unprecedented achievement has been accomplished by Professor See, an American just in the prime of life.

The two New Sciences which he has established are:

COSMOGONY, dealing with the Creation of the Heavens;
GEOGONY, which treats of the Creation of the Earth.

The New Sciences are as distinct and clearly defined as the problems of the development of the Heavens and of the Earth, respectively; and taken together they unfold the majestic panorama of the Creation of the entire Universe. There is thus opened to the mind a vision almost divine!

The marvelous story of how these unparalleled discoveries were made by a young man of penetrating intuition and steady purpose, working independently, *and thus absolutely free of entangling alliances*, without other than his own moderate means, in an age characterized by increasing restriction of individual freedom incident to growing centralization and vast expenditure, ostensibly for scientific investigation, cannot fail to be of interest to a great and increasing circle of readers in both hemispheres.

It is often lamented that the simple life and individual independence enjoyed by the pioneer investigator is passing away with the complexity arising from the centralizing consolidations of modern industrialism, by which the individual is reduced to a mere cog in the wheel of a vast machine.

It is therefore very reassuring to have a concrete proof, in Professor See's discoveries, that *the time will never come when* INDIVIDUAL INDEPENDENCE AND FREE INITIATIVE, *which characterized the philosophic habits of Aristotle and Plato, will not bear fruit in the modern, as in the ancient, world.* Indeed the *failure* of many contemporary Scientific Institutions is due to disregard of the mature and wholesome truths taught and practiced by the wisest of the Athenian Sages.

We are thus impressed with the wholesome doctrine that great discoveries cannot be made by the methods of the factory, the counting-house and the department-store, which have well-nigh destroyed the *creative efficiency* of some of our most liberally endowed and best supported scientific institutions.

Professor See is universally recognized as the most intrepid and indefatigable of the explorers of Nature; and since the death of Poincaré and Sir George Darwin, in 1912, occupies easily the first place among living natural philosophers. These eminent men were in fact mathematicians rather than investigators of the physical universe; and thus were not so careful in their premises as is usual with discoverers of the first order.

In vain does the mathematician strive after the laws for the unfolding of the mysteries of the universe, so long as the premises underlying his reasoning are insecure. It is one of Professor See's greatest services to Science to have emphasized impressively this great weakness in much of our contemporary thought; and the lesson thus taught can not be read too often by those who are interested in the progress of Truth.

I first came into close relations with Professor See a quarter of a century ago, while serving with Hon. Champ Clark on the

Legislative Committee for the Investigation of the University of Missouri. The student then foremost in the University has now become foremost among men of Science; and naturally I have followed his triumphant career with pride and unabated enthusiasm.

While preparing a biography of Hon. Champ Clark, Speaker of the National House of Representatives, in 1911, I decided to undertake the more ambitious work of popularizing the discoveries of Professor See. Several learned colleagues of this eminent savant, in Missouri and elsewhere, have helped to lighten the burden thus assumed. It was further decreased by Professor See's kindness in granting permission to reprint several articles and addresses of great interest, including the paper on the Origin of the Himalaya Mountains presented to the American Philosophical Society in April, 1913. Grateful acknowledgments are due for priviliges of reprinting extended by this illustrious Society.

I am especially indebted to Professor L. M. Defoe and Professor Harris Hancock, close friends of Professor See at the University of Missouri and the University of Berlin, respectively; and to the Historical Society of Montgomery County, Missouri, for the loan of a copy of the "Records of the See Family of Virginia," which furnishes authentic genealogical data dating back to 1734, when the early members of this Family came to America from Prussian Silesia.

W. L. WEBB.

INDEPENDENCE, MISSOURI,
June 6, 1913.

SKETCH OF PROFESSOR SEE'S BIOGRAPHY.

(From *Who's Who in America*, 1912.)

SEE, THOMAS JEFFERSON JACKSON, astronomer, mathematician; born near Montgomery City, Mo., Feb. 19, 1866; son of Noah and Mary Ann (Sailor) See; A. B., L.B., S.B., University of Missouri, 1889; A.M., Ph.D., University of Berlin, 1892; married Frances Graves of Montgomery City, June 18, 1907. In charge Observatory of University of Missouri, 1887-9; volunteer observer Royal Observatory, Berlin, 1891; traveled in Italy, Egypt, Greece, Germany and England, 1890-2; organized and had charge of Department of Astronomy, and aided in organization of Yerkes Observatory, University of Chicago, 1893-6; astronomer Lowell Observatory in charge Survey of Southern heavens, 1896-8; with 24-inch Clark refractor at Flagstaff, Arizona, and City of Mexico, examined about 200,000 fixed stars, in zone between 15 and 65 degrees south declination, which led to discovery and measurement of about 600 new double stars and remeasurement of some 1,400 double stars previously recognized by Sir John Herschel and other observers. Professor of Mathematics, U.S. Navy, since 1899; in charge 26-inch equatorial telescope, U.S. Naval Observatory, 1899-1902; Professor of Mathematics, U.S. Naval Academy, 1902-3; Naval Observatory, Mare Island, California, since 1903; lecturer on Sidereal Astronomy, Lowell Institute, Boston, 1899. During 1901-2 investigated diameters of planets and satellites by daylight, deducing their constants of irradiation and absolute densities. Published researches on Laplace's Invariable Plane, and on the internal densities, pressures, temperatures, rigidities, and moments of inertia of the principal bodies of the planetary system, 1903-6. Observed earthquake at San Francisco, April 18, 1906, and proved that world-shaking earthquakes and mountain formation depend on leakage of oceans and expulsion of lava, producing great wall along margin of sea, as in typical case of the Andes. During 1908-9 established laws of the Formation of the Solar System, showing that the planets and satellites were not detached from the bodies which now govern their motions, as supposed by Laplace, but have all been captured, and have since had their orbits reduced in size and rounded up into almost perfect circles under the secular action of a resisting medium. The moon is thus shown to be a planet captured by the earth, and not a detached portion of the terrestrial globe, as held by Sir George Darwin and earlier investigators. Carried out also important researches on the eclipses of the past 3,000 years, and the moon's secular acceleration, the rotation of the earth and other planets, the formation of lunar craters, origin of comets, cause of variable and temporary stars, thus founding a new science of cosmogony, since adopted by Poincaré and other eminent authorities. During 1911 investigated the depth of the Milky Way, improving and extending the forgotten methods of Sir William Herschel, and showed that this depth is several million light-years, and thus about a thousand times greater than astronomers have recently believed. This confirmation of the neglected theories of Sir Wm. Herschel led to a movement for the republication of his collected works by the Royal Astronomical and Royal Society of London. Has computed about sixty orbits of double stars. Fellow or member of many scientific societies in United States and abroad. Author: Die Entwickelung der Doppel-Stern Systeme, Berlin, 1893; Researches on the Evolution of the Stellar Systems, Vol. I, Lynn, 1896; Vol. II, The Capture Theory of Cosmical Evolution, 1910; Researches on the Physical Constitution and Rigidities of the Heavenly Bodies, Kiel, 1904-6; Researches on the Physics of the Earth, and especially on the Cause of Earthquakes and Mountain Formation, Proc. Am. Phil. Soc., Philadelphia, 1906-8; Determination of Depth of the Milky Way, Proc. Am. Phil. Soc., 1912. Also double star catalogues and about 250 contributions to technical journals and magazines. Address: Mare Island, California.

CHAPTER I.

1866–1872.

ANCESTRY AND CHILDHOOD.

SPECULATED ON THE SUN, MOON AND STARS WHEN ONLY TWO YEARS OLD.

THE nature of genius always has been deeply mysterious, and heretofore philosophers have labored in vain to account for its appearance. It seems to be an accentuation of the usual endowments of the individual, combined with a power of concentration which produces the maximum efficiency, and doubtless is an extraordinary gift of Nature designed for the protection and improvement of the race. At least this is the purpose which genius serves in the economy of the world.

But as genius is the culmination of the more normal creative effort, and appears only under favorable conditions, we may remark that to understand the forces that produce a great man one has to look into the *environment* of his individual life, and also examine the *ancestry* of his family. Taken together these two influences, in some mysterious way, determine the mental and bodily powers and tendencies, always a very important factor in those labors which make for high achievement. It takes generations of good stock to produce the best type of man, just as it does to produce the best types in the rest of the animal kingdom.

For although it is a recognized maxim of the most eminent historians, as Thucydides and Tacitus, Gibbon and Grote, Ranke and Niebuhr, Mommsen and Curtius, that the importance of ancestry often is overrated, yet the Southern saying that "blood will tell" holds true in our History; and nowhere is this steadying influence more effective than in the persistence required for the higher intellectual life. To develop the noblest products of the human mind, such as discoveries which lay the foundations of new sciences, the forces must all be strong and well balanced and the mental intuition clear and penetrating. When these conditions are favorable Nature occasionally supplements her ordinary creative efforts by examples of the extraordinary type called genius.

Needless to say the ancestry of Professor See is of the sturdiest kind, and marked by great strength of character for many generations, on both sides of the family. His talents have been very largrly inherited, but they are also original gifts of Nature, which have been developed by industry and favorable environment.

The earliest American ancestor by this name was Adam See, a Protestant and an adherent of a sect of Baptists, who fled from Prussian Silesia, with the colony of Schwenkfelders in 1734*, and settled first in Bucks Co., Penn. Adam See's wife was named Barbara, and he had an elder brother, Michael Frederick See, whose wife's name was Catherine. They were all quite young at the time of the immigration from Germany, to escape from religious persecutions†; and the Adam See family continued to use German Bibles to the third generation.

---

* This was the same year in which the Moravian Evangelists first came to Pennsylvania, but their first temporary settlement and mission to the Indians was at Savannah, Ga., 1735. In 1740 these Moravians moved to Pennsylvania, and with Count Zinzendorf and others from Herrnhut, Saxony, founded Bethlehem, 1741.

†The persecution under which the Schwenkfelders fled from Prussian Silesia is described in the *Encyclopedia Britannica*, ninth edition, Article *Schwenkfeld*, as follows: "In Silesia they formed a distinct sect, which has lasted until our own times. In the 17th Century they were associated with the followers of Jacob Böhme, and were undisturbed until 1708, when an inquiry was made as to their doctrines. In 1720 a Commission of Jesuits was despatched to Silesia to convert them by force. Most of them fled from Silesia to Saxony, and thence to Holland, England and North America. Frederick the Great of Prussia, when he seized Silesia, extended his protection to those who remained in that province. Those who had fled to Philadelphia in Pennsylvania formed a small community under the name of Schwenkfeldians; and Zinzendorf and Spangenberg, when they visited the United States, endeavoured, but with little success, to convert them to their views. This Community still exists in Pennsylvania, and according to information obtained from their ministers by Robert Barclay they consisted in 1875 of two congregations of 500 members, with three meeting houses and six ministers."

THE RETURN OF THE GREENBRIER CAPTIVES, AFTER THE CLOSE OF THE FRENCH AND INDIAN WARS, 1765.
(From an old History).

HON. CHARLES MICHAEL SEE.

One of the most widely known and highly respected citizens of Central Illinois. Mr. See has a notable record in the Union Army, 1861-65; and a remarkable service of 40 years as Station Agent of the Illinois Central Railroad, at Alma. He took up the study of the Family History, about 1880, at the suggestion of Judge Silas Bryan, who had long known the Sees in Virginia.

RESIDENCE OF HON. CHARLES MICHAEL SEE AT ALMA, ILL.

From a photograph taken about 1905.

In 1745 they moved from Pennsylvania to the Valley of Virginia, and settled near the present town of Moorefield, in Hardy County. Here Adam See became a prominent planter, and lived till about 1790. About 1760, his elder brother and family moved on to Greenbrier settlement, where he was killed in the Indian massacre of July 17, 1763, and the family, consisting of wife and four children, carried captive to Old Town (Chillicothe), Ohio. After the treaty of peace, at the close of the French and Indian Wars of 1765, they were all restored to their people, except John See, a child of seven, who had been adopted in an Indian family, and, as the captives were leaving, ran back and stayed with the Indians, till ransomed by his Uncle Adam See some years later.

John See then grew up with his Uncle Adam's son George See, and both fought in the Revolution, John being so badly wounded at Brandywine that he was pensioned by the government in old age. He lived to be ninety, dying near Peoria, Ill., in 1848. When he was very old he gave a detailed account of the early history of the family to his grandson, the Rev. Michael See, of Wyman, Iowa, who was appointed a member of the Sanitary Commission by President Lincoln during the Civil War. The Rev. Michael See gave this account to Hon. Charles Michael See of Alma, Ill., who took up the study of the family history about 1880, at the suggestion of Judge Silas Bryan, father of Hon. Wm. J. Bryan, and later gave the data thus gathered to Hon. Noah See, father of Professor See; so that all the records are authentic and preserved in enough detail to make an interesting history.

Adam See seems to have had a family of one or more daughters, and the son George mentioned above. Before the Revolution, probably about 1767, George See had married Jemima Harness, by whom he had a family of nine children: Adam, Michael, George, Charles, and John; and the daughters: Barbara, Hannah, Elizabeth, and Dorothy. The history of the family of this generation is fully kept, but most of it need not be given here.

It suffices to say that the second Adam See was a student at Dickinson College, and afterwards became an eminent lawyer, a senator at Richmond during the War of 1812, and a member of the Virginia Constitutional Convention of 1829.

His brother Michael See married Catherine Baker, and raised a family of nine children, the names of the six sons being: Adam, Anthony, Jacob, John, Solomon, and Noah; and of the daughters: Mary, Elizabeth, Barbara. This Noah See, the youngest child, and the most talented, was the father of Professor See, the subject of this Biography. His grandfather, George See, and son Charles had been killed by lightning while stacking hay, about 1794; and the two brothers, Adam and Michael, with their families, then moved to Randolph County, Va., about 1795, where Noah See was born September 19, 1815. Michael See served in the War of 1812, while his brother Adam was a Senator at Richmond.

In 1837 Noah See visited the West, traveling on horseback through Ohio, Indiana, and Illinois, and finally settled in Montgomery County, Mo., whither his father, mother, and three brothers and two sisters soon followed, so that the See family has been prominent in that part of Missouri for three quarters of a century. Michael See lived as a highly respected citizen of Montgomery County till his death in 1857.

Noah See was educated in the High School at Beverly, Virginia, and trained as a cabinet-maker. He also became an architect and civil engineer, having built a bridge over the Cheat River in Virginia before he was twenty-two. In these early days he also studied land surveying, which he afterwards followed as a life-long profession, having been twice elected county surveyor of Montgomery County, and generally considered one of the finest surveyors in Missouri. The profession of architect he also kept up, having built a great many houses still standing in Montgomery County; while his talents as an engineer caused him to be chosen as bridge commissioner of the county for nearly thirty years. His conduct of these several offices was always marked by great

THE RESIDENCE OF HON. MICHAEL SEE, IN RANDOLPH COUNTY, VIRGINIA.

Noah See was born here Sept. 19, 1815. From a photograph taken about 1900.

THE RESIDENCE OF HON. JAMES SAILOR, ON LOUTRE, 1872.

This house was built by Cyrenus Cox, a hunting companion of Daniel Boone, in 1832. It was here that Mr. and Mrs. Noah See were married Oct. 18, 1853. From a drawing in India Ink, by Mr. E. E. See, 1906.

HON. NOAH SEE.

Professor See's Father, as he appeared when about sixty years of age. He was born in Randolph County, Virginia, Sept. 19, 1815, and died in Montgomery County, Missouri, Feb. 9, 1890. Owing to his experience as a Civil Engineer, Surveyor, and Architect, he served as Bridge Commissioner of the County for over 30 years.

MRS. MARY A. SEE.

Mother of Professor See, from a photograph taken in 1899, when she was 67 years of age. Mrs. See was born in Montgomery County, Missouri, Jan. 14, 1832, and has always resided in the County.

fidelity to the interests of the community. By virtue of natural abilities and strictly legitimate industry he became wealthy and influential, and for fifty-two years was one of the most highly respected citizens in the county.

On October 18, 1853, Noah See married Miss Mary A. Sailor, daughter of James and Sabina (Cobb) Sailor. The Sailors were a highly respected family which came from near Mt. Sterling, Montgomery County, Kentucky*, but were originally from Virginia. The earliest American ancestor by this name, John Sailor, born about 1750, was an Englishman, who settled in Virginia about 1772, and afterwards fought in the Revolution. He moved to Montgomery County, Ky., about 1790, and resided near Jackson's Mill, on the Licking River, being by profession a skilled machinist. He had a family of six children — five sons: John, Emanuel, Mathias, Jacob, and William, and the daughter Sarah, who married Samuel Cobb, a brother of Phillip Cobb. His second son, Emanuel Sailor, with his wife and family of three sons, James, John and Thomas, settled in Montgomery County, Mo., in 1824, and their descendants have always been highly respected citizens of that part of Missouri. Emanuel Sailor's wife, at the time of their marriage, was a widow, her first husband having been Dr. James Geary, of Ohio, and her maiden name Ann Hollett, of New York City.

Mrs. Noah See, mother of the famous astronomer, still lives at the old home near Montgomery City, and is one of the most remarkable women in the United States. The family consisted of nine children, of whom eight are still living, one daughter having died in childhood. Mrs. See has long been noted for her devotion to the family, and for her energy and force of character. She has always been greatly beloved by the whole community, as such model mothers usually are. The names of the children in order of age are: Anna Maria, Millard Filmore, Missouri Virginia, Robert E. Lee, Lucy Elizabeth (died at age of two and

---

* The State of Missouri was settled by Virginians and Kentuckians, and Professor See therefore is a typical Missourian in every sense.

half years), Thomas Jefferson Jackson*, George Washington, Sylvester Clay, Edward Everett.

From this list it will be seen that the astronomer is the sixth child and third son in a family of nine, all of whom are talented. All the boys were raised as farmers, and most of them have adhered to the family tradition. Three of Professor See's brothers, namely, M. F. See, Geo. W. See, and E. E. See have decided scientific tastes, however, and could have become eminent professional men; while the eldest sister, Anna Maria (Mrs. A. M. Weeks) has extremely varied talent. The other living sister, Missouri Virginia (Mrs. S. T. Weeks) has the domestic taste of her mother and has raised a family of nine children. Robert E. Lee See is a farmer and land surveyor; while S. C. See is one of the best and most prosperous farmers in Montgomery County. The little sister Lucy Elizabeth, who died in childhood, was very talented, and already showed a remarkable sense for music.

As a further account of Professor See's brothers it may be stated:

1. That the eldest, Millard Filmore, is a great reader of scientific literature, having made a careful study of such celebrated philosophers as Darwin, Spencer, Haeckel, Huxley, John Stuart Mill; and of late years has given much attention to astronomy and cosmogony, along the lines marked out in Professor See's "Researches." His mind is noted for its scientific turn, and he has practical talent as a builder, and inventor of mechanical appliances. Moreover he is well read in law and public administration. His son, Russell See, is a distinguished graduate of the Missouri University, and now a civil engineer in the U.S. Reclamation Service.

---

* Originally named in honor of the famous Confederate General Stonewall Jackson, but as the name Jonathan in the General's name did not seem the most suitable, it was replaced by Jefferson and the new name then considered as representing three celebrated men: *Thomas* in honor of Thomas Jefferson, *Jefferson*, in honor of Jefferson Davis and *Jackson* in honor of Stonewall Jackson. Professor Newcomb once remarked to Professor See in Washington that his father must have been a great admirer of American history to have given him such a distinguished name.

2. The intellectual tastes of George W. See are about equally pronounced. He made a good record at the Missouri State University, including a year in the Law School; and has been quite active in public affairs. In 1898 he represented Montgomery County in the State Legislature, and served on important committees. He has long been a warm friend and trusted adviser of Speaker Champ Clark; and in 1912 was designated by the State Central Committee a Presidential Elector at Large on the Democratic Ticket, to fill a vacancy, but did not serve, owing to subsequent ruling of the State Supreme Court sustaining the claims of the first nominee, whose legal right to act as Elector was in doubt.

3. The youngest brother, E. E. See, was a promising student at the Missouri State University, and made notable progress in biology, under the celebrated Dr. Howard Ayers; and his subsequent studies have included geology, astronomy and cosmogony. All of Professor See's brothers take a deep interest in his discoveries, and Edward also has artistic talent.

Missouri Virginia's husband, Judge S. T. Weeks, was a man of high standing and liberal attainments. He was elected county Judge of Callaway County, and afterwards State Senator; and aided in important legislation looking to the betterment of the State. The offices which he held came to him quite unsought. While Senator he was a trusted advisor of Governor Francis, whose administration is reckoned among the best in the history of Missouri.

Before dismissing the subject, it may be remarked that Professor See's Uncle, Jacob See, was in his time also a leading citizen of Montgomery County. He was elected sheriff, and afterwards represented the county in the Legislature, during the session of 1876-7. But his greatest fame was won as a raiser of fine stock. The celebrated ox, "Stonewall Jackson," weighed 4,300 pounds, and was by far the largest animal of the kind in the world. This mammoth ox was exhibited in many cities of the Union, and finally taken to the Centennial at Philadelphia, where it was crippled and died.

Jacob See's son, Randolph E., was twice elected sheriff of Montgomery County, and later was appointed marshal of the Supreme Court at Jefferson City. Under Governor Folk, Randolph See became chief assistant warden of the Penitentiary, where he rendered such eminent services, on the occasion of an outbreak of the prisoners, that his widow was voted the sum of $2,000. by the Legislature, in recognition of bravery which shortened his life, owing to the extreme exertions then made in the discharge of his duties to the State. His death soon after this heroic conduct was viewed as a public calamity.

From these indications it will be seen that the prominence attained by the See family in Virginia was not temporary, but has been much increased in Missouri during successive generations, and in several branches.

Returning now to the subject of this biography we notice that Professor See was born at the "Prairie Place," a large farm of some six hundred acres, three miles northwest of Montgomery City, Mo., Feb. 19, 1866. This was just after the close of the Civil War, and when the terrible days of test oaths and reconstruction were coming on. During that fearful conflict, Noah See was an outspoken Southern sympathizer, and was persecuted accordingly. He had owned two or three slaves before the war broke out, but they were well treated and remained faithful to their old master during these terrible times, and continued to live near him after the close of the war.

Having a growing family of small children, Noah See could not well leave them when the country was so overrun with marauders, who carried away live stock and provisions and pretty much everything in sight, and often burned houses and towns, and committed many cold blooded murders. Thus Mr. Hamp Logan, an innocent and unoffending young man, was killed by licentious and drunken soldiers within a mile of Noah See's home. By these depredations Mr. See lost property during the war worth at least sixteen hundred dollars.

Much of the time he had to keep in hiding, to come to his family in time of need, and to provide for the devoted wife and

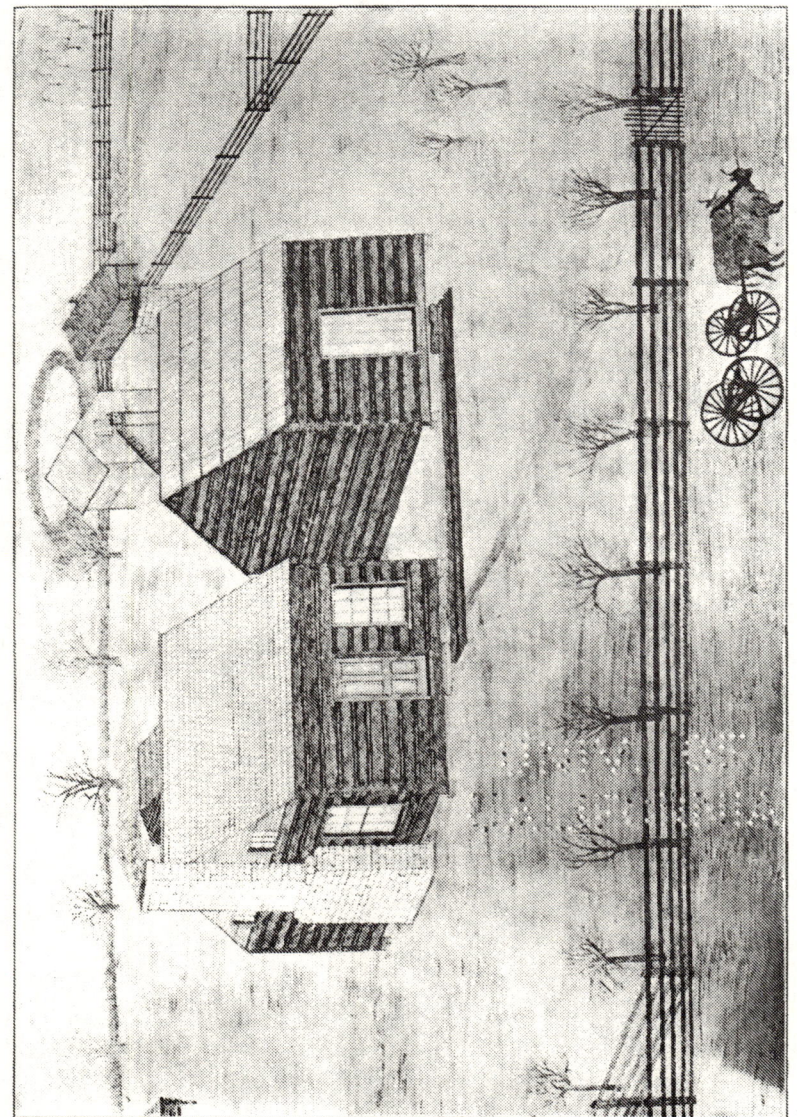

THE PRAIRIE PLACE.

As it appeared when Professor See was born, Feb. 19, 1866. From a drawing in India Ink, by Mr. E. E. See, 1906.

children. For two or three years, at times of greatest danger, he camped in the creek bottoms, often sleeping in caves, or in ravines or hollows, with nothing but a low canvas over his head as a shelter against the wind and snow.

First one set of raiders would come, and then another. On two or three occasions he narrowly escaped capture at the hands of desperate and drunken soldiery. Finally he was captured unexpectedly, and detained as military prisoner in Danville, where he worked as carpenter, building the block house which was used as a fort by the Federal troops. He always had good friends among the Union sympathizers, and they secured his safety. After some months he escaped and ran away, while the guard was inattentive, but was again apprehended, though not long detained; and he was then allowed to remain at liberty, as one of the inoffending Southerners.

Noah See had in fact never taken any part in the war, and was persecuted by a few envious individuals of the community just because he was prosperous and well-to-do. Those who were trifling and penniless made the war a pretext to spy on their prosperous neighbors, and aid in parceling out their property. It was just such lawlessness as this that ruined the Federal cause in the eyes of the best citizens of Montgomery County. The town of Danville lost standing in this way, and after it was burned during the war never recovered. As a law-abiding and peaceful citizen, persecuted and thus compelled to camp out during the war, much like Daniel Boone, in his conflicts with the Indians, Noah See has related that he used to lie awake at night, with nothing but the stars overhead, and wonder if there could be a God governing the world, who would permit the triumph of such injustice and wickedness. Few men ever went through a more trying experience than the future father of the famous astronomer, who was destined to be born a year after the close of the war.

It is worth recording in this connection, that Mrs. Noah See, while her husband was in seclusion, or detained under military guard in Danville, was under the necessity of managing the farm as well as the household, and with very little help. A part of the time her younger brother, John T. Sailor, then a boy of twelve or fourteen, helped her about the place, and around the house. But oftentimes the militia would come at night in their search for firearms, and stay so long, by the comfortable fire, that they would burn up all the wood in the house, and leave none for use next morning.

They stole and carried away flour, bacon, lard, sugar, coffee, live stock, hay, cattle, sheep and hogs, as well as horses and mules. On one occasion they tried to kill one of the only yoke of oxen on the place, wanting to shoot the ox while yoked to the feed wagon. But Mrs. See was brave as a lion, and emphatically ordered them off the place, using very strong language in laying down the law. As she got between their guns and the ox, and simply would not yield, they finally desisted, and went elsewhere for beef.

During several of the winters of the war the snow was very deep, and the cold intense; yet Mrs. See herself had to yoke the oxen and attend to the feeding, besides caring for a family of five children, several of them quite small. If ever a woman deserved a place in Missouri history it is Mrs. Mary A. See, the mother of the great astronomer. No heroine of the American Revolution ever went through more trying experiences than this noble and good woman.

It was from such sturdy stock, tested in the crucible of bitter experience during the war, that the future illustrious scientist was to be born. And strange to say, he first saw the light on the birthday of Copernicus (1473–1543), the founder of modern astronomy, Feb. 19, 1866. This date of birth might be an accident, but the believers in astrology will find in the career of Professor See and his revolutionary work in astronomy so much to remind them of his great predecessor, as to cause many to think that after all our destinies are shaped by the stars under which we are born.

As a baby, the future astronomer was large and vigorous, weighing nearly ten pounds. He suffered from no important illness in childhood, except a croupy tendency, which however was relieved without much difficulty. He was a quiet child, but bright and inquisitive as soon as he developed to the talking age. As soon as he could walk about the house, he was fond of following his mother around, and asking all kinds of questions, such as why do you do this, and why that, etc.

It is authenticated that when not more than two years of age, he would count the leaves on the trees, and the wild geese flying in flocks overhead; and cry out: "Geese, geese! how many? A hundred, or a thousand?" This showed a mind for numbering all things; and naturally it extended to the stars lighting up the sky at night. They too had to be counted before the little boy closed his eyes in sleep. Nor was the Moon, as the chief ornament of the nocturnal sky, overlooked. On the contrary, it was his special pet, and he used to debate whether it could not be brought down to the earth, like a plate on the table.

The little boy of three never dreamed in this happy childhood that some day he was to be the one astronomer who could enlighten the world regarding the origin of the Moon. Yet all these tendencies in childhood marked the boy as a born investigator, and his questions ran all the way from who made the Sun, Moon and Stars, to who made God. Even in childhood he was every inch a natural philosopher.

On August 7, 1869, a total eclipse of the Sun took place, the path of totality passing over Iowa, Missouri, Kentucky and North Carolina. It was so dark in eastern Missouri that the cows came home, as in the evening, lowing for the calves, while the chickens went to roost, and the cocks crowed, as at night. The little boy, under the safe keeping of his good mother, observed all this, and it produced a lasting impression on his childish mind. He went out to look at the Sun when covered by the Moon, but finding it almost as dark as night, with only a halo of rays about the Sun, due to the corona, he hastened back into the house and hid under the bed, till all danger was passed.

As a child, Professor See learned his letters so early that no teacher was required. Without instruction, he learned to spell, probably from the example of the older children. He first went to a district school, in a log school house, where his mother had acquired the elements of her education years before. This school house is shown in the accompanying picture. It had slabs for seats, which were without any backs; and was heated by a fireplace, and thus as primitive, as in the time of Andrew Jackson, the neighborhood having undergone but little change in the forty years since his mother's birth, Jan. 14, 1832. But the place was safe, and in this rural Arcady the little boy passed an ideal childhood.

His first teacher was Professor Benjamin Elliot, who still lives in Montgomery County, and is naturally very proud of the great man now grown out of the little "Tommy" See of six, who came to him to learn the elements of reading, writing and arithmetic, forty years ago.

In a letter dated Mineola, Mo., January 8, 1906, Professor Elliott wrote Professor See regarding these early days at school as follows:

"I am in receipt of your favor of recent date (regarding the mathematical researches on the constitution of the Sun), which I read with the greatest pleasure. You can not conceive the gratification it is to me to know of the success you have had in your chosen field of labor. Well do I remember the first day that you were under my care at school. The methodical manner, in which you took up the duties assigned to you, attracted my attention; for even in childhood you employed system in everything you did; and this led me to conclude, and rightly, that I had found the ideal boy. And I never had the least cause to change my first impression, as long as we were together in school.

"I had thought to give some recollections of those days, but there are so many pleasant ones that present themselves, that to write even a small part of them, would make this letter too long. There is ever a warm place in my heart for you, and an earnest

MR. BENJAMIN ELLIOTT.

Professor See's earliest teacher, as he appeared when about 70 years of age. From a photograph taken in 1906.

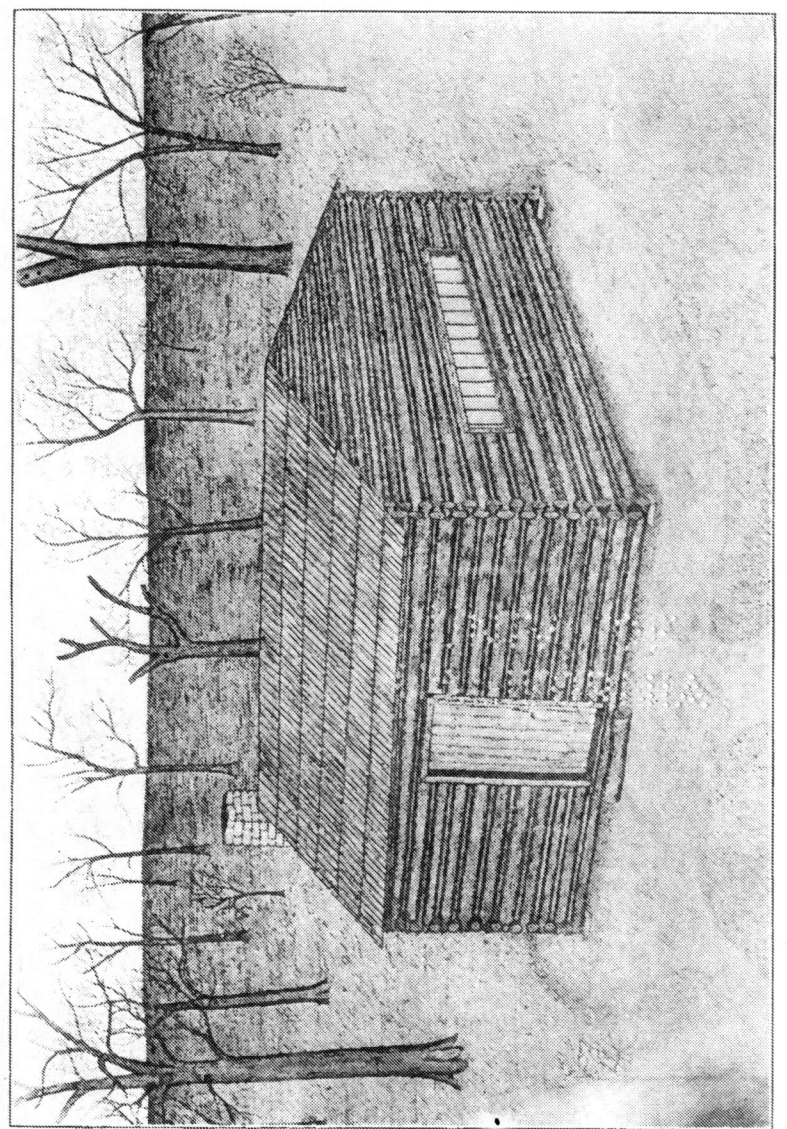

THE OLD LOUTRE SCHOOL HOUSE, 1872.

Here Professor See first attended school as a child of six. From a drawing in India Ink, by Mr. E. E. See, 1906.

wish that you may succeed in all your undertakings; for it seems to me that your success is my success. I claim part of it anyway.

"I have no photograph at present, but shall have some made soon, and send you one. I met your mother at the Old Settlers' Reunion last August, the first time I had seen her since the family moved from Loutre. Was real glad to meet her, as I am to meet any of the old-timers. Be sure to visit me when you come to Missouri next time."

Something in these earliest days led little Tom See to learn by heart the familiar poem:

> "Twinkle, twinkle, little star,
> How I wonder what you are,
> Up above the world so high,
> Like a diamond in the sky.
>
> "When the blazing sun is set,
> And the grass with dew is wet,
> Then you show your little light,
> Twinkle, twinkle, all the night.
>
> "And if I were in the dark,
> I would thank you for your spark;
> I could not see which way to go
> If you did not twinkle so.
>
> "And when I am sound asleep
> Oft you through my window peep,
> For you never shut your eye
> Till the sun is in the sky."

It was observed that he had a prodigious memory, and he used to repeat such poems at play time, to the delight of all the pupils. Little did his associates then imagine that the little boy with methodical methods and brilliant memory was to become the greatest astronomer in the world, and one of the greatest of all time!

CHAPTER II.

1879–1884.

BOYHOOD AND EDUCATION PREPARATORY TO COLLEGE.

KEEN INTEREST IN SCIENCE SUPPLEMENTED BY ARTISTIC TASTE
AND BY THE STUDY OF DRAWING AND PAINTING.

BEFORE proceeding with the story of Professor See's boyhood, it is advisable to dwell briefly on his father's activity at this period. We have already related that Noah See was a man of remarkably keen mind. He was rather stocky in build, about five feet eight inches in height, but active as a farmer, builder, engineer, and surveyor, till within a few years of his death in 1890. He was a good business man, and acquired in time an independent fortune. He invested his savings chiefly in land, and thus the estate finally included some eight thousand acres. Accordingly in the latter years of his life Noah See was one of the largest land holders in northeast Missouri.

In the early days, from 1840 to 1870, Mr. See acquired land little by little. He entered some of it himself, and in other cases bought it from others who wished to sell. In the forties and fifties the whole country from Montgomery City to Palmyra, in Marion County, was an open prairie, with grass as high as a horse's back. The flies were so bad that people could not live in the prairie, and the early settlements had therefore all been along the creek bottoms and in the timbered regions, where water also was more accessible than in the prairie country.

But Mr. See himself moved to the Prairie Place, three miles northwest of Montgomery City, about 1852, and settlers began to enter the prairie land also. At this time they had to go to Palmyra to obtain the land patents, and thus had to ride about sixty miles through the high grass. It was impossible to travel by day,

A VIEW OF PROFESSOR SEE'S COUNTRY PLACE, STARLIGHT ON LOUTRE.

Showing the bridge over Loutre Creek, and the sycamore and other trees on both sides.   From a photograph by Torbett, Feb., 1913.

because the flies were so bad on the horses, and the custom was to travel by night. Many times did Noah See traverse this stretch of open prairie with nothing but the stars to guide him. As he was a surveyor, he knew how to reach his destination by the shortest route, which often decided who got the land offered for patent by the Government. Guided by the stars he would ride all night, and rest his horse by day, under a cover to protect the animal from the flies; and then on the second night reach Palmyra by the light of the morning stars.

Most of Professor See's country place on Loutre, was entered by his maternal great grandfather, Phillip Cobb*, from whom Noah See purchased it in 1837; but he calls it *Starlight*, in memory of the nightly journeys of his father, who thus acquired so much of his land by entry at Palmyra. Besides the name *Starlight* is very appropriate for the home of an astronomer, who first learned to study the heavens in this most beautiful region of Montgomery County.

After his marriage in 1853, Mr. See gave up building and constructing houses for others, but as he had acquired several farms of his own, he continued to improve them with buildings, barns, and tenant houses. And he continued to act as bridge commissioner for the county till after 1880. While Noah See always took a keen interest in public affairs, and was so patriotic in his feelings that he named his sons largely after the Presidents, he did not like political life, as it is carried on. Hence he made it a rule not to hold public office. But upon the solicitation of friends he was persuaded to be a candidate for county surveyor twice in the seventies, and was each time elected by good majorities.

---

* The Cobbs, like the Sailors, were of English origin, having settled in Virginia before the Revolution. After participating in that struggle some of them moved to Montgomery County, Ky. Phillip Cobb settled in Montgomery County, Mo., in 1823, and his daughter Sabina married James Sailor, Dec. 28, 1828. Among well known descendants of the Cobbs of Virginia are Professor Collier Cobb of the University of North Carolina, the celebrated Confederate Statesman Howell Cobb, Justice A. J. Cobb of the Supreme Court of Georgia, and others.

For many years he was accustomed to ride about the County on bridge inspections, surveying, and other work; and often attended court at Danville to hear speeches by the more eminent lawyers. He would also attend political meetings, to hear Senators Vest, and Cockrell, or Champ Clark. In earlier days he heard ex-Senators John B. Henderson, and Waldo P. Johnston, and predicted eminent careers for both of them. He had been a great admirer of Henry Clay, but said that he was too honest to be elected President.

On account of these habits Noah See was accustomed to be much away from home during the day, but seldom stayed over night, and when he did it was with some of the substantial citizens. Occasionally his surveying work took him to remote parts of the County, and he might be gone a week; but this was exceptional. He knew everybody in the County of any standing, and had a strong personal following, and very few enemies. His fondness for riding and his activity about the farm, in spite of severe weather, kept him in fairly good health till within a year of his death in 1890.

As Noah See always lived on large farms in the country, only the district schools were available for the education of his children, except when special arrangements were made for their stay in town, or at the University, after T. J. J. See went there in 1884. In Professor See's boyhood the family lived at the Loutre place, about seven miles west of Montgomery City. The father might go to town on business, every day or every few days, but the rest of the family stayed close at home, and were actively occupied with the work of the farm, the children being in school about four months during the winter. This was the common country school, very good as far as it went, but usually not going beyond the elements of reading, writing, arithmetic, grammar, history, geography, and in a few cases the elements of physics, geometry and physical geography.

With only four months of the year devoted to school, it is clear that advancement could not be very rapid. Each year the

THE NEW LOUTRE SCHOOL HOUSE, BUILT BY HON. NOAH SEE IN 1878

From a photograph by Torbett Feb., 1913. As a boy of twelve, Mr. T. J. J. See aided his Father in building this school house, and attended school here during the winter of 1878-9.

pupils got a little further than the year before, and the brighter ones took up new studies. Noah See was "good in figures" or a good mathematician, and he taught his son Thomas some of the most important processes of arithmetic. Usually, however, the children depended upon the teacher, and the older children who had gone over the ground before. But, on the one hand, if the schools were limited and somewhat short and inadequate, yet on the other they were not crammed with such a mass of stuff as to confuse both teacher and pupil, as they so often are nowadays.

Thus Professor See's early educational advantages were limited, but such as to give a clear understanding of what he did study. Professor Benjamin Elliott was his earliest teacher, and he was a good mathematician, and clearheaded in all that he did. Professor See's later instructors during the years at Loutre, included his sister Mrs. A. M. Weeks, who was an excellent teacher, and especially good in arithmetic. From his earliest studies it was observed that Tom See always stood at the head of his classes. Good in everything, he would spell down every one in school, the teacher not excepted; and it was the same way in arithmetic. If there was any problem which no one could solve, in such books as Ray's Arithmetic, it was put up to Tom See, and not once did he fail.

The old Loutre school house was burned down during Christmas week of 1875, and a new frame school house built by Noah See for the district, on a tract of land donated by him for the purpose. It is now called *Starlight*, and is included within Professor See's country place. It was here that Tom See as a boy of twelve and thirteen went to school during the winter of 1878 and 1879. He won the first prize for scholarship, a beautiful picture, and on the last day of school surprised everybody by solving a very difficult problem in Ray's Third Part of Arithmetic, which Professor Elliott and many others believed could not be solved.

In these early school days, which were characterized by few but excellent books, Tom See became familar with Longfellow's "Psalm of Life" by hearing this famous poem recited from time to time:

"A PSALM OF LIFE."

"What the Heart of the Young Man Said to the Psalmist."

"Tell me not, in mournful numbers,
　　Life is but an empty dream!—
For the soul is dead that slumbers,
　　And things are not what they seem.

"Life is real! Life is earnest!
　　And the grave is not its goal;
Dust thou art, to dust returnest,
　　Was not spoken of the soul.

"Not enjoyment, and not sorrow,
　　Is our destined end or way;
But to act, that each to-morrow
　　Finds us farther from to-day.

"Art is long, and Time is fleeting,
　　And our hearts, though stout and brave,
Still, like muffled drums, are beating
　　Funeral marches to the grave.

"In the world's broad field of battle,
　　In the bivouac of Life,
Be not like dumb, driven cattle!
　　Be a hero in the strife!

"Trust no Future, howe'er pleasant!
　　Let the dead Past bury its dead!
Act,— act in the living Present!
　　Heart within, and God o'erhead!

"Lives of great men all remind us
　　We can make our lives sublime,
And, departing, leave behind us
　　Footprints on the sands of time;

"Footprints, that perhaps another,
    Sailing o'er life's solemn main,
A forlorn and shipwrecked brother,
    Seeing, shall take heart again.

"Let us, then, be up and doing,
    With a heart for any fate;
Still achieving, still pursuing,
    Learn to labor and to wait."

It is undeniable that even in the boyhood period Tom See had such pride that he dreamed of some day becoming a great man. Thus the stanza:

"Lives of great men all remind us
    We can make our lives sublime,
And, departing, leave behind us
    Footprints on the sands of time."

seems to have sunk deep into his soul — how deep, perhaps only the record of his unrivaled achievements in mature manhood can adequately tell. At any rate the fire of youthful ambition thus enkindled by Longfellow's inspiring song never wholly died out; for even in deepest adversity he still remembered vividly those

"Footprints, that perhaps another,
    Sailing o'er life's solemn main,
A forlorn and shipwrecked brother,
    Seeing, shall take heart again."

Thus it is believed that such poems, taken earnestly and sinking deep into the subconscious mind, had a great influence in moulding Professor See's career. The two conditions necessary for this effect were a serious and earnest view of life, and a prodigious memory — both of which Tom See had in the highest degree. And with all he had resolute purpose to adhere to plans once formed, and thus triumph over all difficulties, like the heroes we read about in history.

While living at Loutre, within half a mile of the beautiful river by this name, two astronomical events especially impressed the boy Tom See. On the evening of January 1, 1877, the family had retired early, after an active day about the farm, when, to the terror and consternation of mother and children, a great meteor suddenly appeared in the west and traversed the heavens with a rapid flight towards the northeast. It was so bright as to cast a brilliant light through the windows, and the shadows on the floor moved rapidly around with the flight of the meteor, so that the effect was very terrifying. Some thought it was so near as to hit the barn, but a moment's observation showed it to be very far away. Subsequent reports declared that it passed over central Iowa. A blazing train was left behind, and a thundering noise followed sometime after the meteor had disappeared.

At the time of this occurrence Noah See was absent from home, on surveying work, and spending the night with Mr. Black, near Wellsville. He saw the phenomenon and knew immediately that it was a meteor. Needless to say, he watched its flight without alarm, just as he had the brilliant star shower of Nov. 12, 1833, in Virginia. He described the train of the meteor as equal to the Moon in width, and ten times as long as it was broad, so that the light was very intense. Great pieces of fire seemed to fall from the meteor as it traversed the heavens, with dazzling splendor, inferior only to the light of the Sun; and the earth was so lighted up that the smallest objects could be seen on the ground, even in a forest. The suddenness of the phenomenon and its great brilliancy inspired general terror and not only in human beings, but even in animals of all kinds, which were awakened from their slumbers as by an earthquake, and for some time could not be quieted.

The other event of special astronomical interest was the solar eclipse of July 29, 1878, which was total in Colorado and Wyoming. It so much cut down the sun's light in Missouri as to give the afternoon the appearance of moonlight. The See boys were at work in the fields, and on coming home found the rest of the family and Squire McLoughlin of Williamsburg looking at the Sun through a smoked glass. This eclipse interested the boy Tom See almost as much as that of 1869 had the child, though the darkness was only a great reduction of the Sun's light, the belt of totality not having crossed over Missouri.

Loutre Creek is noted for its fine fish, and in those days the See boys were great fishermen. At the end of the week, when the farm work was done, they would go to the Creek for some good sport. Noah See had built a boat, for use on the large hole of water near the school house, and this added to the safety and pleasure of the fishing, in which the boy Tom See was no laggard. He liked to fish, though he cared little for hunting.

The Loutre region is hilly and heavily timbered, and the work of the large farm included the felling of trees, rolling of logs, and all manner of hauling, as well as plowing, planting and cultivating the corn and other crops. Tom See participated in all such work, and as this kept him in the healthiest of outdoor activity it probably gave him the physique requisite for the hard mental work he has since done in science. But for the work on the farm, in boyhood and young manhood, it is practically certain that he could not have achieved what he has in the way of discovery.

It is a common belief that discovery is a matter of genius, and so it is; but genius itself is chiefly a matter of hard work and everlasting perseverance. It was long ago remarked by Michael Angelo, the celebrated Italian painter, sculptor and architect, that genius consists in eternal patience. Another great authority says it is the ability to do hard work. Professor See himself says that genius is a combination of all these and more besides: "It is the ability to do hard work, combined with eternal patience and the faith that moves mountains." Without all these qualities genius of the highest order does not exist; and the rarity of the combination is the reason why we have so little genius of the first rank. Modern society, as now organized and conducted, does next to nothing to support the labors of genius; and therefore we should wonder not that we have so little genius, but that we have any at all, especially in those branches of human effort which are without profit, such as scientific discovery. Professor See's decision to be a scientist was a matter of gradual development, as more fully set forth in the next chapter. In his boyhood he could not forsee the opportunity, which came later, for devoting his life to scientific research.

In the month of October, 1879, the See family moved to the large farm of 920 acres on Elkhorn Creek, three miles southeast of Montgomery City, where the mother still lives. While feeding the turkeys one winter morning of 1878–9, Noah See fell on the sloping ground, about the Loutre residence, and fractured the bones in his left foot, which confined him to the house for a time. This led him to think of the greater safety of the level prairie for an elderly person. Then too, it happened that the eldest son, Filmore, was already feeding cattle on an extensive scale at Elkhorn, where the pasture of nearly a thousand acres was at hand. Mr. See and the eldest son were in partnership, and as the other boys were nearing manhood, it seemed that the prairie offered the best opportunity for the future. The family therefore quit Loutre and settled permanently between Montgomery City and New Florence.

Before parting from Loutre in this narrative, however, we may remark that a terrible tornado visited that region, Jan. 1, 1876, just a year before the great meteor appeared. Many of the strongest trees were uprooted, and twisted to pieces, fences swept away, and even crab apple bushes torn from the ground. In the case of rail fences not even the ground rail was left in its bed. This storm came unexpectedly about one o'clock in the afternoon when the family had just finished dinner. Jacob Stewart, Esq.,* of near Wellsville, an old time Virginian and a tried friend of the terrible days of the Civil War, was stopping at the house, having come on foot the day before to pay his taxes at Danville, and remained over to recall the stories of narrow escapes which had

---

*A first Cousin of Margaret (Stewart) See, wife of John See, and Sister-in-Law of Noah See.

enabled him and Mr. See to live through that desperate conflict.

As soon as it was realized that a storm was breaking, Tom See and his brothers ran to the windows, only to behold the largest oaks whirling and falling before the blast of the tornado. The whole forest for a mile was in an uproar; but the center of the cyclone had missed the house and passed nearer Loutre Creek. The family immediately scattered to look after the animals on the farm, now unrestrained by any fences, and Mr. Stewart, fearing for the safety of his own family near Wellsville, struck out for home. This terrible storm produced a deep impression on the mind of Tom See, then a boy ten years old, but it is remarkable that no fatalities resulted from the tornado, because the region was thinly populated. The force seems to have spent itself on the forests of Loutre hills, and but little damage resulted elsewhere. Yet some of the large trees blown down had turned up immense rocks as much as eight feet high, attached to their roots; and for years the travelers along the public road wondered at the scene of devastation presented to their eyes, and used to inquire the particulars from Tom See and his brothers.

Aside from the occasional appearance of a comet in the heavens, and floods of Loutre Creek, following terrible storms of thunder and lightning, which are very common there, the natural phenomena of most significant character have now been recorded.

It should be remarked, however, that little Tom See from childhood had a great fondness for large trees, and especially for trees of beautiful shape. Trees with snags or irregularities in their limbs were considered by him very ugly, and he was constantly devising ways and means to get rid of them. Once the family went to church, when Tom was about three years old, and he happened to sit near the window, where he could look out into the neighboring forest. The snags on the trees interested him much more than the sermon; and if he did not have a swinging lamp to study, as young Galileo had in the Cathedral at Pisa, he kept his mind on the improvements needed for beautifying the symmetry and regularity of the grove of trees about the Church. It is probable that this craving for regularity and symmetry in the trees was an expression of the mathematical talents then latent in the mind of the child. His mother had always been very fond of trees, and Professor See to this day dearly loves a fine forest, and will not allow any timber to be destroyed on his country places.

At the large estate of Noah See on Elkhorn, the school facilities were no better than on Loutre. The boys were occupied with the business of the farm, and as before school did not extend over more than four months. During the winter of 1882-3, Tom See missed school entirely. His eldest sister, Mrs. A. M. Weeks, was much disturbed about his lack of suitable opportunity for extending his education. It happened that the Montgomery City School was being improved, under a superior teacher, Professor A. L. Jenness, who had been a student at Amherst, but had not graduated. Mrs. Weeks now besought her father to let Tom go to the town school, by riding back and forth on horseback. After considerable effort this plan was fixed upon, and Tom made the best of his opportunities.

In this place it may be noted that the teachers of Professor See, during boyhood and youth, prior to his entrance at the Montgomery City High School, Sept., 1883, were as follows:

> 1872– 3, Benjamin Elliott,
> 1873– 4, Benjamin Elliott,
> 1874– 5, Benjamin Elliott,
> 1875– 6, Lafayette Brelsford,
> 1876– 7, Miss Mattie Phipps,
> 1877– 8, Benjamin Elliott,
> 1878– 9, Mrs. A. M. Weeks,
> 1879–80, Miss Rhetta Lens,
> 1880–81, Miss Helen Huddleston,
> 1881–82, Miss Helen Huddleston.

MR. T. J. J. SEE, AS HE APPEARED WHEN A YOUTH OF SEVENTEEN.
From a photograph by Varnum, Montgomery City, Mo., 1883.

THE PRESENT RESIDENCE OF MRS. MARY A. SEE, NEAR MONTGOMERY CITY, MO.

This photograph was taken on June 6th, 1907, and shows Professor See next to his mother, and near his aunt, Mrs. Maria Keele; Mr. M. F. See and his family appear on the left.

This was the last house built by Hon. Noah See, in 1883. As a youth of seventeen Mr. T. J. See aided his father in hauling the lumber from Loutre, ten miles distant, and also took part with his older brother, Robert, in building the house.

At the Montgomery City High School, 1883–4, Professor See's teachers were the principal, Professor A. L. Jenness, and Miss Lillian Jones, first assistant.

The arguments used by Mrs. Weeks with her father were to the effect that Tom was so talented that he ought to have a good education. Others had made similar arguments before, and she merely emphasized the current view. Senators Vest and Cockrell, she said, could not always serve Missouri in the Senate; and Colonel A. H. Buckner would need a successor in Congress (this was of course before the days of Champ Clark.) Noah See had a poor opinion of the legal profession, as now carried on, and did not wish any of his sons to adopt a profession in which he could not be honest and preserve a good conscience. He had such a high opinion of Tom's abilities and steady qualities that he was inclined to think he would make a great man, if given an opportunity; and as others in the community told him the same thing about the promise of this son, he gradually came to favor more elaborate education for him.

There were some other favorable circumstances which came to Tom's support. About 1882 his father had purchased at low price a large tract of land in Vernon County, by which he made considerable money. Former United States Senator Waldo P. Johnson of St. Louis said that Noah See made $10,000 by this trade. It may have been more. And he added to it other tracts of land also purchased at low price, till he had about 4,000 acres in southwest Missouri. The increase in the value of this property made Mr. See feel that his large family eventually would be well provided for. When his older children were of school age he had not been so well off, and could not so easily provide for their education, as he now could for Tom's. There was some jealousy in the family over this outlook, but it was felt to be right to provide for Tom even if such full provision had not been made for others when circumstances were less favorable.

There was one other more powerful reason than any other why Tom had his way, namely, he was always a most industrious and efficient worker, and his father saw that he would not waste money or neglect opportunities. By strict attention to business Tom came to enjoy his father's confidence more than any other of his sons. He therefore entered the Montgomery City School in the autumn of 1883, and kept going from home daily till May, 1884. Tom See was now seventeen, and quite tall, being almost a six footer*. He was poorly trained in comparison with some of the town boys, but they did not have the industry and determination which Tom had, and before spring came around he stood first in the school.

He distinguished himself especially in geometry, physics, and astronomy. For although there was no regular course in astronomy, Tom had obtained at Jas. R. Hance's store a copy of *Steele's Fourteen Weeks in Astronomy*, and read it with such absorbing interest that at the close of the term he delivered an original composition on astronomy, which led Rev. Henry Kay to remark that he saw in the effort made indications like those noticed by the sculptor who saw a beautiful statue in a rough block of marble.

It must not be supposed that this year at the Montgomery City School was without its trials and hardships, and serious ones at that. But the significiant fact was that the country boy of energy, ambition and purpose, though entering but poorly prepared, had distanced all his city competitors in the race for scholarship. Tom See had made good in the general estimation of the school and in the eyes of his teacher, and won the support of his father to such other educational career as he might wish to enter upon. He missed only two days of the school year, when the creeks were beyond their banks and impassable; and on each of these occasions he notified the teacher by U. S. Mail why he was detained. No wonder his efforts commanded confidence, even among doubting Thomases! Such serious and determined effort had not been expected by anyone. At first the town boys had

---

* His present height is six feet four inches, and weight about 240 pounds, so that he is a man of very commanding presence.

been inclined to laugh at the simple farmer from the country; but before the year closed they saw their mistake, sighed that they had lost in the race with him, and were in a more serious mood.

Before closing this account of Professor See's boyhood days, mention should be made of the fact that he always had great taste for art. While still occupied on the farm he would spend his evenings with books, or in drawing and copying pictures. He drew a good picture of the great comet of 1882, which in 1910 was engraved in the second volume of Professor See's monumental work, *Researches on the Evolution of the Stellar Systems*. His artistic work included portraits, done with pencil, and resembling steel engravings. Water color work was one of his favorite labors. and he painted flowers and fruit after the manner of veteran artists. This was all done without any teacher, and at such moments as he could snatch from daily outdoor life on the farm. Some of his drawings gained prizes at the Montgomery County Fair; and when he entered the Missouri University in the autumn of 1884, Professor Diehl, the Professor of Art, told him that they showed great originality and artistic power. Since he became a scientist Professor See has found no little use for his talent, by way of drawing and illustrating, though naturally he has not cultivated art in a professional way. Yet this childhood and boyhood tendency to seek the true and beautiful gives the key to the labors of his life.

CHAPTER III.

1884–1889.

FIVE YEARS AT THE UNIVERSITY OF MISSOURI.

FIRED WITH ENTHUSIASM BY THE STUDY OF HUMBOLDT, NEWTON, LAPLACE AND HERSCHEL, YOUNG MR. SEE GRADUATES AT THE HEAD OF HIS CLASS, WITH HIGHEST HONORS IN ASTRONOMY.

WE have already pointed out that Professor See as a youth of seventeen had some difficulty in securing an opportunity to attend the Montgomery City High School, but he made good to such a degree that he fixed his eye on the State University at Columbia, and none there were to oppose his going. Accordingly soon after the High School closed in May, 1884, young Mr. See visited Columbia on a tour of inspection, to see what the University looked like. He had a letter of introduction, from a Mr. Lovelace, a former student of the University, to Professor Paul Schweitzer, of the Department of Chemistry.

Columbia, in the first days of June, always wears a gay aspect, in honor of the commencement week; but on arriving there young Mr. See only looked about the town, walked over to the University, inspected the buildings, attended some services in the Chapel, met and conversed with Professor Schweitzer, was introduced to Dr. Laws, the President, who advised him to study agriculture and return to the farm. It is a curious fact that Dr. Laws did not encourage young Mr. See in the idea of a scientific career, nor did the young man himself at that time think it prudent to discuss his inmost hopes beyond a mere hint that he was interested in science. Yet he satisfied himself that the University was an important center of learning, representing the State of Missouri, and that it offered ample opportunities for his present needs. Accordingly, after a stay of two days at Columbia, Mr. See return-

THE MAIN BUILDING OF THE UNIVERSITY OF MISSOURI.

As it appeared in the student days of Professor See, prior to its destruction by fire, Jan. 9, 1892.

Univ. of
California

MR. T. J. J. SEE AS HE APPEARED AT THE AGE OF TWENTY

Then a student at the University of Missouri.   From a photograph by Douglass,
Columbia, Mo., 1886.

ed to his home at Montgomery City, to wait for the opening of the University in the autumn.

A few words must now be added to explain Mr. See's early interest in natural science. While attending school under Professor Benjamin Elliott, during the winter of 1877–8, he had taken up the study of physical geography in a very elementary way. He used Monteith's Geography, which included an outline of the theories of the interior of the Earth. *Molten matter* and *volcanic action* henceforth were familiar to the boy's mind. The taste was further developed during succeeding winters, and the name of Humboldt was so often quoted that he longed to see his *Cosmos*.

During the winter of 1882–3, when Tom See was out of school, he corresponded with a book agent, having advertisements in the *Journal of Agriculture*, St. Louis (a Mr. A. E. Wardner, of Perry, Mo.), who procured for him a copy of the Bohn translation of the *Cosmos*, nicely bound in half calf, for $17.00. It was understood to have been purchased in Chicago. Mr. See tried to read it, but of course most of it was beyond his grasp; yet he did get a great deal of inspiration from it, and some idea of the extent and variety of the physical sciences. The subsequent study of physical geography in the Montgomery City High School was more thorough, and enabled him to better appreciate Humboldt. But little could the young man then have dreamed that twenty-two years later he would himself become an authority of the physics of the earth greater than Humboldt or any other naturalist of former times.

Now when Mr. See was in his first session at the University, in December, 1884, a teachers' conference was in progress, and who should he meet there but Mr. A. E. Wardner of Perry, Mo., who had procured him the copy of Humboldt's *Cosmos?* The meeting was very agreeable, and Mr. Wardner encouraged the young man to go on with his studies. Mr. See had found himself well prepared for some studies at the University, and poorly trained in others. Geometry presented no difficulty, but algebra was more troublesome, owing to a confusion in the use of the signs, arising from defective teaching at the High School. The mathematical work of the first college year was thus carried through, but not with entire satisfaction. And during the next summer, while at home, Mr. See found time to review his algebra thoroughly, so as to master every step; and from that day on he never once encountered a seroius difficulty in any branch of mathematics. He believes that mathematics naturally is an easy subject, and that most people find it difficult only because the processes are not made clear as the student goes along.

Among the fortunate events of Mr. See's first year at the University must be counted his instruction in Latin under Professor J. C. Jones, who advised him to take up also the study of the Greek language. During the second semester, therefore, he entered the class in Greek, and came under the influence of Professor A. F. Fleet; and it turned out later that this entry upon the comprehensive study of the classics, as the best educational basis for a profound knowledge of science, alone made it possible for Professor See to take high rank among the great scholars of history.

In an account of his stay at Berlin during the winter of 1787–8, Humboldt recalls that he applied himself in emulation of his industrious Brother Wilhelm, afterwards founder of the University of Berlin, more assiduously to Greek; and in the following May he writes to his friend Wegener that he works hard under Bartholdi's instruction, and finds the study of the language a pleasure. "The more I know of the Gereek language, the more I am confirmed in my preconceived opinion that it is the true foundation of all the higher branches of learning. It was certainly very ill contrived of me to build my house on mere sand; yet the foundations of so temporary a structure as mine may easily be relaid, and therefore it does not distress me that I am only learning to decline ἐχιδνα in my nineteenth year." (Bruhns' Life of Humboldt, transl. by Lassell, Vol. I, p. 54).

Similar reasoning evidently was employed by young Mr. See, for he too first learned Greek in his nineteenth year, because he conceived that it was indispensable to a thorough mastery of the sciences. Mr. See never had occasion to alter this impression of his early student life at the University; and he remains to this day a firm believer in the high value of Greek to the scientific investigator. In the opening sentence of Chapter XXII of his *Researches*, Vol. II, 1910, pp. 625, he says: "The Science of the physical Universe begins with the Greeks, and it will therefore be of interest to examine their theories of the Milky Way, although it would be unreasonable to expect more than sound fundamental principles from the greatest philosophers who lived before the invention of the telescope."

It may have been this classic standard of scholarship as well as his admiration for Humboldt and the most assiduous industry in the pursuit of scientific truth that caused Mr. See to be frequently spoken of at this early period of his undergraduate life as the "Humboldt of the University." At any rate he acquired this name among the students; and now it almost seems as if the saying that great events cast their shadows before them had a prophetic basis of truth.

Humboldt's charm of style is due to his classic training, and modern readers notice the same elegance and beauty of style in the writings of Professor See. These literary accomplishments are comparatively rare among men of science, and it is unfortunate for science that it is so; because elegance adds to the beauty and artistic finish of even the greatest works. Among modern scientists who are noted for elegance and simplicity in their writing, one recalls especially Laplace and Sir John Herschel, Lord Kelvin and Sir George Darwin, Newcomb and Poincaré; but the combination of a classic style with scientific thought is sufficiently rare to occasion remark.

Thus after the appearance of the second volume of Professor See's famous *Researches*, in 1910, Professor W. B. Smith of Tulane University, New Orleans, writes with enthusiasm how fortunate it is that America had produced such an astronomer who is also in learning and spirit a Hellenist. It is not wonderful therefore that Professor See has always shown great appreciation of his early instruction under Professor J. C. Jones, and Professor A. F. Fleet, who awakened his love for the classic languages.

During Mr. See's first year at the University it happened that his studies did not include physics or natural philosophy. That department was in charge of Professor B. F. Thomas, who at the end of the year resigned to go to the University of Ohio; while Professor W. B. Smith of Central College, Fayette, Mo., was called to the University to fill the chair of physics. This seems to have been especially fortunate for Mr. See. For Smith was a most inspiring teacher, and both his learning and charm of manner set up an enthusiasm for knowledge which carried several of the Missouri students into high professional careers as investigators, among whom See and Defoe are the most famous.

But before dwelling on the influence of Smith, it may be pointed out that Professors Ficklin, Cauthorn, and Tindall, in the department of mathematics, had confirmed Mr. See more and more in his enthusiasm for geometry and the related mathematical studies. Ficklin was a quiet man, of slow methodical habits, but an excellent teacher, and a very clear-headed mathematician. He was kind and gentle, but not very intimate with the students. When, however, he came to know the serious turn of a student he would take a deep interest in him; and thus it was that Ficklin heard of the promise of Mr. See in the geometry class of Professor Cauthorn.

The second year of Mr. See's career at the University was one of the most important of the five. He had then entered upon his studies with zeal and enthusiasm, and during the year obtained a good start in mathematics, physics, and chemistry, as well as in German and the classics.

As already mentioned Professor W. B. Smith held the chair of physics at the beginning of the session of 1885–6, and he continued to occupy it till Professor Ficklin's death in the summer of 1887, when Smith was given charge also of mathematics, and later formally made professor of mathematics. Mr. See's studies in mathematics were therefore first under Ficklin and his associ-

PROFESSOR PAUL SCHWEITZER.

Head of the Department of Chemistry, one of the most eminent Professors of the University of Missouri. He was born in Berlin, Germany, in 1840, and died at Columbia, Mo., in 1911, after 40 years service to the University. He was strict, but very just, and always much beloved by the students, a firm friend of Professor See, and among the first to recognize his great discoveries in Geogony and Cosmogony.

ates, and subsequently under Smith. The students whom Professor Smith had enthused by his labors in the department of physics now followed him to the department of mathematics. He was the center of thought and inspiration in the University — the one member of the faculty who could fill with credit and success any chair, from Greek and logic to mathematics and physics.

We shall not go into the details of Mr. See's studies, further than to say that his work in physics, chemistry and mathematics had its foundation laid in the years 1885–7, and was more fully rounded out during the last two years at the University. The department of chemistry under Professor Schweitzer was especially fine. It was in this department that See broke the record, making the best grade since the foundation of the University. Professor Schweitzer wanted him to be a chemist, but his mind was already set on the study of the stars. Mr. See has always said that his inspiration in science was especially due to Smith and Schweitzer, both of whom were greatly beloved by the students, because they really tried to develop the young people by a personal interest in their intellectual progress.

Many students at college grope in the dark and waste time, merely finding the way to knowledge, because no one of greater experience is approachable as a guide to them. On account of this need of *competent guidance*, President Woodrow Wilson, while at the head of Princeton University, introduced a system by which all students were brought into close personal contact with the members of the Faculty, each professor and instructor being assigned responsible advisory power over a small group of young men, and all of them thus cared for systematically. This is an educational reform of the first magnitude, and will have to come into universal use before our Universities can be made really efficient. The problem of developing professors of the highest class is not yet solved, and presents great difficulty in view of the inadequate rewards of intellectual effort. In our modern universities, overcrowded with numbers, this condition is greatly aggravated; but at the University of Missouri, in Mr. See's day, the numbers were not so great, and close personal contact with the professor was possible. And it happened that the quality of some of the professors was so high that it could hardly be improved on anywhere. Thus Ficklin was a good teacher, clear-headed, just, honest and candid in all his work; while Smith and Schweitzer had all these high qualities, and besides were attractive to students and inspired them with energy and ambition for high scholarship and research.

At that time the Missouri University was, properly speaking, only a college, but it was a good college; because the elective system had not weakened the vigor of the college curriculum. The courses for degrees were prescribed, and such as might properly be considered appropriate, though some of the studies gave only an introduction to the different subjects.

It was in this second year also that Mr. See made a great discovery in the University library — a copy of Bowditch's Translation of Laplace's *Mécanique Céleste*, bound in boards, with the leaves uncut. Apparently it had never been used by anyone, or, if at all, very little. Of course no other student had ever thought of looking into this great work. But no sooner was the discovery of the monumental work made by Mr. See than he sought access to it daily. At first the work could not be withdrawn from the library, and could only be read during office hours, but by the time the session of 1886–7 came around Mr. See was sufficiently established in the confidence of everybody that the librarian allowed him to take volumes of the precious work home with him.

Mr. See's enthusiasm over the *Mécanique Céleste* of Laplace knew no bounds. It was his subject of meditation day and night, Sundays and holidays. The other students might go in for sports or games, but he would be found working at the *Mécanique Céleste* of Laplace of the *Principia* of Newton. Mr. See purchased a copy of Newton's *Principia* in the autumn of 1886 and studied it zealously. The Bowditch translation of the *Mécanique Céleste* was much more expensive and difficult to get. But he could not rest content without it, so that in the summer of 1887 he had the Columbia book store of Kirtley & Phillips advertise for it in New York, and in November, 1887, they obtained for Mr. See a copy originally purchased by Dr. John Sage, of Sag Harbor, Long Island, at the time of publication (1839), and left by him to his cousin, Wm. S. Pelletrean, of Southampton, Suffolk Co., New York.

This great work is directly responsible for Mr. See's becoming an astronomer — it was the determining factor in fixing his career in science. Prior to this time Mr. See had been aroused to enthusiasm for science by the writings of Humboldt and Newton; but as the nebular hypothesis had interested him from boyhood, since his purchase of *Steele's Fourteen Weeks in Astronomy* (Oct. 1, 1883) it only required the greatest work of Laplace to make him supremely happy*.

Probably it was his secret hope that he might sometime add to Laplace's work, but he never dared to believe that his own researches in cosmogony, twenty years later, would supplant those of Laplace. Naturally there was a vast difference between *reading a work of Laplace, and meditating over his ideas, and devising mathematical proofs and methods to supplant the theories of the great French geometer.* This was to be Mr. See's labor during the next twenty years, and well was it worth this effort, since it has now given us an entirely new theory of the formation of the heavenly bodies. To the State of Missouri has come the imperishable honor of discovering the laws of the development of the solar system, which will mark an epoch in astronomy not inferior to those made by Copernicus, Kepler and Newton.

During the summer of 1887, Professor Ficklin died, after an illness of some months, from a kind of dropsy. He had already seen Mr. See grapple with the different branches of Mathematics, through calculus and analytical geometry, and also Astronomy. He was so impressed with Mr. See's earnestness and reliability

---

* Mr. See was always a very active worker in the Athenean Literary Society, and wrote numerous essays on scientific subjects, especially on the discoveries of Laplace relating to the Mechanics of the Heavens.

that he gave to this undergraduate student the keys to the Observatory, and invited him to make free use of all the instruments. Considering how tenacious Ficklin was in holding on to the personal supervision of the Observatory this was a remarkable testimonial to the esteem in which young Mr. See was held. It used to be said by the students of the University that by hard work during his first three years See had made such a reputation for high standing and scholarship that after that time any Professor would give him the highest grades without question. But of course Mr. See never ceased to work, any more than he has since leaving the University.

During the summers of 1887 and 1888 he remained in Columbia, hard at work in the Observatory, returning to his home at Montgomery City only for short visits. He began the work under Ficklin, and after his death carried it on under Smith, who was later given charge of the department of mathematics and astronomy. Thus for two years before graduation Mr. See was actually in charge of the Observatory, and did all kinds of work, from determining the latitude, with the altazimuth, to observing the planets, comets, sun spots and prominences, with the $7\frac{1}{2}$-inch equatorial.

Among the first objects which especially interested Mr. See were the double stars — gigantic systems of double suns revolving about one another under the Newtonian law of gravitation. Having once seen such double stars as Mizar in the Great Bear, he never afterwards lost sight of these systems, but kept them constantly in mind, and in 1889 wrote his graduating thesis on the "Origin of Binary Stars" to which was awarded the Missouri astronomical medal.

Mr. See took to the problems of cosmogony, on account of his interest in Laplace's Nebular Hypothesis, from boyhood days. Professor George H. Darwin, of Cambridge, England, had recently modified Laplace's theory to some extent; and Mr. See's undergraduate effort was to consider the influence of tidal friction on systems such as the double stars. The thesis was very notable,

MR. T. J. J. SEE, AS HE APPEARED AT THE AGE OF TWENTY-TWO.

From a photograph by Douglass, Columbia, Mo., 1888, about eight months before Mr. See graduated at the head of his class.

THE LAWS OBSERVATORY OF THE UNIVERSITY OF MISSOURI.

Here Professor See first studied Practical Astronomy. He had charge of the Observatory for about two years before he graduated in 1889, with the highest honors in Mathematics and Astronomy, including the Missouri Astronomical Medal, for an original thesis on the Origin of Binary Stars. This was the beginning of the more celebrated work, at the University of Berlin, which at length was so extended as to constitute the foundations of an entirely New Science of Cosmogony, embracing all classes of the celestial bodies, from satellites and comets to clusters and star-clouds of the Milky Way.

as a beginning of the more celebrated researches since carried out at the University of Berlin, and in his monumental work, *Researches on the Evolution of the Stellar Systems*, Vol. I, 1896, and Vol. II, 1910.

During the period of his student days, Mr. See was always the most respected and influential student in the University. He was the one whose work had weight with both students and faculty; yet in a student assembly he was not so popular as some of the more reckless talkers, and on one or two occasions they were preferred over him, as editors of the college paper. While Mr. See was open and democratic in manner, he was dignified and a little austere by his high standing as a student. Then, too, he was a Greek fraternity man — a member of the Phi Delta Theta — and that tended to set an element of the "Barbarians" against him. He had positive convictions and dared to express them, so that, as usually happens with positive characters, he had very devoted friends, and a few enemies among a class whose methods were none too scrupulous.

The events of the last year, 1888–9, showed his unquestioned supremacy in the most conclusive manner. There were a series of crying abuses in the University, now growing noticeably worse, and Dr. Laws, the President, had been there so long that he was set in his way, and would do nothing to alleviate the dissatisfaction. The complaints ran all the way from incompetent professors to injustice to students and general lack of progressiveness, and in some cases involved bad faith with the people of the State. Senator Morton of the visiting board appointed by the Governor reported to the Legislature early in the year that things were not satisfactory at the University. A great commotion followed among the students, and then a special committee of the Senate and House of Representatives was appointed to investigate the University, at the head of which Hon. Champ Clark was placed, because he was the recognized leader in the Legislature.

The committee visited the University, held a long and searching investigation, with the result that the Legislature reorganized the Board of Curators and removed Dr. Laws, by a rider attached to the appropriation bill. Above all others, Mr. See was the student on whom the insurgents at the University had to rely for the management of their fight for the overthrow of the old regime. He desired to keep out of the fight, but could not do it, with the faculty split, and most of his devoted teachers on the side of the insurgents.

Rather than desert his devoted teachers, to whom he owed so much, he took the side against the president, who had very antiquated methods and had much outlived his usefulness. When the contest began in earnest, the students came to Mr. See and said: "Now, See, you must come to our support. You have influence and prestige here and you alone can save the day for us." With great reluctance, but from a sense of duty, Mr. See went over to the cause of progress, and did the hard work of making the movement a success. Everyone trusted See, and he gathered all the data, drew the questions, and conducted the prosecution for the students.

Hon. Champ Clark conducted the inquiry from the legislative point of view, and afterwards carried through the heavy work of reorganization in the House of Representatives. And a wonderfully able effort he made. It saved the life of the University, and enabled it to enter upon a period of progress and greatly increased usefulness. By this well nigh incomparable service to the State, Mr. Clark earned the title of "Founder of the University," in distinction from the College, which it had been before, and of which Major James S. Rollins was justly entitled to be called the Father.

It is not necessary to say anything more about Mr. See's college days, except to include here the commencement program, which tells its own story:

Forty-Seventh

ANNUAL

COMMENCEMENT.

Missouri State University,

Thursday Morning,

JUNE 6. 1889.

Statesman.

Program.

Music—Prayer—Music.

Thesis, - - - - - - John Locke and His Theories of Education.

RICHARD GEORGE HADELICH, Pe. P.

English Prize Essay, - - - - - - - The Poetry of Browning.

CHARLES HENRY STUMBERG, A. B., L. B.

MUSIC.

Stephens Medal Oration, - - - - - - - The World's Heroes

GEORGE FAUST YOUMANS, S. B.

Astronomical Prize Thesis, - - - - - Origin of Binary Stars.

THOMAS JEFFERSON JACKSON SEE, A. B., L. B., S. B.

MUSIC.

Valedictory Address of Law Class.

BYRON BUCKINGHAM BEERY, LL. B.

Valedictory Address of Academic Classes.

THOMAS JEFFERSON JACKSON SEE, A. B., L. B., S. B.

DELIVERY OF DIPLOMAS AND PRIZES.

Stephens Medal, - - - - - - GEORGE FAUST YOUMANS.

Astronomical Medal, - THOMAS JEFFERSON JACKSON SEE.

McAnally Medal, - - - - - CHARLES HENRY STUMBERG.

Appleton Prize, - - - - - - - JAMES HENRY COONS.

M. C. Lilly Sword Prize, - - - - - LUTHER YAGER KERR.

A Salute of Forty-Two Guns by University Cadets,

LIEUT. E. H. CROWDER, U. S. Army, Commandant.

GRADUATES OF 1889.

ACADEMIC COLLEGE.

First Rank (Av. grade 90-96.)

Thos. Jefferson Jackson See, A. B., L. B., S. B.
Charles Henry Stumberg, A. B., L. B.
Curtis Fletcher Marbut, S. B.
Louis Elmer Pitts, A. B.

Ulie Belle Denny, S. B.
George Faust Youmans, S. B.
Samuel David Gromer, S. B.

Second Rank. (Av. grade 70-90.)

Myron Alfred Corner, S. B.
Charles Breckenridge Faris, L. B.
James Thaddeus Dick, S. B.

Elston Holmes Lonsdale, S. B.
Mitchell Cross Shelton, A. B.
Sterling Price Dorman, L. B.

LAW COLLEGE. (Degree of LL. B.)

BACHELOR OF LAWS,
cum laude.
Byron Buckingham Beery.
George Alvin Dabbs.
BACHELOR OF LAWS.
William Kennedy Amick,
Rudolph Bahn,
Marion Richard Biggs,
Robert Alexander Brown,
James Peddicord Chinn,
Eugene Warrington Couey.
Thomas Jefferson Dickson,

Robert Terrel Haines.
Frank M. Howell,
Thomas Henry Jenkins.
Charles Fielding Keller,
William Echols Rainey,
Joseph Johnston Reynolds.
John Fletcher Sharp.
William Henry Utz.
Samuel Newton VanPool,
Conrad Waldecker,
Sam Mason Wallace.
John Samuel Wash.

William Henry Young.

ENGINEERING COLLEGE.

John Thomas Garrett, C. E.
Alexander Maitland, C. E.

William Florian Seidel, C. E.
Kirby Calhoun Weedin. C. E.

Orville Hickman Browning Turner, Top'l Eng'r.

CERTIFICATE IN SURVEYING.

Oliver Neal Axtell.
Charles Alden Bonfils.
Edgar Fisher Fielding.
Bernard Wilbern Hays.

Charles Decatur Potts.
Samuel Girard Ratekin.
Samuel William Shinkle.
Theodore Arthur Stumberg.

MEDICAL COLLEGE (Degree of M. D.)

[Eighty-three young men were graduated from section No. 2 (Missouri Medical College, St. Louis,) in March. Of this number, those given below received the joint Diploma of section No. 1 and section No. 2.

Arthur L. Eagle.
George J. Field.
George E. Gray.
Gustave A. Keehn.
John L. McGhee.
Alford R. McLeod.

Roscoe W. Maintz.
John D. Prowell.
Robert W. Renwick.
Rufus B. Schofield.
James H. Smith.

AGRICULTURAL COLLEGE, (Degree of B. A. S.)

Thomas Doss.

NORMAL COLLEGE.

Degree of Pe. B. (Bachelor of Pedagogics.)

Ulie Belle Denny, S. B.
Samuel David Gromer, S. B.
Myron Alfred Corner, S. B.

James Thaddeus Dick, S. B.
Elston Holmes Lonsdale, S. B.
Sterling Price Dorman, L. B.

Charles L. Mosely, L. B. '82.

Degree of Pe. P. (Principal in Pedagogics.)

Richard George Hadelich.
Una Verda Peters.
Anna Colvin Payne.
Minnie Ann Pettingill.
Eva Liggett.
Anna Maud Reed.
Carrie Maurer,
Maggie Chapman Maupin.
Ida May Knepper.
Wilber Fisk Johnston.
Gilbert Newton Harrison.
Ellen Winchester Dorsett.
Georgie Olive Nagel.

Fannie McNutt.
John Charles Storm.
Noah Elsworth Sutton.
Walter Caldwell Cox.
Jennie Lorena Hall.
Annie Margery Byrne.
Lula Graves.
Ida Orissa Post.
Eva Levy.
Ruby Moss Westlake.
Ella Bowden.
Amanda Bay Rucker.
Brookey Ann Yowell.

Sallie Pierce.

MASTER'S DEGREES. A. M.

Thomas L. Rubey, A. B. '85.

Edgar D. Watson, A. B. '86.

L. M.

Payne A. Boulton, L. B. '85.

Edward E. Longan, L. B. '86

S. M.

Wm. Wallace Clendenin, S. B. '86.

Ida May Clendenin, S. B. '86.

Honorable Mention.

1888-9.

All students, who have finished the work of any department, and who have reached in it an average grade of 96 to 100, shall be named by the Professor in charge of such department in his annual report to the President of the University for HONORABLE MENTION in the catalogue; this fact of honorable mention shall likewise be stated on the Commencement programme in the case of graduates. —[From rules for grading students, adopted April, 1884.]

DEPARTMENT OF CHEMISTRY.

MYRON ALFRED CORNER.
CURTIS FLETCHER MARBUT.
THOMAS JEFFERSON JACKSON SEE.
GEORGE FAUST YOUMANS.

DEPARTMENT OF ENGLISH.

CHARLES HENRY STUMBERG.
THOMAS JEFFERSON JACKSON SEE.

DEPARTMENT OF GEOLOGY AND MINERALOGY.

ELSTON HOLMES LONSDALE.
CURTIS FLETCHER MARBUT.
MITCHELL CROSS SHELTON.
THOMAS JEFFERSON JACKSON SEE.

DEPARTMENT OF HEBREW.

THOMAS JEFFERSON JACKSON SEE.

DEPARTMENT OF LATIN.

THOMAS JEFFERSON JACKSON SEE.
CHARLES HENRY STUMBERG.

DEPARTMENT OF METAPHYSICS.

JAMES THADDEUS DICK.
CHARLES HENRY STUMBERG.

DEPARTMENT OF MATHEMATICS AND ASTRONOMY.

THOMAS JEFFERSON JACKSON SEE.

DEPARTMENT OF BIOLOGY.

THOMAS JEFFERSON JACKSON SEE.

THE JAMES S. ROLLINS UNIVERSITY SCHOLARSHIPS.

These scholarships have been awarded as follows:

College of Arts, A. B. Course..............................JAMES HENRY COONS.
College of Arts, S. B. Course.........................CHARLES PAGE WILLIAMS.
College of Agriculture.......................................JOHN LEWIS TANDY.
College of Law..JAMES L. NICHOLAS.
College of Medicine...JOHN GARTH RUCKER.
College of Engineering, C. E. Course.... ....FRANK BLAIR WILLIAMS.

Next session begins September 10th.

On account of the action of the Legislature in reorganizing the University, this commencement was notable. Some weeks before it occurred Dr. Laws had spoken before the Legislature, in Jefferson City, but finding the tide there too strong for him, he had presented his resignation to the Governor, who held also the resignations of all the Curators. The Governor thereupon appointed a new Board of Curators, met with them at Columbia, and had them accept the resignation of the President of the University. This carried out the decree of the Legislature, and the University began to enter upon a new period of growth and greatly increased usefulness.

Governor Francis was always capable of doing the best thing, and is known as the best Governor Missouri ever had. By his presence at the Commencement he raised the spirits of everyone, and delivered the diplomas to the graduating class, at the head of which stood Mr. See, a great admirer of the Governor. When Mr. See had delivered the Valedictory address and received the Medal for his Thesis in Astronomy, the Governor remarked that he was the hero of the day; afterwards introduced him to Mrs. Francis, and offered him an official letter of introduction with the Seal of the State of Missouri on it, and duly countersigned by the Secretary of State, which proved of great value during his studies and travels abroad.

CHAPTER IV.

1889–1892.

THREE AND A HALF YEARS AT THE UNIVERSITY OF BERLIN.

POSTGRADUATE RECORD DISTINGUISHED FOR SCHOLARSHIP AND THE PUBLICATION OF FAMOUS THESIS ON THE ORIGIN OF DOUBLE STARS.

IMMEDIATELY after graduation at the University of Missouri, June 6, 1889, Mr. See returned home for a short visit, and then proceeded to Berlin, where he spent the next three and a half years in postgraduate study. Noah See naturally was greatly rejoiced over the high honors which his son had won, as the result of five years of hard work at the University of Missouri, and cordially approved his plan for study abroad. He realized the high promise of eminent distinction which the career of his son held out, and he desired to support him in every possible way. The visit home, however, was saddened by the father's failing health. It was considered very doubtful if he would live to see his son return from Germany, for the stay abroad was to extend over several years.

Yet with characteristic fatherly affection Noah See desired his son to go on with his educational career, which promised eventually to shed such renown on the family name. Accordingly he explained to his son the provisions of his Will, which made special arrangements to enable him to complete his education in Europe; and the executors were carefully enjoined to see that this trust was faithfully executed, the money thus advanced to Thomas J. J. See to be deducted from his share of the estate, on final settlement. With this provision for his financial support assured, Mr. See could go abroad with definite hope of completing his course of postgraduate study and obtaining the degree of Doctor of Philosophy, which would give him a favorable start in the world.

Young Mr. See was very loath to leave his father, in his feeble condition, but as the latter was well cared for at home, he finally started for Europe, his father merely cautioning him not to work too hard, and to "Remember that Rome was not built in a day." After reaching Berlin he corresponded with his father regularly till within a few weeks of the latter's death, which came earlier than had been expected, Feb. 9, 1890. Noah See showed a constant interest in all that his son did, and was very proud of the great name he was making in the world of science.

One of Mr. See's chief teachers at Berlin was the celebrated Professor Helmholtz, and the young man sent a picture of this master of science to his father, who had it framed and hung on the wall of his room. If Noah See could have foreseen that his son twenty years later would have become even more famous than the great Helmholtz, what is there that he would not have done for him? His cup of joy would have been filled to overflowing! Yet it is certain that his father must have expected for his son a great career, since from boyhood T. J. J. See made good in everything which he undertook, and even surpassed the expectations of his best friends. It was this characteristic of young Mr. See which enabled him to triumph over all difficulties, and to gain a decisive victory where others would have failed.

On the way to Europe, Mr. See spent several days in Washington, D. C., and saw the large telescope of the Naval Observatory, visited the Johns Hopkins University at Baltimore, where he met Professor Rowland; then stopped at Princeton, for a day with Professor Young; sailing from New York on the *Etruria*, June 22, and landing at Liverpool, June 30. From there he proceeded to London, but only remained overnight, and then visited Paris, for four days at the Exposition; and finally started for Berlin, July 5, and reached his destination next day.

The ocean passage on the *Etruria* was uneventful, but London impressed Mr. See as very noisy and as full of rush as New York

City.   Paris had the charm of great works of art, and magnificient buildings and monuments.   Mr. See saw as many of these as he could in four days, with a guide who knew the city.   The Arc de Triomphe, Napoleon's Tomb, the Louvre, the Pantheon, various museums, the Exposition, the National Observatory, and the Père la Chaise Cemetery and the grave of Laplace (found to have been removed) all claimed his attention.   At the Observatory Mr. See saw the beautiful statue of Leverrier holding the planet Neptune in his hand.   As he was not yet recognized as a professional man of science, but was still a student, he did not seek introductions to the French astronomers and mathematicians.

When Mr. See went to Europe, he did not know a living soul in that part of the world.   His loneliness therefore was considerable, and he desired to be at the University of Berlin as soon as possible.   When he reached there July 6, he found the summer semester of the University about to close, and hence he could do nothing till the autumn, except perfect his knowledge of German, and accustom the ear to the accent, so that he could follow lectures when the winter semester opened, in October.   He located at 97 Zimmer Strasse, about half a mile from the University, and an equal distance from the Royal Observatory.   This was a Pension, or boarding house with meals, and was kept by Frau Kähm. And while many of the boarders were transients, coming and going from time to time, others were there for whole seasons, and some for several years.   Members of the nobility, such as counts and barons, and diplomats, as well as high ranking officers of the German army dined there, and attended the dances held in the Pension occasionally.   And whilst Mr. See was too seriously occupied with his studies to take part in such gay functions, he saw something of them, and became acquainted with citizens of various countries — France, Russia, Sweden, Norway, Denmark, England, Italy, and Austria, but naturally the Germans predominated.

Very soon after his arrival in Berlin Mr. See had called on some of the leading professors of the University, to find out what studies he ought to take up preparatory to the lectures.   Thus he called on Helmholtz, Weierstrass, Fuchs, Foerster, and several others of the more renowned of his future teachers. It turned out that Professor Weierstrass was ill, but this illustrious mathematician received him with great kindness, and carefully advised him regarding the books which should be read, and then referred him to Professor Fuchs, as he (Weierstrass) had little hope of being able to lecture again. In their turn Fuchs and Foerster proved equally kind and helpful. Helmholtz too was approachable, and kind, but a man of few words, from a habit he had learned in childhood; and thus not easy to get much out of. Lord Rayleigh told Mr. See when he visited London in 1892 that he had once entertained Helmholtz in England, and found the same difficulty in conversing with him.

The lectures of Helmholtz were on mathematical physics, and naturally of the finest quality; for in the lecture room he had to talk. The finest lecturer in physics, however, was Professor Kundt, who was also a delightful man to work with in the laboratory. In mathematics the best lecturer was Fuchs, who had a slow methodical way which enabled the student to follow every step with entire clearness. Other important lecturers in mathematics from whom Mr. See profited were Knoblauch and Schwartz; and in astronomy, Foerster, Tietjen, Lehmann-Filhés, and Brendel.

In practical astronomy Mr. See was working with Professor V. Knorre, at the Royal Observatory, and for several months during the summer of 1891, in charge of the 9-inch equatorial telescope, just as he had formerly been in charge of the $7\frac{1}{2}$ inch telescope at the University of Missouri. This 9-inch telescope is famous as the one which Dr. Galle used in discovering Neptune, Sept. 23, 1846. Mr. See used it for measuring double stars, and his results were later included in one of the volumes of the Royal Observatory.

The fact that Mr. See, as an American student, had these priviliges showed the entire confidence and esteem in which he was held by the German professors. He had access to the Observatory Library, and a key to the building, so that he could come and go when he chose. When observing with the 9-inch telescope in 1891 Mr. See used to work till daylight, and Professor Foerster, Director of the Observatory, was more than once surprised to see him going home after the members of his own family were preparing for breakfast. It was by such serious effort that Mr. See made such a great reputation at the University of Berlin. Coming there in 1889 without a friend, he left there in 1892 with everyone his friend and unwilling to part with him.

Once in 1892 Emperor William visited the Observatory. While entertaining His Majesty, Professor Foerster told of the fine work being done there by a young American, Herr See. In this way Mr. See's fame spread to every department of the great University, and in fact all over Germany, and even to Italy, France, Russia, and England. It happened that in going back and forth to the University Mr. See would pass the Emperor almost daily, driving in his carriage, and dressed as a General of the German army. The Emperor always returned the salute, in military fashion, of those who greeted him on the street; and thus Mr. See became accustomed to this military salute, but of course he had no occasion to be presented to the Emperor.

When the Emperor of Russia visited Berlin, in 1891, Mr. See was admitted to the Ministry of Education, and thus obtained a close and excellent view of the great military parade, with the Emperors of Germany and Russia, Bismarck, and other high officials. These great military parades are one of the striking features of life in Berlin, and as the parades pass right in front of the University, the students naturally see much of them.

The study of the art treasures in the museums of Berlin was one of the chief delights of Mr. See's stay abroad. Sunday was free to all, and on many Sunday afternoons Mr. See would wend his way to one of the museums or to the National gallery, to study archælogy, statuary, painting, or some other form of the fine arts.

The course of lectures in the history of Greek philosophy under the renowned Professor Edward Zeller was especially attractive to Mr. See, for he revered Zeller as a kind of modern Plato, then nearly eighty years of age, but working on with the unabated

THE MAIN BUILDING OF THE UNIVERSITY OF BERLIN.

The statues of Wilhelm and Alexander von Humboldt are shown in the foreground. Professor See was so gratified with the high ideals maintained at this noble institution that he has often said that he could not recall one unfavorable incident during the three and one-half years he spent there. Accordingly it is well known that he looks back to the University of Berlin with increasing veneration.

ALEXANDER VON HUMBOLDT.

(From the portrait by Schrader, in possession of Albert Havemeyer, Esq., New York; Guyot's *Physical Geography*).

It was in May, 1802, that Humboldt was exploring the great volcanoes and other peaks of the Andes about Quito, and forming the impressions which so powerfully influenced his writings. Exactly 104 years later, May, 1906, an interest in earthquakes and Volcanoes which Humboldt and his writings had awakened in boyhood, enabled Professor See to discover the true laws of Earthquakes and Mountain Formation, as a result of the earthquake at San Francisco, and the revival of early studies in the Physics of the Earth.

zeal and enthusiasm of youth. The great Zeller literally lived for truth, like Plato in ancient times, and was so revered by all that Mr. See was especially proud to have this venerable and good man as one of his examiners, when he made his doctor's degree, December 10, 1892.

Before such examinations are held the candidate for the degree, in evening dress and white gloves, calls on the Professors chosen as his examiners, by consent of the university dean, and invites them to be present and take part in the examination. When Mr. See called on Professor Zeller he found the venerable philosopher in his study, with a book in hand, but with sight so defective that it had to be held at very close range. If an aged professor has such enthusiasm for "Light, more Light," as Goethe said, how much more zeal, thought Mr. See, ought a young man have for the advancement of truth? The effect of Zeller's example on Mr. See was profound, though no one ever had need to tell him to work; yet in adversity it is said that this recollection has more than once sustained him.

One other very inspiring influence was Mr. See's visits to the country seat of Alexander von Humboldt, at Tageldorf, a suburb of Berlin. Here the student who read the *Cosmos* in boyhood beheld the homes of the Humboldt brothers — Wilhelm, the founder of the Berlin University, and Alexander, the great naturalist — and often visited the graves of these illustrious men in the pine forest north of the house, to pluck an ivy souvenir, or to view the beautiful park about it, with the tawny deer playing among the bushes. As Alexander von Humboldt had been the inspiration of Mr. See's boyhood days, and now, by good fortune, he attended the University founded by Wilhelm, and he himself wished to be an investigator of the physical universe, the pilgrimage was natural and appropriate. Besides, Mr. See's old teacher Professor Paul Schweitzer, had been born in Berlin, and had acted as assistant to Gustave Rose, the eminent chemist who accompanied Alexander von Humboldt on the trip to Central Asia. Thus he was drawn to the home of the Humboldts by ties of peculiar interest, while his own thoughts were centered on the study of the physical universe.

During the stay of three years at Berlin, Mr. See often visited Potsdam, to see the palaces, and the astrophysical observatory; so that he formed an intimate acquaintance with all the surroundings of the German capital. Mr. See was especially impressed with the classic style in art and architecture so generally followed by the Germans; and with the classic spirit in the University of Berlin, which was originally introduced by Wilhelm von Humboldt and his contemporaries and firmly maintained in more recent times. Without a classic education Mr. See would have been out of sympathy with his beautiful surroundings, but as he had wisely pursued those very studies before specializing in science, he could in spirit visit Athens or Rome any Sunday afternoon, by going to the museum.

This awakened in Mr. See a profound interest in classic things, and led him to visit successively Italy, Egypt, and Greece. The trip to Italy was made in company with Professor D. W. Shea of the Catholic University, Washington, D. C., in March and April, 1890; and included stops at Basel, Turin, Milan, Pisa, Naples, Pompei, Vesuvius, Baiae, Pozzuoli, Rome, Florence, Orvieto, Venice, Verona, Munich, and Leipzig. It would take up too much space to describe this wonderful journey, and we must be content with saying that it included the objects of highest intellectual interest in each place. Thus, at Naples, Vesuvius was ascended, owing to Mr. See's life-long interest in volcanoes, while Pompei was visited for the best available insight into the Roman cities of the first century, A. D. At Pisa and Florence on the other hand, special attention was paid to the things associated with Galileo,—such as the leaning tower, and swinging lamp at Pisa, and the first toy-like telescopes and other relics preserved at Florence. The grandeur and inspiration of the scenes and antiquities at Rome simply beggar description. It must suffice to say that here one is on holy ground, and in the Roman Forum the traveler still walks on the very same stones on which Caesar's legions trod nearly 2,000 years ago.

KAULBACH'S PAINTING OF HOMER AND THE GREEKS, NATIONAL GALLERY, BERLIN.
One of Professor See's favorite objects of study.

The stay in Lower Egypt was limited to about ten days (March 5-15, 1891), and Memphis was as far south as Mr. See journeyed. But it enabled satisfactory visits to be made to the Pyramids and other objects about Cairo; gave good views of the desert, and the clear skies of Egypt, famed in the history of astronomy, as well as of the Southern Constellations, such as the Ship Argus, with the brilliant Canopus, and the stars of the Centaur. At Alexandria effort was made to locate the site of the ancient library and museum, where Hipparchus and Ptolemy labored 2,000 years ago; but so little excavation has been done there that the locations are doubtful, and only the general surroundings of the Alexandrian school of astronomy could be studied with any success. Mr. See recalls that on the morning as the ship from Trieste neared Alexandria the stars appeared very bright, and Venus actually shone by reflection from the waves of the sea.

From Lower Egypt Mr. See crossed over to Athens, for a visit of six weeks in Greece. It would take too long to describe the wonders of this center of Greek civilization, but it may suffice to say that of all the places visited by Mr. See in the old world, Athens is the one he most admires, from the point of view of wonderful skies of blue and violet, and other natural scenery, art and history. As a student trying to make the most of his opportunities he visited the most interesting sights, the ruins about Athens; including all parts of the Acropolis, the temples, and the museums; Mount Pentelikon, Eleusis, Ægina, and the Homeric cities of Tyrins and Mycenae; and also Corinth, Delphi, and Olympia. The olive groves in which Plato taught had an especial charm for Mr. See. The visit to Delphi also proved of very great interest, as well as that to Olympia, where the Hermes of Parxitelles, excavated by the Germans in 1871 is recognized to be the most beautiful statue ever created by the chisel of a sculptor. At Pyrgos, on the way to Olympia, the party* experienced a considerable

---

*Mr. See, two students from Cambridge, and two from Oxford, including Mr. J. L. Myres, now Professor of Ancient History in the University of Oxford.

earthquake, which caused general alarm among the people.   From Olympia Mr. See returned to Berlin by way of Corfu, Trieste, and Vienna.

The spring vacation of 1892 was spent in England, and was of very great importance, on account of the lifelong friendships which Mr. See formed with eminent astronomers and mathematicians. Naturally he visited the great universities of Oxford and Cambridge, and the principal places of interest about London, such as the British Museum, Natural History Museum, Westminster Abbey, the House of Parliament, the Royal Society, Royal Astronomical Society, Royal Observatory, etc.   He met and was entertained by Professors Darwin and Forsyth in Cambridge, and by the fellows of St. John's College.   He was also entertained in London by Sir William and Lady Huggins, the founders of *Astrophysics*; Miss A. M. Clarke, the historian of astronomy; and Mr. A. C. Ranyard. a well known astronomer, who had a private observatory.   In traveling to England via Rotterdam and returning via Antwerp, Mr. See was enabled to enjoy a bird's-eye view of Holland and Belgium.

Mr. See had now remained in Germany so long that he was anxious to return to America as quickly as possible after his examination. His *Inaugural Dissertation*, was printed in advance of the examination, except the title page, and on December 10, 1892, he was granted the degrees of Doctor of Philosophy and Master of Arts, with high honors.   His thesis at once made a great reputation, and was much discussed all over Europe. At the public disputation in the aula of the university, when the degree was conferred, it was remarked by several of Dr. See's professors in attendance, that it was one of the most beautiful ceremonies that they had ever seen, and that Dr. See spoke German almost as fluently and accurately as a native, which is seldom true of the foreign students taking degrees in Germany.   It is now twenty years since Dr. See left Berlin, but it is well known that he still speaks German fluently, and often delights his German friends by conversing with them in their own language.

CHAPTER V.

1893–1896.

FOUR YEARS AT THE UNIVERSITY OF CHICAGO.

ESTABLISHMENT OF THE DEPARTMENT OF ASTRONOMY — STARTING
OF THE YERKES OBSERVATORY, AND PUBLICATION OF THE FIRST
VOLUME OF RESEARCHES ON THE EVOLUTION OF THE STELLAR
SYSTEMS.

IMMEDIATELY after graduating at the University of Berlin, December 10, 1892, Dr. See sailed from Bremen for New York, December 13, on the North German Lloyd steamship *Saale*. He landed at New York Christmas day, the passage having been slow and so stormy that the ship was four days late, and general alarm felt for her safety, when at last she was sighted covered with snow and ice. The New York newspapers of Christmas morning had scare headlines: "Where is the Saale?" This was of course before the days of wireless telegraphy, and at that time a ship had to be observed before its arrival or whereabouts could be ascertained.

While traveling in Egypt, Mr. See had met at the Hotel de Nile, in Cairo, March 6, 1891. Professor Eri B. Hulbert of the old University of Chicago. The meeting was quite accidental, but Dr. Hulbert liked Mr. See so well, after traveling with him about Cairo, that he entrusted to him some pictures of their party taken on camels at the Pyramids; and said that after his journey to the Holy Land, he would visit Berlin and claim the pictures. At that time Mr. See only knew Mr. Hulbert was from Chicago, but had no inkling that he was connected with the University. What was Mr. See's surprise, when his traveling friend reappeared in Berlin, claimed his pictures, and then told him that he (Hulbert) was a professor at the University of Chicago, a colleague of Dr.

Harper, the president of the new university, and wanted See to join the faculty at Chicago when he finished his studies in Berlin? Dr. Hulbert then said that he had written to Dr. Harper about Mr. See, and that he (Harper) would be in Berlin that winter (1891–2). At that time little was thought of the matter, but later sure enough Dr. Harper came to Berlin, as Dr. Hulbert had said he would; and of course Mr. See met Dr. Harper at the home of Rev. Dr. J. H. W. Stuckenberg, the pastor of the American church in Berlin, who kept open house once a week, for the American colony. It was generally known that Dr. Harper was buying books and libraries and selecting professors for the new university; and he had therefore consulted with Dr. Stuckenberg and others, but Mr. See made no application for any position at Chicago, nor had he talked with Dr. Harper about the plans the latter was developing.

It turned out, however, that Dr. Stuckenberg had recommended Mr. See, just as Dr. Hulbert had done, and therefore when Mr. See was at length in sight of his doctor's degree, and he wrote President Harper at Chicago that he would be seeking a position later for 1893, the president immediately replied, wishing Mr. See to join the faculty at Chicago, and aid him in securing an observatory to cost from $200,000 to $300,000. This was in July, 1892, before anything had been done about the Yerkes observatory. Things moved rapidly at Chicago, however, and before the negotiations with Mr. See were concluded, Mr. George E. Hale, who had a private observatory in Chicago, was brought into relationship to the University; and Mr. Hale and Dr. Harper together prevailed on Mr. Yerkes to buy the 40-inch glass discs, then lying unground in the shops of Alvan Clark & Sons, Cambridgeport, Mass., for the lenses of what has since become the great telescope of the Yerkes Observatory. It seems that Mr. Hale had written Mr. Yerkes a letter asking if he would *consider buying the discs*; and when he replied in the affirmative, Dr. Harper and Mr. Hale secured his promise of the required funds, about October 1, 1892. This was the beginning of the Yerkes Observatory.

PROFESSOR E. B. HULBERT, MR. T. J. J. SEE, AND MR. H. K. WHITE,
At the Pyramids, in Egypt, March 14, 1891.

When Dr. See reached Chicago the day after Christmas, 1892, many of the departments of the University, which had opened October 1, were just being organized, some of the classes meeting in sheds, stores, and other temporary buildings. His first business was to organize the department of astronomy. As he was familiar with the work in astronomy at the great universities of Berlin and Cambridge, he naturally tried to plan similar work at Chicago, though its full development could only come gradually. His first classes in the calculation of orbits of comets had about eight graduate students, which was very satisfactory, considering the attendance of only about two hundred students at the University.

Up to July 1, 1893, the fees from students allowed Dr. See, as Docent, were only about $150.00; and it was therefore arranged to advance his position to assistant, which would pay $800.00 per annum, and be self-supporting for a young man. The work of the department was rapidly developed and it was not long till it was recognized everywhere as one of the best in the country.

Meanwhile the mounting of the large telescope was finished by Warner & Swasey of Cleveland, Ohio, and exhibited at the World's Fair, about two miles from the University. The grinding of the glass discs, on the other hand, was a much slower process than making the mounting, yet this optical work was making some progress. During the winter of 1893-4 Mr. Hale was abroad for study and some solar observations on Mt. Aetna. Everything seemed to hang fire about the observatory, and no progress seemed to be in sight, beyond what had been done by Warner & Swasey, and the grinding of lenses by Alvan Clark & Sons.

It should be said in this connection that Professor S. W. Burnham, long famed as the greatest double star observer in the world, had quit Lick Observatory in California, in August, 1892, and thus he was in Chicago when Mr. Yerkes agreed to give the funds for the glass discs, October 1, 1892. He held a very lucrative, and not very onerous but very responsible position as clerk of the United States Court, and had his offices in the old post office building. Burnham thus had no connection with the University, but it was understood that he was to have such connection as soon as the Observatory was built. Naturally in his private situation he could do nothing to promote the progress of the Observatory. In the summer of 1894 Professor Hale returned from Europe, and took steps to establish the *Astrophysical Journal,* and yet there was not the least sign of any progress about the Observatory. The site had not been selected, no buildings had been started, and it looked as though it might be years before anything was done.

Now it happened that the promised advancement of Dr. See and Dr. Laves at the University was predicated on the building of the Yerkes Observatory; and as this was hung up, there was a dubious prospect ahead for all concerned — Burnham, Hale, See, and Laves, as well as those whom it was hoped to have associated with the Observatory later, of whom Professor Barnard was the most famous.

In this state of general paralysis, about October 1, 1894, Dr. See called to interview President Harper as to the cause for the apparently indefinite delay in the building of the Observatory. He was told that the running of the Observatory was estimated to cost $30,000 per annum, and there was no avaiable source of income adequate to meet this demand, nor likely to be any during the rest of the present (19th) century — thus there was nothing in view but waiting for six years at least. "I like to get gifts for the University, but I am worried to death to find funds for the maintenance of the Observatory after it is built!" pathetically cried President Harper. Dr. See assured him that he could show him how to start the Observatory on the available income of the University; and, at the president's request, submitted a plan, a few days later, which accomplished this object, so that the building began immediately.

Dr. See's plan consisted in cutting down the inflated budget, on the principle that necessities come before luxuries, and a child must crawl before it can walk. So also if an Observatory can get started, and make a record for efficiency, it too should grow and prosper; while by planning for the impossible it might be delayed

THE YERKES OBSERVATORY OF THE UNIVERSITY OF CHICAGO.

Professor See aided in establishing it in 1894, when the plans were about to fail.

for many years, or never get started at all. Mr. Yerkes died in 1905, and if it had not been built during his life-time, the whole matter probably would have fallen through and come to nothing. Accordingly whatever the Yerkes Observatory has accomplished must be ascribed largely to the timely help of Dr. See.

As the outcome of this forward movement Burnham at once became officially connected with the University as professor of practical astronomy, while still holding his office in the court. Barnard was called to Chicago from Lick Observatory in California, and the site selected and work rushed forward at such a rate that the Observatory was opened for observations and formally dedicated in September, 1897, with an address by Professor Simon Newcomb of Washington.

The importance of this founding and opening of the Yerkes Observatory for American science has been considerable; for it has now had sixteen years of creditable activity, and that many years of the life of Burnham and Barnard have been usefully employed, whereas they were likely to be largely wasted, under the unfortunate conditions existing prior to 1894 both at Lick and at Chicago. Moreover enlarged opportunities have been opened for Frost, Ritchey and others. Dr. See also was rewarded for his untiring efforts, but not at Chicago.

It is well known that President Harper greatly appreciated the services of Dr. See at the University, yet he ungratefully let him leave, probably hoping thereby to placate the jealously of Professor Hale, who is said to have blamed Dr. See for the reduction of the inflated budget, which alone made possible the building of the Yerkes Observatory. It might be unfortunate that the University could not better provide for the support of the Observatory; yet it was obviously better to have a half loaf than no bread, since with half a loaf it was possible to live and struggle for more, whereas without it even the struggle could not be kept up.

We must now dwell on Professor See's scientific work at the University of Chicago. It has already been pointed out that from the first he had a goodly number of students, including some of very great promise, such as the late Mr. George K. Lawton, Professor F. R. Moulton, and Professor Eric Doolittle, and thirty or forty others now holding responsible positions in various colleges, universities and observatories. Dr. See's work and department stood high at the University, but he felt that he labored at a great disadvantage because of his rank being only that of instructor, whereas many members of the faculty of nothing like his qualifications and experience were given the rank of assistant professor, associate professor, or even professor.

Accordingly when Professor Percival Lowell, early in 1896, offered him an opportunity to make a survey of the Southern Heavens for the discovery and measurement of double stars, Dr. See accepted it. President Harper then offered him leave of absence, with the rank of assistant professor, but Dr. See insisted that for obvious reasons it should be associate professor, the same as that held by Professor Hale. When President Harper could not see his way to grant that, Dr. See declined the assistant professorship and merely went away, on leave, yet not expecting to return, because it was evident that at the University of Chicago nothing was being done on merit.

Soon after coming to Chicago in December, 1892, Dr. See had come to be closely associated with Professor S. W. Burnham, the greatest known authority on double stars. See would frequently visit Burnham each week, and sometimes every few days, to get a list of observations, for the calculation of the orbits of particular double stars; for it was found in 1893 that all the published orbits required revision, on the basis of recent observations, and by the shorter and simpler methods which had been worked out by Burnham and See.   This work finally included the revision of the orbits of forty double stars, and occupied Dr. See about three years, from the summer of 1893 to 1896.

It was also made to embrace a critical mathematical investigation into the action of central forces, with a new spectroscopic method for testing the law of Newtonian gravitation among the stellar systems. This latter work was published in July, 1895, and attracted universal attention, because it had been held by such authorities as Professor Asaph Hall of the Naval Observatory, at Washington, (cf. article in the *Astronomical Journal*, Vol. VIII) that it would never be possible to really test or prove the operation of the Newtonian law among the double stars, but that we could merely make it more and more probable, by adding to the number of orbits investigated.

Dr. See had been occupied with this question at Berlin in 1890, and had then prepared a small paper on the subject, and now he gave it the final form, showing that a real test is actually possible, with the highest degree of rigor attainable in the observations of the fixed stars, by means of the combination of the micrometer and spectrograph. The latter instrument is a photographic spectroscope for determining the motion in the line of sight, by the method of slight displacement of the spectral lines, developed by Huggins in 1868. Dr. See thus completed the methods for testing the validity of the Newtonian law of attraction throughout the sidereal universe, and they have since been used by Professors Campbell and Wright of Lick Observatory, on Alpha Centauri, Sirius, and other double stars.

During the month of April, 1895, Dr. See was making observations at the Leander McCormick Observatory of the University of Virginia, and in August at the Washburn Observatory of the University of Wisconsin, to secure the latest positions of the companions of certain double stars. With the assistance of his postgraduate students Lawton, Moulton and Doolittle he was rapidly completing the forty orbits, which were to be made the basis of the first volume of the famous *Researches on the Evolution of the Stellar Systems*. President Harper had agreed to have this work published by the University when finished.

Finally, in the spring of 1896, all was ready for the press, but the excuse was made that no funds were available, for the University to do its part with; and so Dr. See had to publish it at his own expense. About the time Dr. See was disheartened by this breach of faith on the part of the University, after all his labor in doing the work, he received a telegram from Professor Percival Lowell to undertake the survey of the double stars of the Southern Hemisphere with the 24-inch telescope at Flagstaff, Arizona, and at the City of Mexico. The first volume of Dr. See's *Researches* appeared in January, 1897, while he was at the City of Mexico, surveying the brilliant region of the ship Argus, Centaurus, and the Southern Cross, in which many important new double stars were discovered.

As this volume of *Researches* was essentially finished at Chicago, and only the proof read at his home in Montgomery City, and later at the Lowell Observatory, we may state here that the volume was everywhere recognized as setting a new standard in double star astronomy. The enthusiasm over the work was general throughout the scientific world. Thus Lord Kelvin wrote Dr. See as follows:

The University, Glasgow, March 20th, 1897.

Dear Dr. See:—

I thank you very much for your letter of January 7, and the accompanying copy of your new work "On the Evolution of the Stellar Systems," which you have kindly sent me and which I duly received. It is a splendid book and full of matter most interesting to me.

Double star astronomy has always been exceedingly interesting in giving us some fundamental information of systems in different parts of the Universe analogous to our Solar System in respect to orbital motion under gravitational force but different from ours in that grand detail of two suns instead of one. And the interest is now greatly enhanced by the revelations of physical properties and of velocities relatively to our system which spectrum analyses have given us within the last thirty-three years.

I enclose an extract from a letter which I received from Tisserand only a few months before his death, by which you will judge how eagerly I looked to your Chapter 3, §4, and how interested I was

LORD KELVIN, (1824–1907)

From a photograph by Falk, New York, 1902. The most eminent British Natural Philosopher of the past century, and one of the foremost of all time. He was one of the first British authorities to adopt See's discoveries on the Constitution of the Sun and on the Cause of Earthquakes and Mountain Formation.

PROFESSOR G. V. SCHIAPARELLI, OF MILAN. (1835–1910).

The most eminent Italian astronomer since the time of Galileo, and one of the first to adopt Professor See's Theories in Cosmogony and Geogony. He was so impressed with the discovery of the Cause of Earthquakes and Mountain Formation, that, although at an advanced age, he addressed young Professor See as "Revered Colleague."

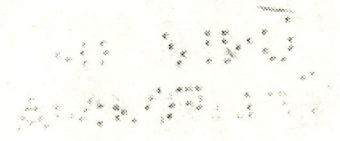

to find in it the italicized paragraph on page 251. The physical cause of the great eccentricities of the orbits of double stars is certainly a very important subject for investigation or speculation.

I hope the continuation of your work may prosper and that before very long we may have a second volume.

Believe me, with kind regards, yours truly,

KELVIN.

From Milan the illustrious Italian astronomer Schiaparelli wrote that Dr. See's *Researches* "would constitute the third great epoch in double star astronomy since those of W. Herschel and W. Struve." To understand this fully we should recall that Sir William Herschel first discovered and proved the existence of double stars by the observations made with his great telescopes from 1780 to 1802; while the celebrated William Struve of Dorpat, Russia, first carried on a systematic campaign for measuring over three thousand double stars, 1825–1837, and published the results in his famous *Mensurae Micrometricae*, Petersburg, 1838. Thus Herschel had found out that double stars exist, and proved that some of them are in motion; while Struve had investigated the motions on an extensive scale, with a view to determining their orbits. These were the two great epochs in double star astronomy, and Schiaparelli declared that the third great epoch (troisième grande époque) would be made by Dr. See's *Researhes on the Evolution of the Stellar Systems*, by which the origin of these wonderful systems would be explained.

What Schiaparelli predicted, in 1897, is now a matter of history. For it is now universally recognized that Dr. See's *Researches* have marked the third great epoch in double star astronomy, and that it is fully as important as the original epoch made by Sir William Herschel, or the later great epoch made by the systematic observations of W. Struve, at Dorpat, and subsequently at Poulkowa. The classic achievements of Herschel and Struve have been repeated in the different and much more difficult line of Cosmogony by America's famous astronomer, T. J. J. See.

CHAPTER VI.

1896–1898.

TWO YEARS AT THE LOWELL OBSERVATORY, FLAGSTAFF, ARIZONA, AND AT THE CITY OF MEXICO.

SURVEYING THE DOUBLE STARS OF THE SOUTHERN CELESTIAL HEMISPHERE. — LECTURES ON SIDEREAL ASTRONOMY AT LOWELL INSTITUTE, BOSTON, 1899.

UP to the time Dr. See joined the Lowell Observatory he was known chiefly as a mathematician and calculator of orbits of double stars. As astronomers are in many cases, unfortunately, either mere observers with the telescope, and almost without knowledge of the mathematical branches of the science, or, on the other hand, mere mathematicians and equally devoid of a practical knowledge of the heavens as derived from the use of the telescope, Dr. See became impressed with the view that to obtain a really deep knowledge of the universe as it is, one must be both a mathematician and a telescopic explorer of the heavens.

Accordingly after careful consideration he deemed it advisable to accept Professor Lowell's generous offer of an opportunity to survey the Southern Heavens. Some of the mathematicians, such as Dr. G. W. Hill, of New York, probably thought that Dr. See was making a mistake to give up his mathematical researches, even temporarily, to do telescopic work; but Dr. See had before him the example of the two Herschels, and wisely decided that intimate knowledge of the heavens was as necessary now as it was a century ago. He rightly believed that it is the one-sidedness of most modern investigators that prevents them from obtaining the breadth of view required for the greatest advances in science. Since Professor See's revolutionary work in

THE TOWN OF FLAGSTAFF, ARIZONA, WITH VIEW OF THE SAN FRANCISCO MOUNTAINS TO THE NORTHWEST.

They are situated ten miles to the north of the Lowell Observatory, which is to the left of the town as shown here. The mountains rise about 13,000 feet above sea level, and thus 6,000 feet higher than the Observatory. The tops of the mountains usually are covered with snow, and bear still flourish in the surrounding forests.

establishing a New Science of Cosmogony (1910), it is certain that his intuition of 1896 was right; for no one but an astronomer of the widest experience could have sustained this comprehensive creative effort, which marks one of the greatest epochs in the history of astronomy.

Before joining Professor Lowell at Flagstaff, Arizona, about August 1, 1896, Dr. See spent some three months, May to July, at his home near Montgomery City. Prior to leaving Chicago he had planned for the work of the department of astronomy, during his absence, and had the work of instruction divided between Dr. Laves and Mr. Moulton. Mr. Moulton was considered by Dr. See one of his ablest students, and President Harper had appointed him (Moulton) upon Dr. See's sole recommendation, without even seeing the young man — so great was the President's confidence in any recommendation submitted by Dr. See.

While visiting his Mother at Montgomery City, in June, 1896, Dr. See suffered a mild attack of typhoid fever. It lasted some twenty days, and left him weak, and somewhat emaciated, though not extremely so. Accordingly when he first joined the Lowell Observatory he had not yet fully recovered, and had to begin heavy work by easy stages.

Professor Lowell was accompanied to Arizona by two assistants, Mr. A. E. Douglass, and Mr. D. A. Drew; Alvan G. Clark, the telescope maker; a secretary, Miss W. L. Leonard; and Dr. See and his assistant, Mr. W. A. Cogshall, who were occupied with the double star work. Mr. Clark went along chiefly to see that all was right with the lens as finally fitted in its cell. The party reached Flagstaff, over the Atchison, Topeka & Santa Fe Railroad, during the last week in July,— Dr. See and Mr. Cogshall coming two days later than the rest, owing to arrangements for the shipping of books which he had to be made in Chicago, where the party first assembled.

The town of Flagstaff is in a desert, on the high plateau of Northern Arizona, about 7,000 feet above the sea, and the observatory is on Mars' Hill about a mile west of the town. The astronomers had to live at some of the hotels*, and climb the hill of some four hundred feet elevation in going to their observations. The observatory is surrounded by a magnificient pine forest and the location is beautiful, except for the dryness, which, however, is necessary for the best conditions in the investigations of the heavenly bodies. All astronomical observations have to be made through the terrestrial atmosphere, and in order to secure steady seeing the observatory ought to be in a dry climate, and also on a high plateau, which is above the densest part of the atmosphere. Such was the site selected by Professor Lowell for his Observatory in Arizona, at which so much famous work has been done.

The citizens of Flagstaff were very appreciative of the Lowell Observatory, in fact it was the pride of the whole territory. People came from all over the southwest to visit the observatory, as well as from Chicago, New York and Boston, and even from Europe.

Professor Lowell had great enthusiasm for his favorite study of the planet *Mars*. Thousands upon thousands of drawings and sketches were made and afterwards digested and discussed in the *Annals of the Lowell Observatory*, as well as in more popular books. In this way Professor Lowell not only made his observations, but got them before the world in an impressive form. Accordingly ever since 1894 Lowell has been generally recognized as the highest authority on the observations of the surfaces of the planets.

Dr. See's work consisted in sweeping the southern heavens for the discovery of new double stars. His zone of work began at about fifteen and extended to about sixty-five degrees south declination. Accordingly it included over half the southern celestial hemisphere, but of course a period of two years was not enough time in which to make the survey exhaustive. The southern most part of the work could only be done at the City of Mexico. The

---

* While living at the Grand Cañon Hotel Dr. See had the serious misfortune to lose his library, valuable correspondence and many personal effects by fire, September 14, 1897. He had to flee from the burning building at three o'clock in the morning, carrying the unpublished records of the Lowell Observatory under one arm, and Bowditch's Translation of Laplace's *Mécanique Céleste* under the other—the latter being deemed priceless among the valuable books of the library.

THE 24-INCH TELESCOPE OF THE LOWELL OBSERVATORY, AS MOUNTED IN
THE DOME AT FLAGSTAFF, ARIZONA, 1896.

The telescope is here shown east of the pier, but in the Double Star work of Dr. See usually
was reversed, so as to be on the other side.

observatory was in Mexico city, however, only during the winter months of 1896–7; the observations at that southernmost point being all included within the months of January, February and March, 1897. And hence by far the larger part of the double star work was done at Flagstaff. Yet while at Mexico, the extremely favorable location, within nineteen degrees of the equator, enabled Dr. See to reach all the stars of the Southern hemisphere except those in the small cap within twenty-five degrees of the South Pole; and it is needless to say that every moment of the time available during the three months was utilized to the utmost.

At Flagstaff the double-star work often would begin at sunset, and extend till about eleven o'clock, when the *Mars* work would have preference; and then, when several hours had been devoted to Mars, the double-star work might be resumed again towards daylight. This breaking of the double-star work into two parts made it hard on Dr. See and Mr. Cogshall, but it was not felt so severely except at the City of Mexico, where nearly every night was clear, and no time could be lost, owing to the shortness of the stay in that southern location. Accordingly, at Mexico double stars had to be taken both morning and evening, of every available night, and the observers always went home just as the Southern Cross was fading away on the southern horizon, where it shone with great beauty over the mountains lying in that direction.

The usual practice in the sweeping was for Mr. Cogshall to look through the finder and bring the stars into the field of the large telescope, while Dr. See examined them with various magnifying powers, according to circumstances. It did not take long practice before Dr. See could tell almost at a glance whether a star had a companion or not, but in some cases he had to wait for the image of the star to get quiet, or put on higher power, before he could make out the existence of a companion with entire clearness and certainty. Then it was necessary to revolve the micrometer and measure the position angle and distance at which the companion was seen. While Dr. See was making the measures, Mr.

Cogshall sketched the stars in the field of the finder and recorded the micrometer measures in a book kept at hand for the purpose.

As a rule the dome of the observatory was turned so as to leave the opening pointed a little to the west of south, and the stars were therefore observed just after they had passed over the meridian. This was found to be the most favorable position for work, and by taking the stars as they went by it saved constantly moving the dome, which would have consumed much time and proved to be very troublesome. By working for five or six hours, Dr. See and Mr. Cogshall used often to examine at least a thousand of the larger stars in the region swept over. This usually included a belt of the sky about a degree wide, or twice the diameter of the Moon, and extending one-fourth of the way around the heavens. Such sweeps did not always include every bright star in the region traversed, for in measuring the stars found to have companions, some would pass by and have to be left for another occasion.

At Mexico City the time was so precious that the telescope was pointed first on the naked eye stars, so conspicuously bright in that region, and then on those which were invisible to the naked eye. Among the important stellar systems thus discovered at Mexico City may be mentioned Eta Centauri, Alpha Phoenicis, p Velorum, d Centauri, and many others. Some are pairs of nearly equal stars, lying almost in contact, under the highest telescopic power; others are composed of a faint companion close to a bright star; while still others have excessively faint companions far away, and just barely visible to the keenest eye in the best seeing. About a dozen of these objects looked like planets shining by reflected light. Their color usually was almost black. The double stars thus present an amazing variety of phenomena and some are very highly colored. The tints usually are combinations of yellow or reddish light for the larger stars with bluish or purple companions.

When Dr. See entered upon this survey of the southern double stars but little work of importance had been done there since the

SWEEPING FOR THE DISCOVERY OF NEW DOUBLE STARS, AT THE CITY OF MEXICO.
In this view Dr. See is at the finder and Mr. Cogshall at the large telescope. Dr. See frequently changed place with his associate, in order that the latter might have a chance to share in the work of discovery.

THE DOME OF THE LOWELL OBSERVATORY AT TACUBAYA, MEXICO.

In this view the Dome is turned to the east

memorable survey carried out by Sir John Herschel at the Cape of Good Hope half a century before (1834–1838). But it happened that while Dr. See was working at the Lowell Observatory, Mr. R. T. A. Innes was working also at the Royal Observatory, Cape of Good Hope. Sometimes Dr. See would announce his discoveries to Mr. Innes, after they were already independently noted at the Cape; and, *vice versa*, Mr. Innes would send notice of discoveries at the Cape which Dr. See already had secured sometime earlier at Lowell Observatory. It is agreeable to note that this rivalry always was of the most generous nature, each freely conceding to the other whatever belonged to him.

The survey of Dr. See extended over only two years, the tentative plans for extending it further south, by locating the observatory in Peru, having to be given up, because of a nervous breakdown unexpectedly experienced by Professor Lowell. This illness lasted over some two years, and meanwhile Dr. See had become Professor of Mathematics in the United States Navy, and was in charge of the 26-inch telescope of the Naval Observatory at Washington.

Although not completed, owing to Lowell's unexpected illness, the effect of Dr. See's double-star survey throughout the world was considerable. It stimulated effort in all southern observatories, and even helped the double-star work at Lick Observatory, and at many other places in America as well as at Greenwich, Potsdam, Poulkowa, Paris, Brussels, and other observatories in Europe. In his introduction to Mr. Innes' "Reference Catalogue of Southern Double Stars," published by the Royal Observatory, Cape of Good Hope, in 1899, Sir David Gill, H. M. Astronomer, speaks of this work of See and Innes as follows:

"Up to the present time no general catalogue of the double stars of the Southern Hemisphere has been published. The observer who desired to work in this field of research has, therefore, been compelled either to expend much time in searching for suitable objects in the sky, or to consult and compare many different publications, in order to find the objects most likely to repay labor, with such means as may be at his disposal.

"Greater activity may, in future, be confidently looked for in double-star work, owing to the increased number of suitable instruments recently erected in the Southern hemisphere. A strong additional stimulus will undoubtedly be given by the example of Dr. See's labors in this comparatively unexplored field, and by the publication of his *Researches on the Evolution of the Stellar Systems.*"

Fourteen years after these words are written we find Sir David Gill's predictions fully verified. Mr. Innes for some years has been doing a great deal of double-star work at Johannesburg, in the Transvaal; and Professor W. J. Hussey of the Detroit Observatory, University of Michigan, is now in La Plata, extending his double-star work over the unexplored regions near the South Pole. It is probable that within five or ten years, several thousand more new double stars will be discovered in the Southern Hemisphere. As a sequel to Dr. See's survey at the Lowell Observatory, this is all very interesting, and very encouraging to those who believe in scientific progress. Without this work of Dr. See, as Sir David Gill hints, in the above extract, little or none of this work of exploration is likely to have been undertaken.

At the City of Mexico very considerable public interest was awakened by the location of the Lowell Observatory there. General Diaz, the President of Republic, accompanied by Secretary of State Mariscal, visited the Observatory in state, under a military escort, and spent several hours viewing Venus and Mercury by daylight. All the scientific and literary men in Mexico showed an equal interest, some coming by day and some by night, to view the planets, and especially to observe Mars. This was quite gratifying to Professor Lowell and his associates; and it had the effect of encouraging Science in Mexico, where the Astronomical Society of Mexico has since been established, probably as an outcome of this expedition.

The removal to and from Mexico of all the machinery of the observatory, and its erection in suitable order was a considerable mechanical undertaking. Professor Lowell had a good engineer in Mr. Godfrey Sykes, of Flagstaff, who accompanied the expedition; but in addition to his help, Dr. See, Mr. Cogshall, Mr. Douglass, and Mr. Drew aided in putting up and taking down the buildings and machinery. It was found that the Mexican peon laborers were so wholly devoid of mechanical sense that one American was worth a dozen Mexicans in these building and dismounting operations.

Before leaving Mexico, several of the astronomers, including Dr. See, ascended the volcano Popocatapetl. The trip was very interesting for the view of the country it offered; and for the sight of the sulphur refinery, at an altitude of some 12,000 feet, where the party spent the night.

Professor Lowell was suffering from fatigue and nervousness before he left Mexico for Boston. After reaching home his ailment increased, and although he started again for Arizona, and got as far as Chicago, he had to turn back and take a long rest and treatment before health could be restored. Finally, after two or three years he was himself again, and could conduct the observatory with his old time vigor and enthusiasm.

Mr. W. A. Cogshall who assisted Dr. See most of the time in his work at the Lowell Observatory, developed a good taste for astronomy, and has since attained considerable prominence as professor of astronomy and director of the Kirkwood Observatory, of the University of Indiana. He is an indefatigable worker, and loves to observe the heavenly bodies. The enthusiasm of one worker, as is well known, usually bears fruit in another; and of late years the University of Indiana has produced several promising young astronomers.

After concluding his two years at the Lowell Observatory, Dr. See spent part of the summer of 1898 at his old home, in Missouri, preparing a course of public lectures for the Lowell Institute. These were on the subject of Sidereal Astronomy, and were given during the months of December, 1898, and January, 1899. They included the most splendid illustrations known, and excited generous enthusiasm among the people of Boston. It was generally said that it was the finest and most impressive course of lectures given at the Lowell Institute since the famous course delivered by Professor Benjamin Peirce in 1879.

This course of lectures is important in another way. It impressed Dr. See greatly with the hazy veil of cosmical dust spread over the back ground of the sky in Barnard's magnificient photographs of the Milky Way, which had excited such enthusiasm in Boston. In these lectures and another at Wellesley College, Dr. See pointed out that this dust might be expelled from the stars; and he thus anticipated Arrhenius and others in publicly advocating the modern theory of repulsive forces in nature.

Even before Dr. See gave the Lowell lectures, it was known that Secretary Long and President McKinley were considering his appointment to a Professorship of Mathematics in the Navy, with a view of building up the scientific force at the Naval Observatory in Washington. As soon as his Lowell lectures were finished, and he was returning to his home by way of Washington, he found to his astonishment that he had been appointed by the President and his name already sent to the Senate for confirmation.

While calling on the Secretary of the Navy nobody could have been more surprised than Dr. See to be told, in reply to his remark that he hoped to be considered for a vacancy expected to occur in May: "Professor, I have already made your appointment. The President approved your selection yesterday and your nomination has gone to the Senate. You will of course have to pass a professional and physical examination, but you will have no difficulty about that." Such a pleasant surprise from Secretary Long encouraged Professor See very much. For it looked as if a proper estimate had been put on his strenuous labors of the past six years, since he had returned from Germany.

Naturally his plans of going on to Missouri had to be suddenly altered, and instead he tarried in Washington to pass his examinations, and be assigned duty at the Naval Observatory; after which he obtained leave to arrange his business affairs in the West.

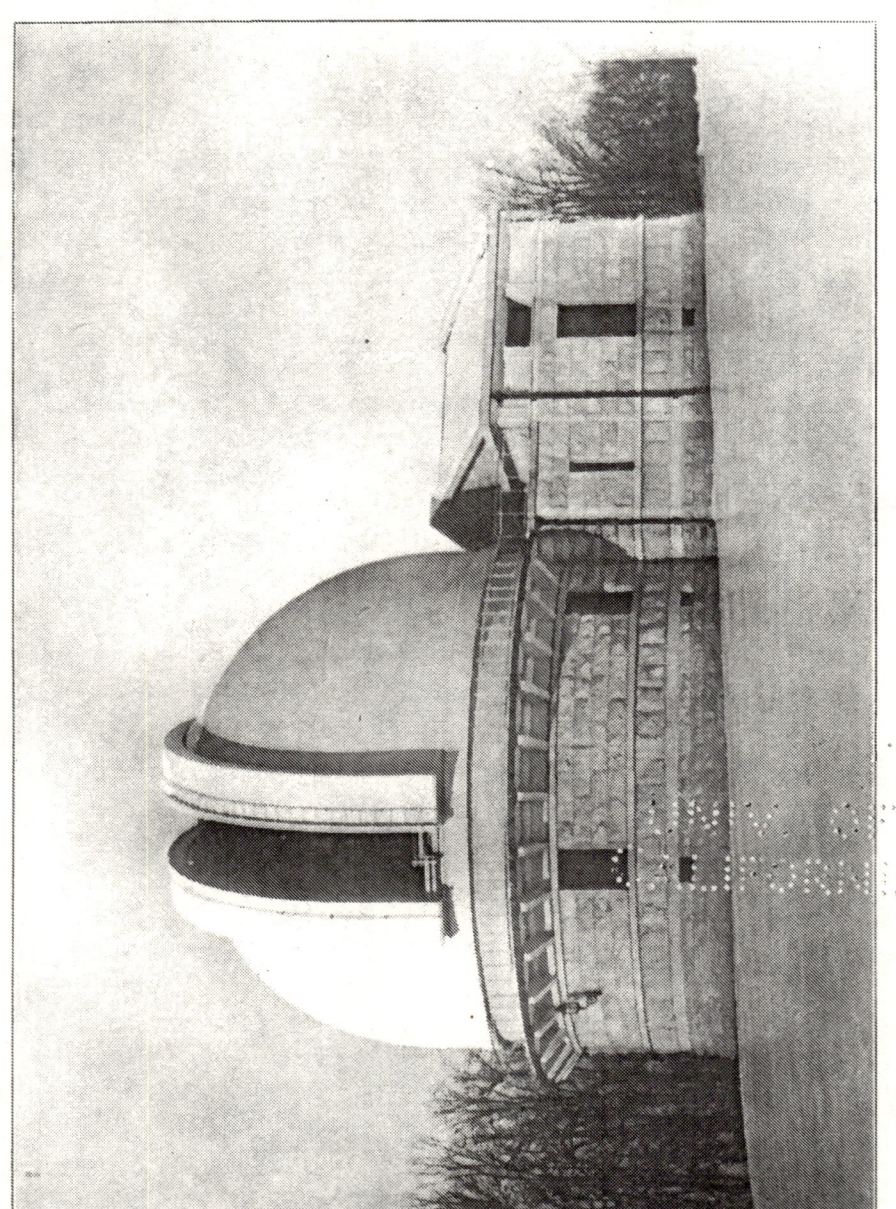

VIEW OF THE DOME OF THE 26-INCH TELESCOPE OF THE NAVAL OBSERVATORY, WASHINGTON.

Taken when the ground was covered with snow

CHAPTER VII.

1899–1902

THREE AND A HALF YEARS AT THE NAVAL OBSERVATORY, WASHINGTON.

OBSERVING DOUBLE STARS AND SATELLITES, AND MEASURING THE DIAMETERS OF THE PLANETS BY DAYLIGHT TO ELIMINATE THE EFFECTS OF IRRADIATION.

ON February 7th, 1899, Dr. See was formally nominated* by President McKinley to be Professor of Mathematics in the Navy, and the nomination confirmed by the Senate on February 10. After a short absence at his home in Missouri, Professor See was regularly on duty at the Naval Observatory in Washington. At first he was occupied with the reduction of the Meridian observations and participating in the observations of the sun, moon, and planets, with the meridian circle. This is an important branch of the observatory work, and Professor See wished to get into close touch with it by actual practice, his previous experience having been mainly with equatorial telescopes of large size. But after the retirement of Professor Edgar Frisbie, U.S.N., in May, 1899, Professor See was given charge of the 12-inch equatorial telescope of the Naval Observatory, till December, when he was given charge of the great 26-inch equatorial, with which he made so many fine observations during the next three years.

The experience gained in the meridian work during 1899 enabled Professor See to effect important improvements in the piers of the new 6-inch transit circle during the year 1901. This instrument had been mounted on marble piers, but the grain of the marble was not symmetrical in the two piers, being tilted in one and horizontal in the other; so that with changes of temperature

---

*To fill the vacancy caused by the retirement of Professor Newcomb, March 12, 1897.

during the day the azimuth of the instrument varied in a troublesome manner. In the summer of 1901 a navy board composed of Professor See, Professor Updegraff, and Assistant Astronomer George A. Hill, recommended the removal of the marble piers, and their replacement by piers of brick, with the result that the instrument afterwards performed with entire satisfaction, and gave results of unrivaled accuracy. This improvement of the six-inch transit circle enable Professor Updegraff to greatly improve the standard of the meridian work of the Naval Observatory.

Professor See's observations with the twelve-inch equatorial were mainly of asteroids, comets and double stars. Professor S. J. Brown, U.S.N., was on the point of giving up the large equatorial telescope to become Astronomical Director of the Naval Observatory, and naturally this powerful instrument was assigned to Professor See as the most experienced astronomer available for this duty.

Early in the month of October, while the twenty-six-inch was still officially in charge of Professor Brown, Professor See began with it a series of observations of the satellite of Neptune. The seeing at this season of the year often is very fine, because it is just before winter comes on, and the air quiet, hazy and smoky, as in Indian summer. These favorable conditions were unusually conspicuous in 1899, and on October 10, while observing the satellite of Neptune, Professor See noticed indications of faint belts on the disc of the planet. They seemed to be bands like those on Jupiter and Saturn, but very much fainter and more indistinct, because the disc of Neptune always appears small even in the largest telescope. The belts on Neptune were observed on several subsequent occasions, and noted also by Mr. Dinwiddie, who assisted Professor See in the work on the great equatorial, so that the existence of the belts is beyond doubt. This beautiful discovery is a severe test of the astronomer's vision, telescope, and atmospheric conditions; and it shows that the planet Neptune is physically of the same type as Uranus, on which belts were discovered by the Henry brothers at Paris in 1884.

VIEW OF THE LARGE TELESCOPE OF THE NAVAL OBSERVATORY AT WASHINGTON.

Showing the mounting, and the elevating floor, by which the observer is brought to convenient height in any position of the instrument.

PROFESSOR SEE OBSERVING WITH THE LARGE TELESCOPE OF THE NAVAL OBSERVATORY.

It was with this fine instrument that Dr. See carried out his delicate researches on the diameters of the Planets and Satellites by daylight and also at night, to eliminate the effects of Irradiation, which had never been done before.

During the first year after Professor See took charge of the large equatorial he was occupied mainly with the measurement of satellites; but later he enlarged the plan of work so as to include in it the determination of the diameters of all the planets and satellites. This was, of course, a considerable program, requiring time, energy and rare mental and physical powers in the observer, but Professor See was able finally to carry it to a conclusion. The satellite observations and those on the diameters of the planets were made simultaneously, without either line of work interfering with the other. And the work on the diameters of the planets was done both at night and by daylight, to eliminate the troublesome effects of the irradiation.

It is a curious fact of history that as many measurements as had been made on the diameters of the planets and satellites by astronomers during the three centuries since the invention of the telescope by Galileo, no one had previously attempted to eliminate the irradiation systematically, so as to get the true diameters of the planets, till Professor See executed this important investigation in 1901 and 1902. The result was a series of planetary diameters which never can be much improved upon. See's determinations have now come to be recognized as standard, and thus occupy a classic place in the literature of astronomy.

It should be explained that irradiation makes all the planets seem to be larger than they really are. It is illustrated by the apparent enlargement of the outer rim of the new moon and by the blunting of the points of the crescent, whereas they should really appear quite sharp. This is owing to the sensation of the light spreading on the retina of the eye; and this enlargement is called the irradiation. There was no previous method for getting rid of this disturbing cause, and Professor See therefore devised the scheme for taking observations by daylight and afterwards by night. It was found that the night diameters were considerably larger than those taken by daylight; and this difference gave the constant of the irradiation, as found by actual measurement, without regard to any theory. Professor See's empirical method therefore is recognized to be safe, and sound; and this doubtless is the reason why his results have been so generally accepted by the scientific world.

When Lord Kelvin was visiting Washington in April, 1902, a public reception by the leading men of science in the city was tendered him at the Cosmos Club. At this reception he took particular pains to inquire of Professor See about the experiments for finding empirical values of the constants of irradiation for the different planets and satellites of the solar system. He dwelt on the problems of irradiation altogether nearly half an hour, and when satisfied with the account given passed on to the problem of a resisting medium and the motions of comets, and their derangement in moving through the system of Jupiter's satellites, which has been considerably studied by astronomers since the earliest researches of Laplace and Burckhardt a century ago.

The other work carried on so unremittingly by Professor See from 1899 to 1902 was the measurement of the positions of the satellites of the solar system. This included extensive observations of eight satellites of Saturn, four of Uranus, and one of Neptune; besides measurements of the diameters of all the satellites which have sensible discs. The satellite program was thus an extensive campaign, and the measures made have since proved to be accurate and well adapted to the determination of precise orbits.

See's observations have been used by Dyson, Bergstrand, Struve, and several other astronomers for improving the theories of the motions of these bodies. The two inner satellites of Uranus proved to be excessively faint; and the same was true of Hyperion in the system of Saturn, but by screening off the glare of the planet, Professor See was able to get an excellent series of measures, when these objects could scarcely be seen by any other astronomer in the world, owing to the low southern declination of Saturn and Uranus, which placed them below the reach of European observers.

Altogether it may be said that the campaign on the diameters of the planets and the positions of the satellites attracted wide and

THE PLANET MERCURY.

As glimpsed by T. J. J. See with the 26-inch refractor at Washington, in June, 1901. It had long been known from photometric observations that Mercury behaved like the Moon, flashing out with great brilliancy near opposition, but otherwise reflecting very little light. If the surface of the planet were very rough and covered with craters and maria, as in the case of the Moon, this behavior would be explained. Professor See was the first observer to glimpse this Moon-like aspect of Mercury at moments of the best seeing. (From See's *Researches*, Vol. II.)

THE PLANET VENUS.

As observed by Professor E. E. Barnard with the 12-inch equatorial Telescope at Lick Observatory, 1889, May 29d, 11h. 12m. A.M. (From See's *Researches*, Vol. II.)

A GENERAL VIEW OF THE EARTH AND MOON AS THEY WOULD APPEAR
FROM A POINT IN SPACE.

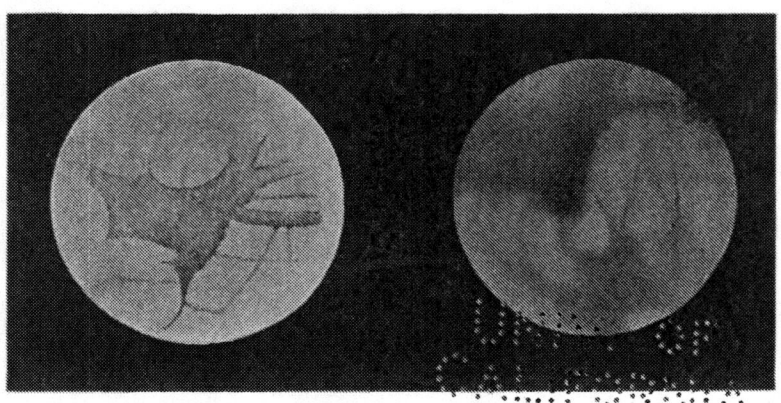

THE PLANET MARS AS DRAWN AND PHOTOGRAPHED BY LOWELL.

The latter view is the drawing made from a number of the Lowell photographs by the skillful hand of Mr. W. H. Wesley, Assistant Secretary of the Royal Astronomical Society.

THE PLANETS, THE EARTH AND MOON, AND MARS.
(From See's *Researches*, Vol. II).

1889, JULY 10ᵈ 8ʰ 45ᵐ P.S.T.
λ = 110°

1889, JULY 9ᵈ 9ʰ 40ᵐ P.S.T.
λ = 353°

1889, JULY 11ᵈ 12ʰ 3ᵐ P.S.T.
λ = 20°

1889, JULY 10ᵈ 10ʰ 2ᵐ P.S.T.
λ = 157°

DRAWINGS OF THE PLANET JUPITER.

Made by Keeler at Lick Observatory, 1889.   (From See's *Researches*, Vol. II.)

THE PLANET SATURN,

As Drawn by Proctor, but modified to take account of the Extension of the Dusky Ring observed by T. J. J. See at Washington in 1901 (*A.N.*, 3768). (From *Researches*, Vol. II, 1910, Plate XXII).

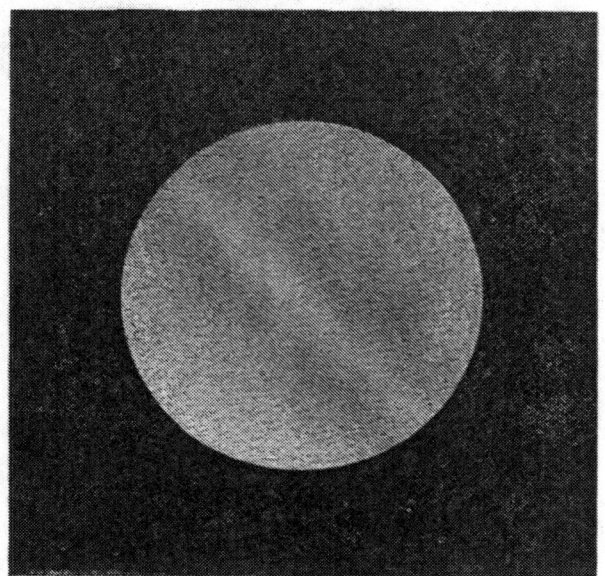

FIG. *a.* THE PLANET URANUS, WITH EQUATORIAL BELTS.

As drawn by the Henry Brothers at Paris, 1884.

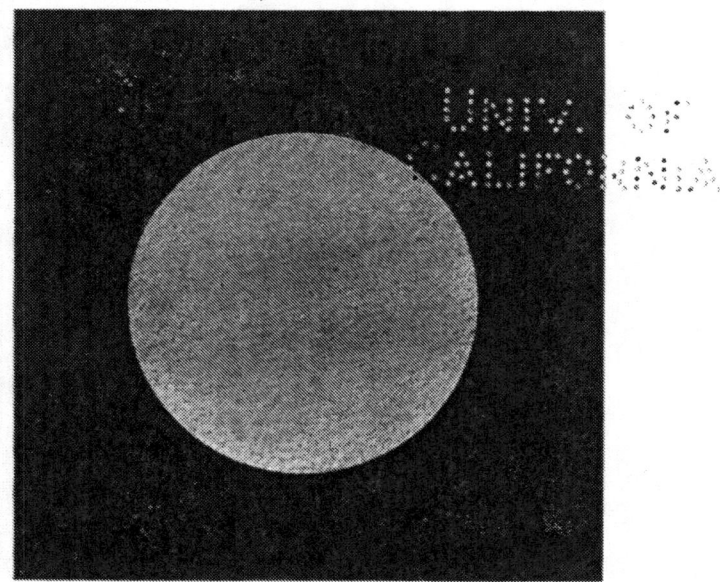

FIG. *b.* DRAWING OF THE PLANET NEPTUNE.

Showing the faint equatorial belts discovered by T. J. J. See with the 26-inch refractor at Washington, Oct. 10, 1899. Views of the planets Uranus and Neptune. (From See's *Researches*, Vol. II.)

favorable notice throughout the world. Professor See's great activity was especially commended by the celebrated French astronomer Callandreau, and by such observers as Schiaparelli, Struve, Burnham, Barnard, and a number of others; while the results of this work naturally were rapidly adopted in the literature of science.

One other very notable feature of See's labors at the Naval Observatory relates to the *improvement of the personnel.* There was a well known advancement in the standard of the Observatory as a whole between 1899 and 1902, and in this upward movement See naturally took a leading part. Young men of promise and ability were encouraged and given opportunity for some distinction, with the result that there was a general advance in the standard and quality of all the scientific work. Accordingly this proof of progress attracted considerable attention not only in America, but also in Europe. The work of this period in the history of the Observatory will always be recognized as one of high promise and proved efficiency.

See had not only worked very hard ever since entering the service in 1899, but also without the usual vacations, and in 1901 was found to be suffering from stomach trouble and sleeplessness, due to disturbance of the digestive processes. He had with difficulty kept up with the heavy program of work in 1901 and 1902; and when he was detached from the Observatory in September, 1902, a leave of absence for some months of rest was found advisable. Full recovery did not follow very quickly, but was a gradual process of some years. The difficulty was somewhat increased by the unfamiliar duties and surroundings at the Naval Academy. Whilst partial recovery was attained at the Naval Academy, full recovery was not possible till several years had been spent at increased outdoor activity in the beautiful climate of California.

The three and a half years which Professor See spent at the Naval Observatory were well employed, and led to beautiful and important results, in the way of measurements with the large telescope; but the work was done at a very considerable sacrifice of health and strength. It was profitable intellectually, but physically exhausting.

In addition to the work of observing with the great telescope See investigated the orbit of the satellite of Neptune; and also the orbits of several double stars. One double star, known as 13 Ceti, was found to be moving very rapidly. The period later on turned out to be only 7.4 years, the second most rapid known visual binary yet discovered.

The double star measures at Washington naturally were taken at odd times, when the planetary observations could not be made. They were thus of minor importance, and yet led to a number of valuable individual results.

In addition to these several lines of work Professor See carried out a critical investigation of the micrometer screw of the large telescope, by an elaborate triangulation of the Pleiades. This requires extremely delicate and accurate work, because all the observations of the large telescope depend on the result obtained. When the measures were all reduced they were found to be very accordant, and ranked See as one of the most accurate of living observers.

In the year 1901 the little planet Eros came very near the earth, and an elaborate international campaign was entered upon for determining the parallax of the sun. The Washington observations were made by See. When reduced in 1908, they proved to be remarkably accurate. They were discussed by Hinks of Cambridge, England, and by the Naval Observatory at Washington, and found to give a solar parallax of $8''.806$, while the standard value most used by astronomers is $8''.796$. It was thus accurate within one-thousandth part of the whole. The work of the Lick Observatory agreed almost exactly with See's work at Washington, and seemed to indicate that after all the true value is a little larger than $8''.800$.

From this survey of Professor See's researches at the Naval Observatory, it will be apparent that he attained eminent success

in every line of inquiry undertaken. This is the real test of efficiency. He who makes a first rank success in the work undertaken, when the work itself is of high quality, is a genuine leader
in science. Other astronomers, as those at the Lick and Yerkes
observatories, had larger instruments than See; but no one of them
has done work of more classic standard. Thus more depends on
the judgement and sagacity of the astronomer in choosing his
work and devising good methods for doing it, than on mere size
of telescope. In other words it is the astronomer at the little end
of the telescope who wins the laurels of science, just as it is the
man behind the gun who wins the victory in battle.

CHAPTER VIII.

1902–1913.

AT THE NAVAL ACADEMY AND MARE ISLAND.

ILL HEALTH AND RECOVERY: BEGINNING OF UNPARALLELED RECORD OF DISCOVERY IN CALIFORNIA.

FOR several months after he was transferred to the Naval Academy, Professor See was too ill for duty, but yet kept active outdoors, hoping to wear off the tendency to sleeplessness. He took long walks in the country daily, and also rowed in a boat on Chesapeake Bay. This was all of some value, but the trouble would yield only in part. The great difficulty was that See was afflicted with a severe internal catarrhal condition approaching a mild form of appendicitis, but even the most experienced physicians were unable to discover the real nature of the disturbance, till a violent attack occurred in 1909, and an operation gave permanent relief.

As soon as he could go on duty at the Academy, in February 1903, he was engaged in teaching the midshipmen mathematics. This work was mainly in algebra, trigonometry and spherical projections; and proved very interesting, because of the charm of manner of the midshipmen. It would have been perfectly delightful if Professor See had not been in ailing health; so that even three hours of instruction caused him considerable fatigue. As it was he enjoyed the work, and formed lasting attachments to the young officers under his instruction, many of whom are now lieutenants.

Pursuing a method different from most of the instructors at the Academy, See would help the midshipmen along when they were embarrassed and likely to fail, by hinting how they might start to solve their problems. The result was that they made rapid headway under him, whereas they would have been disheartened under a less sympathetic teacher. And after a short time the classes which were most deficient in mathematics were assigned to Professor See, so that by his help they could regain their standing. In this way he acquired a great reputation for saving the members of the class who might otherwise have been dropped. Naturally there was general regret at the Academy when it was learned that he was to be transferred to the Naval Observatory at Mare Island, California.

Professor See had remained on duty at the Academy all summer in 1903, and was bringing up the midshipmen who were deficient in trigonometry and spherical projections. The weather had been hot and enervating, and he was seriously afraid of losing his health permanently. The prospect of such duty, without improvement in his physical condition, was far from reassuring; and he hoped for duty in which he could at least recover his health. When he was told that he could have duty at Mare Island, where the climate would be ideal, it did much to reconcile him to life on the west coast. There his health was gradually improved, till he had the full vigor of his early years, except that the tendency to mild appendicitis occasionally produced some inconvenience.

As the method employed by Professor See for restoring his health is of some interest to others, it may be related here very briefly. Ever since settling at Washington in 1899, his sister, Mrs. A. M. Weeks, had lived with him, and thus he had his own household, with food and cooking of the kind desired. The eminent Dr. Franz A. R. Jung, of Washington, had been his medical adviser there, and had given him the necessary instruction in the articles of diet. Suitable bread, however, proved very difficult to obtain, and the problem was not solved till December, 1904, when in desperation over the internal soreness which afflicted him, Professor See began to grind his own flour with a hand-mill. This produced as flour a coarse product of the whole wheat, and when baked as muffins, with egg, salt, soda and butter milk, it gave a bread at once very delicious and very wholesome.

This bread is emphatically superior to anything heretofore known to the medical profession, and several doctors have used it with great benefit to their health.   As soon as the new flour was tried the first time, it was realized that at last they had found Nature's own remedy.   Professor See rapidly recovered and built up his general strength to the ideal point, by living carefully on this muffin bread of coarse whole wheat flour, and taking long walks in the country, about Mare Island.   Sometimes he would go ten miles a day, and seldom less than six.   During 1905, therefore, he was able to carry out the very long and difficult investigations on the sun.   Previously, just before leaving the Academy, he had finished and published an important mathematical investigation on Laplace's Invariable Plane of the solar system.

A more complete account of the several investigations made at Mare Island will be given in the following chapters.   Here it must suffice to note the order of the work, which was as follows:

1.   Researches on the Internal Constitution and Rigidity of the Heavenly Bodies, 1904–6.

2.   Researches on the Cause of Earthquakes, Mountain Formation, and kindred phenomena connected with the Physics of the Earth, 1906–8.

3.   Researches on the Evolution of the Solar System and of Cosmical Systems generally, 1908–9.

4.   Publication of Volume II of the *Researches on the Evolution of the Stellar Systems*, 1910; 735 pages quarto, with fifty-seven full page plates, and other figures in text.   This laid the foundation for a New Science of Cosmogony.

5.   Determination of the Depth of the Milky Way, 1911.

6.   Dynamical Theory of the Globular Clusters and of the Clustering Power inferred by Herschel from the observed figures of Sidereal Systems of high order, 1912.

A study of this order will show that the researches on the sun and planets, in 1904–6, paved the way for those on earthquakes and mountain formation in 1906–8.   But for his recent work on the internal conditions of the planets See probably would not have been able to detect the fallacy in the old theory of earthquakes and mountain formation. On the other hand, this outside work, on the physics of the earth, in 1906–8, gave a rest to his mind, and a freshness, which enabled him to solve the problems of Cosmogony, with rapid and unprecedented success, when they were resumed in 1908. The correct solution of the individual problems of Cosmogony thus gave the basis for a wholly New Science of Cosmogony. And in 1911 See was able to fathom the depth of the Milky Way, by methods of greater certainty than those employed by Sir William Herschel. *He thus found the depth of the Galaxy about a thousand times greater than astronomers have recently believed.*

Lastly, in 1912, he triumphantly confirmed by mathematical methods of a high order the general argument outlined by Herschel a century and a quarter ago to show that the star clusters developed by the drawing together of stars formed separately and originally at much greater distance apart. This enabled Professor See to render the foundations of the New Science of Cosmogony much more secure, and in fact to base Cosmogony on a fundamental law of the sidereal universe, of which a fuller account will appear later in Chapter XV.

On June 18, 1907, Professor See was married to Miss Frances Graves, daughter of the late Dr. James F. and Fannie (Jefferson) Graves, of Montgomery City, Mo. Mrs. See's family came originally from Virginia, but they have lived in the county for some seventy years. Her father was for thirty years one of the best beloved and most highly respected physicians in eastern Missouri. Her mother, who raised a family of ten children, and is one of the most remarkable women in the United States, is the daughter of the late Hon. Booker Jefferson, of the famous Jefferson family of Virginia.

Professor and Mrs. See lead a simple home life, going but little in society, and are both very fond of children. To their infinite grief they had the misfortune to lose their fine infant son, born July 28, 1909.

Mrs. See had some years' experience as a teacher both in Missouri and in New Mexico, and was very successful. Her education at the University of Missouri and in school work gave her the command of exact methods and thorough knowledge of many branches. She is fond of music, well read in literature, and speaks Spanish fluently. Naturally taking a great deal of interest in the scientific work of her distinguished husband, she has proved a tower of strength to him on numerous occasions, but more especially when he was unexpectedly stricken with a violent attack of appendicitis, January 11, 1909.

Fortunately he was in excellent health at the time, and but for that could hardly have survived this terrible attack. For sixteen days the operation was delayed, in the hope of reducing the fever and obtaining more favorable conditions, but finally it had to be made after all this illness. In consequence of the delay the case became so grave that for many days Professor See's life was despaired of. But it was not long after the operation was made till the process of recovery appeared and proved to be so rapid* and satisfactory as to surprise his physicians. Professor See was fortunate to have had the eminent professional services of surgeon H. E. Odell, U.S. Navy. Without very skillful surgical treatment his recovery would not have been possible.

It is worthy of mention here that for weeks, while Professor See lay at the point of death, with the doctors in despair, Mrs. See nursed him, and cooked and brought from home a mile distant, the slight liquid nourishment, which alone is allowable in such grave illness. But for this heroic devotion it seems certain that his life would have been cut short before his greatest discoveries were given to the world. A touching and beautiful tribute to his wife's devotion in this crisis is duly recorded on the last page of the monumental *Researches*, Vol. II, 1910, as follows:

"But of all the persons to whom I am indebted, I owe most to my wife, MRS. FRANCES GRAVES SEE. Without her devotion through a dangerous illness, the author could scarcely have survived to finish the work, and without her constant sup-

---

* Due to life-long habits of total abstinence from liquors or tobacco in any form.

MRS. T. J. J. SEE.

Daughter of the late Dr. James F. Graves of Montgomery City, Mo., and grand-daughter of Hon. Booker Jefferson.

THE RESIDENCE OF PROFESSOR SEE AT MARE ISLAND, CALIFORNIA.
The house is surrounded by an abundance ﹥ flowers blooming throughout the year.

PROFESSOR SEE IN HIS OFFICE AT MARE ISLAND, CALIFORNIA, EXAMINING THE PLANS OF HERSCHEL'S GREAT 40-FOOT TELESCOPE.

It was such studies at Mare Island, in 1909, that started the movement for the republication of Sir William Herschel's Collected Works by the Royal Society and Royal Astronomical Society of London, 1912. It was here also that two New Sciences have been established during Professor See's tour of duty, namely: GEOGONY, *the Science of the Creation of the Earth*, resulting from the researches on Earthquakes and Mountain Formation, 1906-08; and COSMOGONY, *the Science of the Creation of the Heavens*, resulting from the later researches on Sidereal Evolution, 1908-12.

port and encouragement the steadfast labor and sacrifices required for the development and publication of this large volume could not have been undertaken. If it contains any important discoveries I wish it always to be remembered that she contributed in an eminent degree to their development and presentation to the scientific world."

After Professor See's recovery the difficulty of getting the second volume of these *Researches* through the press proved to be enormous. But little of the work was in form for printing when he left the hospital, February 18, 1909. All the work had to be prepared and arranged as fast as the printer needed the manuscript. This proved very difficult, but by July, 1909, Professor See's strength was better than for many years, and this alone enabled him to carry that great undertaking to completion.

After the loss of her infant son, Mrs. See herself was ill, and long required careful attention and treatment. This naturally added to the difficulties under which Professor See labored. Often he would go to the office at five o'clock in the morning, when everyone else at Mare Island was asleep, in order to be free of interruption in writing out the chapters of the second volume of his famous *Researches*. They were thus prepared between numerous and pressing engagements, and yet they have all the finish and elegance characteristic of the most perfect work of the human intellect. It has been justly remarked that See's rapid and remarkable development of the second volume of his *Researches* is comparable only to Newton's writing of the *Principia* in 1685–6; and the two intellectual triumphs equally important and unprecedented.

It will be seen from the list of researches mentioned above that Professor See's activity at Mare Island is by far the most important of his life. Not only are the individual results the most striking, but also the most closely related one to another, giving an unparalleled series of achievements of the very first order. The result of this wonderful activity has been the creation of an entirely New Science of the Starry Heavens, at an epoch so late in the world's history that everyone believed that all the Sciences already had been developed.*

Cosmogony naturally has been a most difficult science to treat, because the Creative Processes are not *directly visible* to the watchers of the skies, but must be *inferred* from the observed order of the universe. Moreover it must harmonize many apparently discordant phenomena, and involves mathematical knowledge of a high order. Obviously all the reasoning must be founded on correct premises; and it happens that these false assumptions are the rocks on which shipwreck was most frequently experienced.

The other fact of importance is that prior to the *Researches* of See there was no deep study of the subject; but in all former efforts the premises of Laplace were assumed, without any critical investigation to determine whether these premises were admissible. At last it is gratifying to find that all such illogical procedure is altered; for a new foundation was found to be necessary, and built up on a basis as solid as a mountain of granite. With this new foundation once correctly laid, the resulting new science is greatly simplified, and all the celestial phenomena easily harmonized, so as to make Cosmogony the latest science of the starry heavens.

It is needless to say that Professor See's life at Mare Island has been one of great activity. In addition to walking in the country, for the contemplation of the beautiful scenery of the earth, sea, and sky, and especially of the mountains, and glorious sunsets of California, he is fond of gardening and all kinds of outdoor exercise. A recent trip to the Yosemite Valley and the Big Trees was the joy of his life. His house is full of fine pictures, including magnificent oil paintings of the Yosemite, Lake Tahoe, the Sierras, and the Himalayas.

As mentioned in Chapter II his natural taste for art dates from childhood. These fine paintings and natural scenery of the mountains seem to inspire his imagination with the eagle-soaring flights required for the development of new sciences of the universe.

---

* The New Science of *Geogony* was also developed at Mare Island.

It is well known that the illustrious Sir William Huggins had a similar taste for beautiful things and delighted in the contemplation of them in his study. Such taste was characteristic of the Greek mind, and as Professor See is thoroughly Hellenic in his feelings for truth and beauty in poetry and art, it may be that Professor Fleet was more of a prophet than was believed when he used to tell his classes that young Mr. See was like the typical Greek.

Since his settlement at Mare Island Professor See has passed in rapid review authoritative judgment upon many of the greatest problems of the universe; and not only summarized the work previously done by others, but added to it *capital discoveries* of his own. It has been generally remarked by eminent men of science that in every line of research his development was amazingly original. Without this spirit of daring, this soaring on the wings of Pegasus, probably it would not have been possible to introduce order into Cosmogony, where only bewilderment and chaos had reigned before.

The small and the timid naturally would be too cowardly to lead in this great enterprise. Fortunately, it is not so with Professor See. He recognized no authority save that of demonstrable truth, based in the centralizing tendency of the force of gravitation and the dispersion of dust from the stars under repulsive forces. This cyclic order in Nature rests on sound sense, and the logic of Mathematics. And having once made sure that he was right in his premises, like Davy Crockett, See dared to go ahead.

As the public often is unable to distinguish between a true cloud of God's firmament, with a plentiful supply of life-giving rain, and a mere mass of dust stirred up by the activity of the envious, we may point out that the evil spirit of professional jealousy is a curious thing. It is in fact nothing but an effort of the weak to pull down the strong, in order that they may keep afloat on the stream of time. To concede frankly the true value of the achievements of the really great would leave the weak without a *raison d'être*; and naturally they like to justify their own existence, even if they are inefficient. Accordingly whenever we see some one very grudging in acknowledging the merits of another, in the same line of activity, we may suspect that he is too small to be generous, or even fair and just. The world is full of this kind of business, and it pervades every walk of life.

It cankers the lives of statesmen, literary men, artists, poets, and scientists alike. Only the really great rise above petty jealousy; for the sun's light is not dimmed by that of a candle. And so it is in the world of science. Only the great feel that they can afford to be fair, whereas as a matter of fact no one can really afford to be unfair, but the small are so narrow that they cannot see the unworthiness of such conduct. It is well known that Professor See is a great comfort to his friends, in that he is never disturbed by outbreaks of jealousy, but quietly pursues the assuring even tenor of his way. Incidents which would distress less calm individuals do not disturb him. In fact he says jealousy is a favorable sign of progress, and advises his friends to be on the lookout for it.

If these weaknesses of human nature are very deplorable, See probably reasons that they do not sway the judgment of history. Only he who is truly great will have his name chiseled upon the sacred walls of her temple. The efforts to inscribe thereon the names of the small and inefficient is vain and fleeting like records written in dust, only to be washed away by the first shower of rain that descends from the clouds of God's firmament.

It is doubly beautiful if the great in ability are also morally great, so as to present the aspect of a really commanding and heroic figure in history, who will shine throughout all time. Many of the most eminent philosophers are of this grand type. Thus the luster of Newton and Herschel grows brighter rather than dimmer with the flight of ages. Every generation has remarked how great were the labors they had to endure, how dear the heart's blood they had to sacrifice! To such wonderful men the world pays no adequate reward. They are beyond all praise and above all price! The very wealth of a nation, great as it is, could not buy them, nor any process of searching for their equals replace them. It has been justly said that great men are the chief assets of nations. They are the crowning glory of the human race!

If it be sad to think how little the greatest men are appreciated during their life time, it is yet comforting to remember that, as was said of the dying Lincoln, *they belong to the ages,* and their light does not go out with their lives. The work of the great philosopher endureth unto all generations, as ageless as the heavens.

Some readers may not realize that the discoveries of Professor See belong to the whole earth, and not merely his native state. They will even outlast the Republic itself, and still be the topic of contemplation for philosophers when many thousands of years have elapsed; just as the works of Aristotle and Plato now belong not to Greece but to all mankind and to all time. It would be especially fortunate for America and her people if she is able to appreciate her great men during their life time; for that would show an enlightened State, and stand to her credit in history. Such biographies as this, it is hoped, may thus be of no small public service.

Since genius of the highest order is wholly beneficial to the State, and men of this type derive little or no pecuniary reward for their efforts, they deserve and ought to have *public appreciation,* since this sustains them in doing the work which the Deity intended them to do. After Newton had struggled along through one disappointment after another, and finally accomplished his great work, not so much by virtue of generous appreciation, as in spite of public indifference, the poet Thomson speaks of him thus:

"Say ye who best can tell, ye happy few,
Who saw him in the softest lights of life,
All unwithheld, indulging to his friends
The vast unborrowed treasures of his mind.
Oh, speak the wondrous man! how mild, how calm,

How greatly humble, how divinely good,
How firm established on eternal truth!
Fervent in doing well, with every nerve
Still pressing on, forgetful of the past,
And panting for perfection; far above
Those little cares and visionary joys
That so perplex the fond impasssioned heart
Of ever-cheated, ever-trusting man."

When will an American poet sing of the labors of the Newton of Cosmogony? This would be a task of no mean order, and require a genius like that of eagle-soaring Pindar. After See, too, shall have passed away, happy will be the few who can boast that they

"Saw him in the softest lights of life,
All unwithheld, indulging to his friends
The vast unborrowed treasures of his mind,"

mild, calm and good, like Newton, but withal having also, like the author of the *Principia*, vigor, and courage, to war against wrong and injustice, whether it be practiced by a King in trampling on the rights of a University, or by a clique of grafters among men of science. Historians have remarked that Newton's whole life was a struggle against injustice; and as for See it is well known that he never shirks his duty in the hard work of this world. After truth has triumphed all seems serene and simple, but establishing it is always a more difficult task, and thus the founder of a new science has to have courage as well as humility.

CHAPTER IX.

1904–1906

POPULAR ACCOUNT OF THE RESEARCHES ON THE INTERNAL CONSTITUTION OF THE SUN AND THE PLANETS.

THE Naval Observatory at Mare Island, California, has no telescope larger than a five-inch refractor, which is a mere pigmy compared to the giant telescopes which Professor See had used at the Lowell Observatory, Arizona, the Naval Observatory at Washington, D. C., and elsewhere. If therefore he was to make any important scientific researches in California, it could not well be with the telescope in use at Mare Island; but rather must be work along mathematical lines, in which nothing but a few books and a clear head is required.

It is to be remembered that in Astronomy all the important discoveries are not made with telescopes, much of the highest work being purely a matter of theoretical research or mathematical calculation. There are telescopic discoveries of facts made by looking through instruments, and others of theoretical or mathematical character, even more important, made by the mind's eye, in the quiet study of the mathematical astronomer.

As Professor See was without large instruments at Mare Island, he naturally turned to account his great abilities as a mathematician. Thus where a mere telescopic observer would have failed, See achieved a triumph of the first order, when in fact no one expected it. When he came to Mare Island in November, 1903, the place was quite unknown to the scientific world; now it is known in the remotest parts of the earth for a series of discoveries of the highest significance.

This brilliant achievement did not come by chance, but resulted from the consummate ability of the astronomer in charge of the Mare Island Observatory. See has always made it a practice to take up those lines of inquiry in which he could attain the first rank — for such is the nature of leadership; and so it was in the unparalleled series of discoveries made in California.

The first of these discoveries related to the internal densities, pressures, and physical constitution of the sun and planets. Prior to Professor See's work in 1904–6 the interior constitution of the planets was a veritable *terra incognita*, a subject on which nothing was yet known; and there was little prospect that anyone would attempt to explore the physical conditions down in the depths of the planets. We cannot descend into the earth or other planets, much less into the sun, and actually observe with instruments what the conditions are in these dark and invisible regions, inside of the heavenly bodies. Many therefore doubtless reasoned that nothing could ever be known of the state of the matter thus inaccessible to our observations. It is scarcely necessary to remark that See did not share this view — he knew too well the power of mathematics!

He had long ago learned to calculate all manner of things from the Newtonian law of gravitation. And he realized that if the arrangement of the law of density within a planet such as the earth could be made out, it would be comparatively easy for the mathematician to calculate the pressure clear down to the center of the globe. Each layer of the globe presses upon the layers beneath it, and the total pressure at the center is the proper sum of all these combined pressures, which can be calculated by the higher mathematical methods known as the Calculus, the first principles of which were invented by Newton in 1666.

Now See set about the following problems:

1. To find the most probable laws of density within the sun and planets.

2. To calculate the resulting laws of pressure in the interior of these bodies, by the methods of higher mathematics.

3. To deduce the physical properties of matter thus imprisoned under tremendous pressure, and high temperature.

And by great labor during the years 1904–6 he gradually

solved all these problems, so as to give us in fact a new science of the interior constitution of the heavenly bodies.

To understand this work, let us first consider the case of the earth. Our globe appears to be solid, and is covered by a rocky crust, but earthquake movements occur; and it is important to know whether these are just beneath the surface, or deep down in the bowels of the globe, as Humboldt believed to be the case three quarters of a century ago.

See first investigated the law of density of the earth suggested by Laplace, and satisfied himself by careful inquiry that it must be either accurate or very nearly so. The proof of this result cannot be given here, but it is a matter on which astronomers are essentially agreed. This law of Laplace makes the density at the earth's center 11.2, that of water being unity, and the average density of the whole earth 5.5. Thus the density of the earth's matter increases quite rapidly as we go down, and at the center becomes equal to that of lead. At the surface the density is 2.55, so that the central density is over four times that at the surface.

Without going into the methods of calculation employed by See, we may say that he found the pressure at the earth's center over three million *atmospheres*, each atmosphere being the weight of a column of quicksilver thirty inches high, as in a barometer, or fifteen pounds to the square inch. This made the pressure at the earth's center over 45,000,000 pounds to the square inch.

To represent this in a simple way, imagine a column of quicksilver — an immensely heavy liquid considerably denser than lead — as long as from St. Louis to San Francisco. Let this column be erected vertically, in a tube strong enough to hold it, and every part of it pressing down just as quicksilver does at the surface of the earth; then the tremendous pressure of this column 1,700 miles in length becomes just equal to the pressure at the center of the earth.

Could any result be more wonderful than this? Yet it is very accurate, and we may absolutely depend upon it. And not only did See find the pressure at the center of the earth, but also the law of its increase as we go downward, from the surface, where it is nothing, to the center, where it becomes equal to the weight of a vertical column of quicksilver as long as from St. Louis to San Francisco.

The outcome of this study was the conclusion that the greater the pressure the more difficult it is for the matter thus imprisoned to circulate or move in any way. Consequently deep down in the earth, where the pressure is very great no motion ever takes place; and the only place where motion can occur is just beneath the earth's crust, as in earthquake movements. In fact it was shown by See that the deep interior of the earth always is absolutely quiescent; and, even just beneath the surface, it takes all the power involved in the throes of an earthquake to enable the molten lava to readjust itself. In this readjustment of lava the crust naturally is terribly shaken, and cities may be laid waste and whole countries devastated.

Accordingly See was able to conclude with certainty that Humboldt was wrong in holding that earthquake disturbances are propagated from deep down in the globe. Measurements by modern seismographs also show that these disturbances are shallow, in no case exceeding a depth of some twenty miles, which is the thickness of the earth's crust. Earthquake phenomena, however, will be more fully discussed in the next chapter, and we must here treat of the interior conditions of the other planets.

In general the larger the body the greater the pressure at the center; so that the sun has at its center by far the greatest pressure of any of the bodies of our solar system. The next greatest pressure is in the center of Jupiter; then comes Neptune, Uranus, and Saturn, the latter coming after the two former because its average density is very small (0.71 that of water).

At the center of the sun the pressure becomes 11,215,540,300 atmospheres, each amounting to 15 pounds to the square inch. This is equivalent to the weight of a colunm of quicksilver about one-eighth as long as from the earth to the sun, when all parts of it press downward, as at the surface of the earth. Truly an amazing pressure!

To form some idea of the physical condition of the matter in the sun, we must recall that it is at a temperature of millions of degrees, and on the other hand held in confinement by this tremendous pressure. Therefore the matter is kept so "tight" as to be highly rigid, though it would prove to be gaseous if the pressure were removed. On this point there is no doubt whatever. Though we cannot experiment with such immense forces, we can calculate them with accuracy and certainty.

A very good comparison of the state of the matter in the interior of the sun was made by Professor Newcomb some years ago, when he said that if the pressure were suddenly relieved this matter would instantly expand, and in fact explode with a violence exceeding that of dynamite or any other known substance. If, for example, gravitation should suddenly cease, the whole sun would expand into a nebula filling the universe. Such a thing as this of course will never happen, yet the picture of such an explosion enables us to realize what dreadful compression and imprisonment matter is subjected to in the sun's interior.

This imprisoned matter is really gaseous, and would expand into a nebula if the pressure were relieved; but in confinement it has the property of a solid, owing to the tremendous pressure at a temperature of millions of degrees. See concluded that at the surface of the sun the temperature lies between 6,000 and 12,000 degrees centigrade; and that deeper down it mounts up enormously, according to laws which he has worked out, and at the center probably lies between 10,000,000 and 100,000,000 degrees, on the same scale of temperature.

Now in dealing with the interior constitution of the earth Lord Kelvin and Sir George Darwin found our globe to be a solid of about the rigidity of steel. In other words our globe is about as hard as a steel globe of the same size would be if the parts of it be imagined to be devoid of the power of gravity. But gravitation exists, and it is in fact the pressure under gravity which makes the earth so highly rigid — the imprisoned matter may be molten or even gaseous, and yet so confined that it is not free to circulate, but actually made to act as a rigid solid.   By careful mathematical calculation See proves that the earth has a rigidity nearly as great as nickel steel used in the armor plate of our battleships.

The nickel steel of moderate grade has a rigidity of about a million atmospheres.   The modern vanadium steel is said to be even more rigid, but we need not extend the comparison.   It suffices to say that by considering the layers of which the earth is made up, and the pressure in each layer, See finds for the earth an average rigidity approaching that of nickel steel.   This result confirms the conclusion of Lord Kelvin and Sir George Darwin, but See's reasoning is much simpler than theirs.   In other words, the rigidity of the earth is due to the pressure which makes the matter behave as a solid; and by the theory of Professor See we may calculate the rigidity of any layer in the globe.   He finds that the rigidity at the surface is equal to that of common granite, which is about one-fourth that of steel; while at the center the rigidity is three times that of armor plate or nickel steel.

One very remarkable thing about See's process for dealing with the rigidity of the earth is the generality of the method, which makes it applicable also to the other planets and the sun; whereas the methods of Lord Kelvin and Darwin apply only to the earth, and cannot be applied to the planets, sun or fixed stars. Thus See's method is one of entire generality, like the law of Newtonian gravitation, whereas the method of Kelvin and Darwin applies only to the earth, and is thus extremely special.   It may be said therefore that See generalized the law of rigidity, somewhat as Newton did the law of gravitation.   For before Newton's work of 1685, Dr. Hooke had proved the law of gravity for the simple case of circular motion; but Newton proved it also for the ellipse, parabola and hyperbola, and thus generalized it for all the orbits described by the heavenly bodies.

Applying these methods of investigation to the sun, See found that the average rigidity of that globe is over 2,000 times that of nickel steel used in armor plate.   Surely a wonderful result! Prior

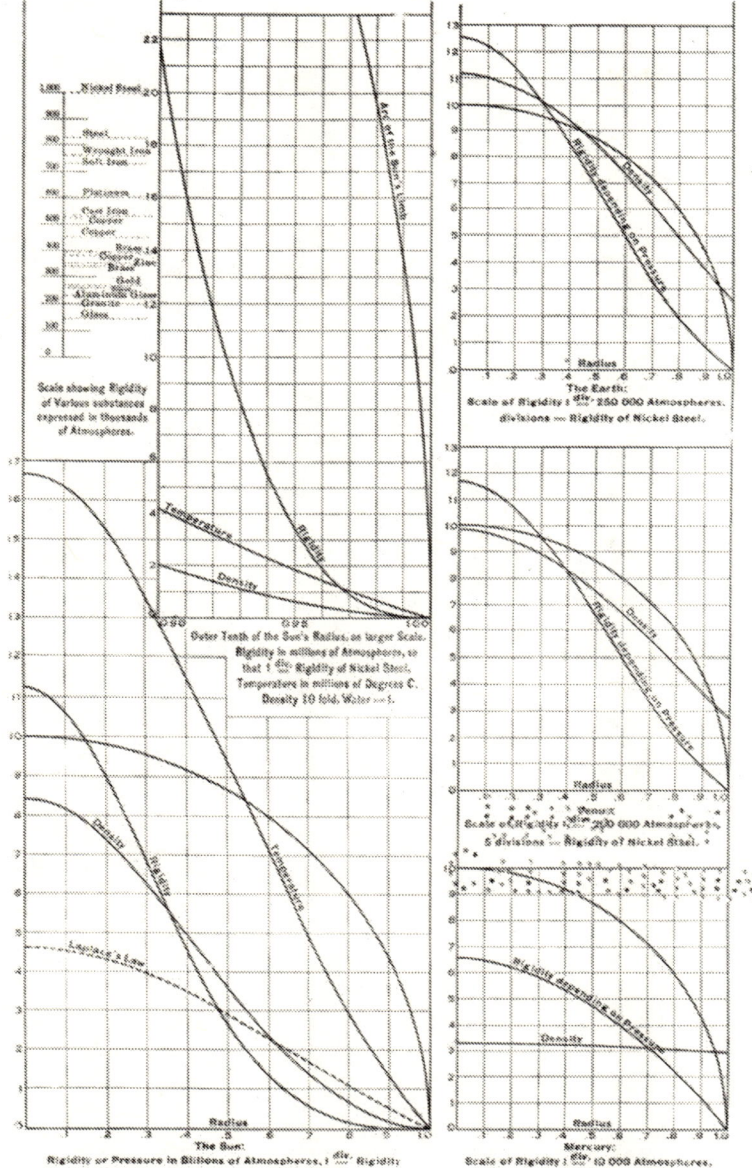

Scale showing Rigidity of Various substances expressed in Thousands of Atmospheres.

Outer Tenth of the Sun's Radius, on larger Scale. Rigidity in millions of Atmospheres, so that 1 div. Rigidity of Nickel Steel. Temperature in millions of Degrees C. Density 10 fold. Water = 1.

The Sun. Rigidity or Pressure in Billions of Atmospheres, 1 div. Rigidity 1,000 times that of Nickel Steel used in Armor Plate. Density on usual Scale, Water = 1. Temperature Scale 1 div. 3 Million Degrees C.

The Earth. Scale of Rigidity 1 div. 250,000 Atmospheres. divisions = Rigidity of Nickel Steel.

Venus. Scale of Rigidity 1 div. 250,000 Atmospheres. 5 divisions = Rigidity of Nickel Steel.

Mercury. Scale of Rigidity 1 div. 10,000 Atmospheres. Rigidity due to Pressure is small, but Planet may be a mass of Solid Rock.

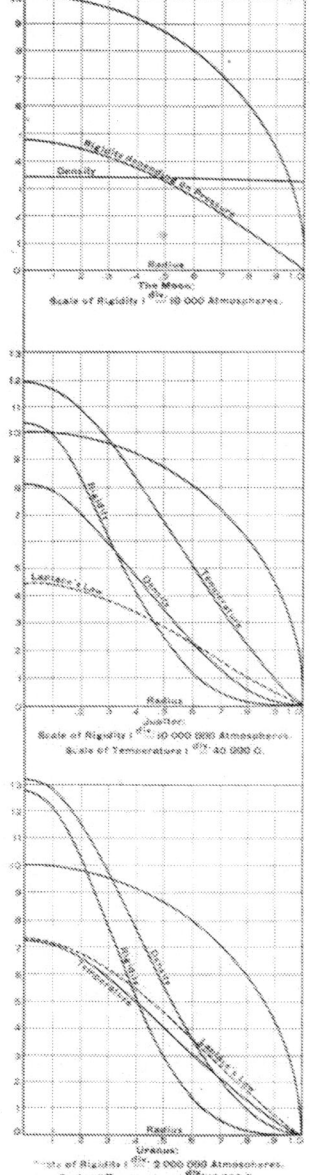

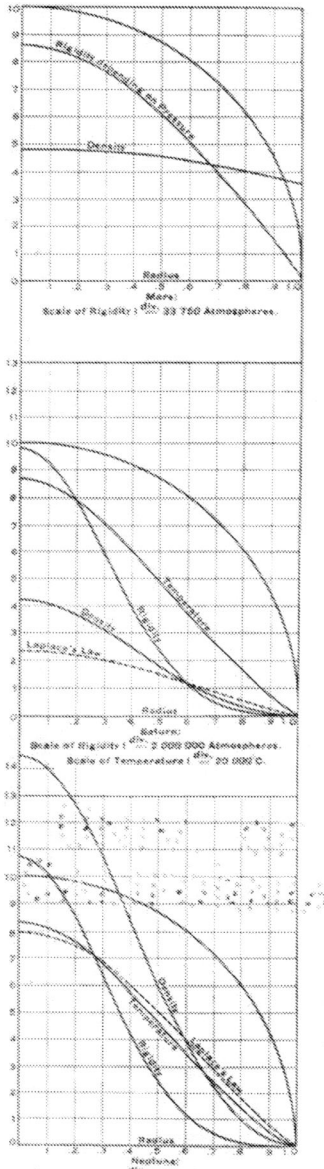

The Moon.
Scale of Rigidity: 1 div. = 10 000 Atmospheres.

Mars.
Scale of Rigidity: 1 div. = 33 750 Atmospheres.

Jupiter.
Scale of Rigidity: 1 div. = 10 000 000 Atmospheres.
Scale of Temperatures: 1 div. = 40 000 C.

Saturn.
Scale of Rigidity: 1 div. = 2 000 000 Atmospheres.
Scale of Temperatures: 1 div. = 20 000 C.

Uranus.
Scale of Rigidity: 1 div. = 2 000 000 Atmospheres.
Scale of Temperatures: 1 div. = 20 000 C.
Scale of Density for all the Planets, Water = 1.

Neptune.
Scale of Rigidity: 1 div. = 2 000 000 Atmospheres.
Scale of Temperatures: 1 div. = 15 000 C.

to See's work of 1904–6, many astronomers had believed that the currents noticed at the surface of the sun extend to great depths, and even to the very center.   This was just like the geologists believing that currents circulate deep down in the earth, which See proved to be quite impossible.   In the same way he showed that circulation at any considerable depth in the sun could not take place, because of the enormous pressure and great effective rigidity of the matter.   At a depth of one-tenth of the sun's radius the rigidity is already twenty-two times that of nickel steel, and hence See argues that all circulation in the sun is confined to a thin layer near the surface, while the great interior globe is quiescent and hundreds and thousands of times more rigid than armor plate.

These profound and original investigations give us new ideas in science, and have revolutionized many of the old theories. Naturally such advancement could only come from a bold and daring leader, who had the courage to lead the way to truth, without regard to traditional opinion.   This power of leadership is a striking characteristic of See.   He is at home in pioneer research, and shows the same courage and independence of mediocre opinion that enabled Archimedes and Galileo to win victories in past centuries.   And just as they triumphed over the jealous opposition of ignorance and mediævalism, so also See has blazed a similar new and luminous path for progress throughout coming ages.

Galileo's opponents often could not refute his arguments, as when he pointed to Jupiter's satellites as verifying his theories; and in this perplexity they could do nothing but refuse to look through the telescope, lest they be convinced.   They did not want to know the truth.   There are still persons of that kind in the world, and no doubt always will be.

One form of the contemptible opposition to Galileo may be recorded here.   When his opponents knew they were beaten, and could no longer make an honest argument against the progress of truth, they tried to get learned societies arrayed against him. Thus it is said that the Academy of Cortona unanimously resolved that the satellites of Jupiter did not exist. Yet Galileo would have shown them to anyone who wished to look through the newly invented telescope. So also there are now people of this type who have fought the progress of See's discoveries till they found out the futility of their efforts. Then they gave up the fight, and now probably they would not admit that they ever opposed the progress of his discoveries, which are in every respect comparable to those of Galileo and Archimedes.

The modern geometer who can devise a method for investigating the physical properties of matter confined under tremendous pressure and enormously high temperature, in the deep interior of the sun and planets, where no instrument or direct observation can ever aid us, evidently is in the same class with the ancient mathematician who could invent burning mirrors, and the principle of floating bodies, as well as deduce the properties of curves and spirals. And hence we have pointed out the parallel between the labors of the celebrated geometer of Syracuse and the famous American geometer whose discoveries have added so much new luster to the American name.

RELIEF MAP OF THE TERRESTRIAL GLOBE.

Illustrating the relations of the mountains to the sea, which has uplifted great walls along the borders of the Continents, by the expulsion of lava from beneath the ocean and its injection under the land. This impressive view of the Earth shows at a glance that the mountains have been formed by the Sea. From Frye's *Complete Geography*, by permission of Ginn & Co., Publishers.

CHAPTER X.

1906–1908.

OUTLINE OF THE NEW THEORY OF EARTHQUAKES.*

By T. J. J. SEE

AMONG all the varied natural phenomena witnessed upon our planet nothing so excites the dread and terror of mankind as an earthquake, which is at once violent and so sudden and unexpected as to alarm the calmest mind. That this direful feeling has prevailed in all ages we are amply assured by the comparisons made in the Bible and other venerable works of antiquity, which make known the consternation inspired among the people by these terrible natural commotions. Thus we read in history that some of the Emperors of Rome, especially Trajan and Hadrian, while witnessing the chariot races at Antioch and other places, found it advisable to withdraw from the amphitheatre and retire into the open spaces, in order to avoid the danger of falling walls. And the history of Greece and Rome abounds in stories of the religious anxiety excited among the people by earthquakes, which were believed to be signs of evil omen, sent from the infernal and marine divinities, but especially Poseidon, "the Earth-shaker," to whom so many temples were dedicated on isthmuses, promontories and other regions in the neighborhood of the sea.

When a great earthquake took place, and was followed by a series of after-shocks, impressively recalling both the terror and the disaster of the principal disturbance, which may have laid waste cities and devastated whole countries, it is not wonderful that the people who had sustained such losses were troubled and wrought up to a high pitch of excitement. In such emergencies

---

* Address delivered at the University of Missouri, May 30, 1907, being Lecture No. 2 of a general course in Natural Philosophy. Reprinted from *Popular Astronomy* No. 154, April, 1908.

the god Poseidon above all others* called forth the veneration of the people; and he was generally held to be the most important of the infernal and marine divinities, because he held both the power of earthquakes and of those dreadful inundations by the sea, which were so often noticed to accompany violent seismic disturbances in the Peloponnesus and elsewhere.

The wide-spread alarm and religious affliction of the inhabitants of the Peloponnesus after the great Achaian earthquake of 373 B. C. is especially remarked by Diodorus Siculus, and other historians. At the same time it is stated that the natural philosophers explain these phenomena by natural and necessary causes, rather than by the wrath of the gods. But during the ages of Greek Polytheism, and even during the earlier centuries of Christianity, such disasters were always believed by the multitude to be a sign of the Divine displeasure. Sometimes they were attributed to the wickedness of an emperor, or to the sins of factional opponents; the heathens charging them upon the Christians and the Christians laying them to the idolatrous conduct of the heathens.

In view of the undeveloped state of Science in former times a modern student can easily understand the great perplexity of the ancients, in the midst of such terrible calamities. The Senate of Rome on more than one occasion did what it could to alleviate the sufferings of the people, which were partly real and partly imaginary. We find several accounts of the sending of formal embassies for the offering of public sacrifices to the angry divinities. If these sacrifices did not quiet the agitating forces of nature, they at least calmed the people and thus allayed their imaginary afflictions and were therefore of service to the State.

It is well known that both the ablest statesmen and generals of antiquity regarded earthquakes as proceeding from natural causes; and I have recently been at some pains to translate the theories held by Aristotle and other leading Greek philosophers.

---

* "Once when an earthquake shook the ground where a Spartan army was encamped, the whole army sang a hymn to Poseidon."
—Article *Poseidon*, Encycl. Britannica, 9th edition.

Aristotle gives the views of those who preceded him, and his own theory was generally adopted by his successors. We may infer this by the way in which it was followed by such writers as Strabo and Pliny.

Aristotle placed his discussion of earthquakes in the book on *Meteorology*, because he ascribed the shaking of the earth to vapor confined within the crust, and agitating to effect an escape, so as to diffuse itself in the atmosphere. He recognized the high internal temperature of the earth from the warm springs observed to break forth in many places, and from the eruptions of volcanoes which he had witnessed in the Aeolian Islands and elsewhere. Both he and Strabo mention eruptions occuring in the bed of the sea, and they also notice the great seismic sea waves which frequently accompany violent earthquakes originating near the sea shores.

Aristotle and Pliny distinctly remark that earthquakes are especially prevalent in maritime districts; and they attribute this phenomenon to submarine passages, conceived as deep conduits, by which air and water obtain access to the heated matter in the bowels of the earth. They held that earthquakes are due to the agitation of imprisoned vapors even when none of it escapes to the surface, but all remains hidden beneath the earth's crust. That the cause is the same when a volcanic outbreak occurs and when only an earthquake takes place without eruption, Aristotle affirmed on the ground of the similarity of the movement in the two cases.

To an unbiased naturalist like Aristotle it did not seem strange that in the one case the vapor should break through and diffuse itself in the atmosphere, while in the other it continued to agitate till movements occurred which gave more space beneath the earth's crust, and was then followed by a cessation of the shocks. Aristotle's view was thus consistent with Newton's rule of philosophy, that the same effects are to be ascribed as far as possible to the same causes; and in marked contrast with the modern method of dividing earthquakes into two arbitrary classes, volcanic and tectonic, according as they are accompanied by eruption, or only by a surface dislocation of the earth's crust along a fault line.

While Aristotle's theory is imperfect in many respects, the general ideas underlying it are essentially sound; and in reading this work written more than twenty-two centuries ago, one cannot but be impressed both by his penetration into the nature of things, and by the vast extent of his knowledge. With characteristic independence he refused to accept the views of his predecessors, but examined *de novo* all questions upon their merits, so far as the existing state of Science would permit. He is thus led to many interesting remarks, and the criticisms which he offers are often as good as can be made to-day.

In view of the great afflictions due to earthquakes suffered by so many countries from the earliest ages, it seems to the modern student truly remarkable that our understanding of the cause of these disturbances has remained so unsatisfactory. Whether we read in Strabo or Pliny that a great earthquake in Syria had laid waste twelve cities in a single night, or turn to the current books and press dispatches, which tell of widespread devastation by modern earthquakes, we are left equally in the dark as to the cause of these calamities. In current discussions we often see it stated that earthquakes may occur anywhere, and that no place is free from the dreadful ravages which they inflict upon large portions of mankind. This statement obviously is not correct, yet it shows that heretofore Science has not reached the true laws of these phenomena.

The main object of Science is the illumination of the human mind, and much of it scarcely admits of application to practical affairs, so as to alleviate human suffering; but if we had a true science of earthquakes it ought to be indeed of the highest humane as well as scientific interest. Shall our cities continue to be devastated and rebuilt without an understanding of the disturbing cause? If so, what advance has our boasted civilization made over that of the Greeks and Romans? Nay, shall we not know even the regions especially afflicted by earthquakes? We could indeed

MOUNT PELÉE.

The Burning Cloud of December 6, 1902, seen from the sea. A most impressive illustration of the vast quantities of steam emitted from volcanoes.

THE SHATTERED OBELISK OF MOUNT PELÉE.

Photographed by Professor Angelo Heilprin. This vast mass of granite rock 1,000 feet high and 500 feet in diameter, was ejected from the volcano with terrific force, but caught and held fast in the orifice, till at length it crumbled to pieces. If steam can eject such a massive column, there is no mountain uplift which it is incapable of producing.

have learned this from the study of Aristotle; but in our time we claim, though not always justly, to have improved on the knowledge of the ancients. If we do not find out the regions especially subject to eartquakes, so as to forewarn the people as to what kind of houses to build and how to protect their cities from fire in the case of an earthquake, of what practical use is Science to the community? Some branches of Science might be very excellent indeed and still be of no use to the multitude of people; yet this obviously is not true of a science which deals with earthquakes imperiling the lives and property of thousands of our fellow citizens.

We must confess that heretofore this knowledge of the cause of earthquakes has not been forthcoming. But as a physicist believing in the existence of natural laws, which, if known, would be of the greatest service to mankind both now and throughout coming ages, I am going to treat of earthquakes and kindred phenomenon connected with the physics of the earth. The theory of which I shall treat has been recently presented to the American Philosophical Society in Philadelphia, and I take this occasion to acknowledge my indebtedness to this illustrious society for the publication of lengthy arguments which can be mentioned here only with the utmost brevity.*

At the time of the great earthquake at San Francisco, I had just finished the researches on the Physical Constitution of the Heavenly Bodies which have been recently published in the *Astronomische Nachrichten*; and as the explanations of the earthquake

---

* 1. The Cause of Earthquakes, Mountain Formation and Kindred Phenomena connected with the Physics of the Earth. Proc. Am. Philos. Society, 1906, issued March, 1907.

2. On the Temperature, Secular Cooling and Contraction of the Earth and on the Theory of Earthquakes held by the Ancients. Proc. Am. Philos. Society, 1907.

3. The New Theory of Earthquakes and Mountain Formation as illustrated by Processes now at work in the Depths of the Sea. Proc. Am. Philos. Society, 1907, issued in March, 1908.

[4. Further Researches on the Physics of the Earth, and especially on the Folding of Mountain Ranges and the Uplift of Plateaus and Continents produced by movements of Lava beneath the Crust arising from the secular leakage of the Ocean Bottoms, Proc. Am. Philos. Soc., No. 189, Sept., 1908.]

then made public by men of science did not seem to me to be well founded, I temporarily laid aside astronomical work in order to take up this problem of the Physics of the Earth. It is not too much to say that the papers which the American Philosophical Society did me the honor to publish have awakened a lively interest in the scientific world; and whilst one can scarcely hope that every difficulty has been overcome, it is evident that at least a good foundation has been laid for the true theory of earthquakes, mountain formation and kindred phenomena connected with the physics of the globe.

Since the processes involved in earthquakes are forever hidden from mortal view, the discovery of the cause involved naturally has been very difficult. But as the effects would become most sensible in earthquakes of the world-shaking class, it was felt at the outset that the investigation should be restricted to the study of these great phenomena. If the study of the greatest earthquakes enabled us to reach the underlying cause, the inquiry could later be made to include the smaller disturbances, many of which are after-shocks of the great earthquakes.

In speaking of earthquakes therefore we shall have in mind primarily earthquakes of the world-shaking class. If we had attempted to study all earthquakes together, the results could only have been hopeless confusion; for we should have been unable to discover the processes even of the greatest earthquakes.

One of the most remarkable results of these inquiries is the conclusion that the earth is not shrinking, as commonly held in all the physical sciences for the past eighty years; but that it may indeed be slightly expanding. Another is that there is a progressive secular desiccation of the oceans, which are becoming narrower and also deeper in many places, so that as the world grows older the intensity of the earthquakes is slowly increasing, not diminishing. But obviously there has been no sensible change within the historical period.

We shall now proceed to state the cause of earthquakes and related phenomena, and after so doing shall resume the considera-

a.   Mountain formation just beginning.

b.   Mountain formation in the middle stages.

c.   Mountain formation in the later stages.

d.   New range rising from the sea.

DIAGRAMS ILLUSTRATING THE SUCCESSIVE STAGES IN THE PROCESS
OF MOUNTAIN FORMATION, BY THE EXPULSION OF LAVA FROM
BENEATH THE SEA AND ITS INJECTION UNDER THE LAND.

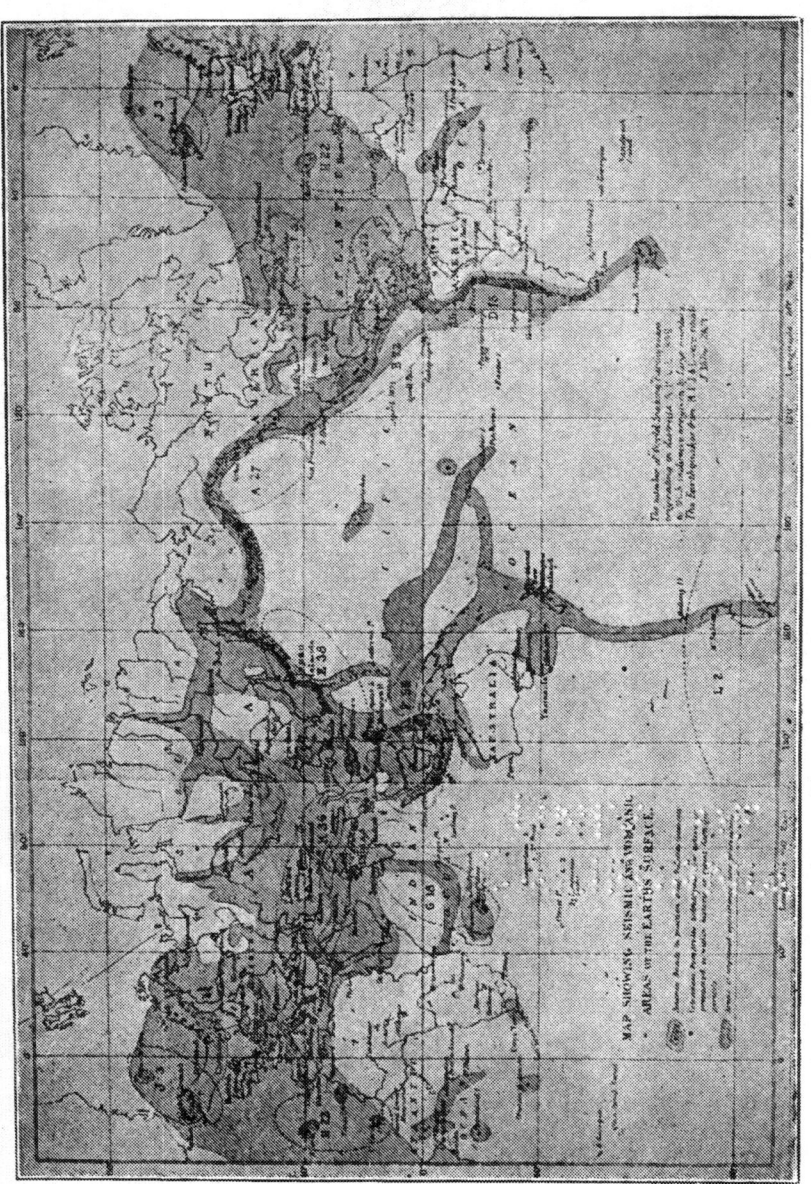

MILNE'S MAP OF EARTHQUAKE DISTRIBUTION.

The darker belts about the borders of the oceans show the regions of greatest seismic activity. The interior of the oceans are relatively blank, because these regions are but little observed.

tion of the other questions connected with the physics of the globe.

1. It is shown that the principal cause of world-shaking earthquakes is the secular leakage of the ocean bottoms, which produces steam beneath the earth's crust. When the pressure has sufficiently accumulated the movement of the underlying molten rock shakes the earth, lays waste cities and devastates whole countries. Much steam is formed under the ocean, but scarcely any under the land, and hence the usual process of movement consists in the expulsion of lava from beneath the sea, and the pushing of it under the land. The crust is thus pushed up and broken along the seashore, and thus forms mountains parallel to the coast.

2. The mountain systems of the world have been formed by this expulsion of lava from under the sea, and not at all by the shrinkage of the globe. Taking account of the mere lay of the mountains relatively to the sea, it is proved by the theory of probability that the chances are at least a decillion decillions to one that they were formed so exactly parallel to the coast by a true physical cause depending on the oceans. Moreover there are other phenomena to be considered of such weight that it becomes an absolute certainty that the mountains are formed by the sea.

3. The coast frequently is noticed to be upheaved during earthquakes, and the adjacent sea bottom is shown to sink, from the way in which the water retires before the inrush of the accompanying seismic sea wave. The sea does not withdraw from the land by the violence of the agitation of the ground during the earthquake, but slowly drains off afterwards, as in the ebbing of a tide, only the withdrawal is more rapid in the case of the movement before the sea wave; and as the sea level near the shore is thus lowered sometimes by forty or fifty feet, so that vessels at anchor in seven fathoms of water are left resting on the ground, it follows that the sea bottom sinks some distance from the shore, and the water rushes in from all sides to fill up the depression. When the currents meet at the center the water is forced up into

a corresponding elevation, above the normal sea level, and the collapse of this aqueous ridge sends a great wave ashore, to add to the horror of the earthquake.

4. If, then, the sea bottom frequently sinks and the coast is simultaneously upraised, it follows that lava is expelled from under the sea and pushed under the land. For in the regular order of nature the sea bottom could not sink unless it was in some way undermined, and the coast could not be uplifted unless something was pushed under it; and as one sinks while the other rises it follows that lava is expelled from under the sea and pushed under the land. Not only is this process now going on along the west coast of South America, and elsewhere, as repeatedly observed within historical times, but we may also affirm that the long continuation of this undermining in the past has sunk the sea bottom down into a deep trough and at the same time pushed such vast quantities of lava under the adjacent mountains that the lofty peaks in the Andes with snow-capped summits now seem to near the stars. There is thus direct continuity between the small movements observed within the historical period and the vastly greater effect of these forces operating over immense periods of time.

5. The process by which mountains and deep ocean troughs are formed is even better illustrated in the Aleutian and Kurile Islands, where the mountains under water are just rising out of the sea and the adjacent ocean trench is very narrow, and runs exactly parallel to them for great distances (see Manual of Tides, Coast Survey Reports, 1900, Part IV, A, by Rollin A. Harris, including maps of the depths of the ocean). This chain is also one of the worst earthquake belts in the world, and many of the mountains have burst open and become volcanoes. The earthquakes are frquently accompanied by great seismic sea waves, showing that the bed of the ocean sinks after lava has been expelled from under it in the formation of mountains. If the process thus made out is a true law of nature, it follows that all the great mountain chains of the globe were formed by this same pro-

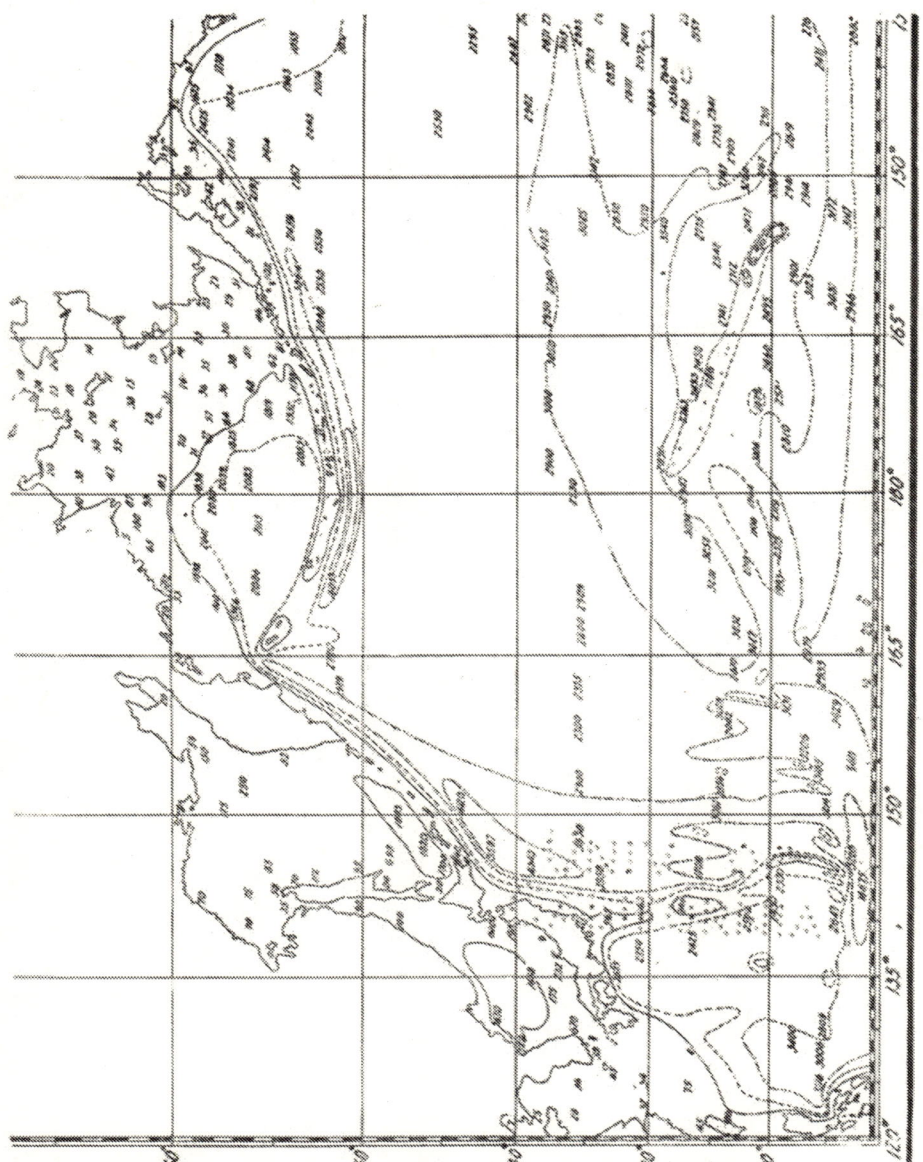

COAST SURVEY MAP OF THE NORTH PACIFIC OCEAN.

4 dots in the contour lines denotes a depth of 4,000 fathoms; 3 dots, 3,000 fathoms; continuous dashes, 2,000 fathoms.

RELIEF MAP OF SOUTH AMERICA.

From Frye's *Complete Geography*, by permission of Ginn & Co., Publishers. Illustrating the New Theory that the Mountains were formed by the oceans, and thus run parallel to the Sea Coast, as in the typical case of the Andes. It was this vast wall along the Western sea-board of South America and the earthquakes afflicting that region that led to the discovery of the cause of Earthquakes and Mountain Formation in 1906. The foundations of the New Science of Geogony were thus laid by Professor See in 1906.

cess, though in some cases the recession of the sea coast due to the movement of the crust by earthquakes, has changed the original shapes of the troughs, and consequently can now be made out only by careful investigation.

6. Our present knowledge of the earth's surface does not enable us to decide just what movement of the land has taken place in each case, but the parallelism of the mountains to the sea coast is sufficiently remarkable to attract universal attention. Heretofore the cause of this phenomenon has been quite obscure, and some have inferred that it is a "coincidence which is only in part casual." It is shown, however, as already remarked, that the chances are at least a decillion decillions to one that the parallelism depends on a true physical cause connected with the sea. It is absolutely unthinkable that the Pacific Ocean could be so effectively walled in by great mountain chains all around, unless the mountains were formed about the Ocean itself, by the expulsion of lava, in the way we have described.

7. In 1899, September 3–20, a terrible earthquake took place at Yakutat Bay, Alaska, during which the coast was elevated for more than a hundred miles, and at the maximum the elevation amounted to forty-seven and one-third feet. Elevations of from seven to twenty feet were common, while small depressions also occurred in a few places. This case was carefully investigated by Professor R. S. Tarr, of Cornell University, and Mr. Lawrence Martin, of the National Geographical Society; and their memoir in the Bulletin of the Geological Society of America, Vol. 17, May, 1906, is illustrated by photographs of the most convincing kind, showing the uplifted coasts, with barnacles still adhering to the rocks. Their investigation is classic and absolutely conclusive. In the confused state of scientific opinion heretofore prevailing, geologists could deny the bodily uplift of the solid land; but after the publication of this memoir, they could no longer legitimately maintain this attitude. And if one instance of elevation by a powerful earthquake could be clearly established, it naturally followed that others could arise from similar causes. Last year

the earthquake at Valparaiso, August 16, 1906, is said to have raised the Chilian coast about ten feet; and many similar movements at other places both in ancient and modern times can be certainly established.

8. The fact that no active volcano exists over about one hundred miles from the sea or other large body of water, and the further fact that according to Geikie 999 in 1,000 parts of the escaping vapor is steam, shows the dependence of volcanoes on the sea. The activity of one hundred and five volcanoes in the Andes within historical time shows that volcanoes are nothing but ordinary mountains broken through by the pressure of subterranean steam. Hence it follows that the same forces which raise the mountain chains and peaks also cause the eruption of some of them.

9. The vapor of steam and no other is the cause of both mountain building and of volcanic outbreaks; for mountain building always takes place in or near the sea, and volcanoes throughout the world develop near the center of the earthquake belts. Volcanoes emit chiefly vapor of stream, and eruptions generally cease when the vapor has escaped into the atmosphere. Thus earthquakes, volcanoes, mountain formation, and seismic sea waves are all due to a common cause.

10. As the expulsion of lava from under the sea causes the earthquakes and seismic sea waves, it follows also that all mountains are underlaid with pumice of various degrees of density, which is simply molten rock inflated with stream and then cooled and dried. The expulsion of such vast quantities of pumice from volcanoes shows that there must be a process for its abundant manufacture in nature, and that it must have been formed under all mountains when they were originally upheaved. The prevalence of pumice in volcanic regions is therefore accounted for in a perfectly simple manner. The grinding up of pumice makes volcanic ashes, and hence arise the vast quantities of this dust blown out of many volcanoes. Pumice and its disintegrated product in the form of ashes, result from the diminished pressure

exerted on steam saturated lava, when it is pushed under the mountains where the crust is broken, and increased expansion of the molten rock takes place.

11.   The formation of islands in the sea and of plateaus on land, is to be explained by elevation of a portion of the earth's crust by the injection of lava beneath.   This lava comes from neighboring areas, which are thus undermined, unless the partial cavity is again filled up by an additional supply of molten rock. Hence plateaus such as those of Titicaca and Tibet are closely associated with the expulsion of lava, which originally caused the uplift of the Andes and Himalayas.   In many cases islands in the sea have depressions near them, showing that the sea bottom was undermined in the elevation of the islands, and afterwards sank down to secure stability.

12.   As all mountains and plateaus exhibit a feeble attraction when measured in geodetic operations, it follows that the cause of this phenomenon is the pumice underlying these elevated portions of the crust, which makes them attract as if they were hollow, or filled with caverns.   This was noted by Bouguer and LaCandamine in their observations on Chimborazo as early as 1738.

13.   When the subterranean pressure becomes great enough to shake the earth's crust, it naturally moves at the nearest fault line, where the rocks are broken, and the resistance is least, *but the movement observed is the result, not the cause of the earthquake.*   It has been customary heretofore to explain earthquakes by the movement of faults, without assigning the cause of the fault movement, or by vague references to the supposed secular cooling of the earth.   Such procedure is altogether illogical, for it does not account for the origin of faults, nor even point out the correct cause of their movement.

14.   If faults were due to the secular cooling of the earth they ought to originate and move in the interior of continents as well as along the ocean shores.   Acre for acre as much heat is being lost by Kansas, or Sahara, as by any sea coast or ocean bed in the world.   Yet no important movements occur inland, while the sea

coast is repeatedly shaken. The constant shaking of the Andes compared to the general quiescence of the Rocky Mountains shows the effect of proximity to the sea, and proves that the secular cooling of the earth is not a true cause of earthquake movements.

15. In the papers published by the American Philosophical Society at Philadelphia it is shown that the effects of secular cooling are wholly inappreciable, and that the earth is not really contracting; but in all probability slightly expanding, owing to the predominant effects of elevations of the land by world-shaking earthquakes, 120,000 of which have occurred since the beginning of the Christian Era. And it is calculated that the effects of elevation may exceed the effects of contraction from ten to one hundred times, so that in all probability the globe is really expanding.

16. It turns out therefore that the doctrine of mountain formation based on the theory of contraction and now held for some eighty years is quite devoid of real foundation. If the earth is not shrinking another cause must be sought to account for the observed elevations of the crust as seen in mountain folds; and it should explain mountain ranges in the sea as well as on the land. The present theory meets this severe test perfectly, and is beautifully illustrated by the phenomena exhibited near the Aleutian and Kurile Islands. Here the earthquakes are raising islands and at the same time sinking down the adjacent sea bottom, as may be confidently inferred from the accompanying seismic sea waves. These long narrow trenches have been dug out by the expulsion process, and it is still going on at the present time. No other interpretation of the observed phenomena is really possible.

17. The whole plateau west of the Rocky Mountains has been raised from the sea in recent geological time. This is shown by the abundant beds of fossils, and by the numerous parallel mountain ranges nearer the Pacific Coast. The San Joaquin and Sacramento Valleys have been recently raised from the sea, and the great earthquake at San Francisco, April 18, 1906, was but one of an infinite number which have raised the Coast Range little

by little and finally lifted California above the ocean level. Earthquakes obviously will recur in California, but no important disturbance is to be expected at San Francisco for at least a generation. This is inferred from the study of other places similarly disturbed during the historical period, and from the nature of the process of ocean leakage, which is very slow and gradual.

18. The cause of the terrible earthquakes in Japan is now perfectly clear, namely, the leakage of the deep sea just to the east of Nipon, known as the Tuscarora Deep. By the expulsion of lava from under this area the whole island of Nipon has been lifted above the sea, and the process still continues with increasing violence. The east coast of Japan has risen considerably within the historical period, and naturally a movement of this kind confirms the theory here developed.

19. The present theory of mountain formation enables us to account for all the principal mountain ranges of the globe, and the more gradual slopes which they exhibit towards the sea from which the lava has been expelled in the process of elevation. In the case of islands the mountains run lengthwise, right through their centers like veritable backbones. In other cases lava escapes under larger submarine areas which will eventually be raised above the sea and formed into larger islands or continents. The principal cause of the movement of the earth's crust is everywhere the same, but we do not yet know the details of all parts of the globe, because most of it is under water, and even that above sea level is very imperfectly surveyed.

20. As land is raised above the sea by earthquakes, it follows that the chief effect of seismic activity is the formation of more land. Since this narrows the oceans, and water is also constantly sinking down into the earth, and only a small part of it again escapes through the vents of volcanoes, it follows that there is a secular desiccation of the oceans, but the process is excessively slow, and not certainly recognizable within the historical period. Yet a portion of the lowering of the strand line noticed in later geological ages may be due to this cause.

21.   In studying the sinking of the sea bottoms in connection with the expulsion of lava for the elevation of coasts and the formation of mountains, the writer took up the problem of the sinking of the Homeric City of Helike, after the great earthquake in Achaia, in 373 B.C., which occurred during the lifetime of Aristotle and Plato.   And it was possible to prove from historical authorities that the subsidence amounted to about one hundred feet, which shows that after that earthquake had pushed lava under the mountains in Arcadia, the bed of the Gulf of Corinth gave down, and carried the shore on which Helike stood down with it, so that, as Pausanias says, only the tops of the trees about the temple of Poseidon remained above the water.   This famous disaster, which happened when Plato was fifty-four and thus at the head of the Academy in Athens, and Aristotle was a boy eleven years old, was therefore due to the expulsion of lava from under the Gulf of Corinth.   Is it not remarkable that after the lapse of so many centuries we should be able to explain by simple principles a calamity which so disturbed the Greek world, and completely bewildered even the wisest of the Athenian sages?

22.   As the result of his researches Aristotle held that earthquakes are due to vapors in the earth, seeking to escape and diffuse themselves in the atmosphere.   This view was generally adopted by the ancients, for we find it clearly stated by Strabo and Pliny, who studied the writings of Aristotle. Strabo also holds the theory that the land is uplifted and depressed by earthquakes.   He seems to have held that not only islands and continents but also mountains are thus produced, which essentially accords with the theory of Aristotle, who had carefully studied volcanic and earthquake phenomena, including several eruptions observed to occur in the sea.   Aristotle had observed that maritime districts are especially subject to earthquakes.   In view of the results of modern observations and the theory now established, may we not justly consider this to be one of the most remarkable inductions of antiquity?

23.   The theory now developed was therefore vaguely outlined by the leading Greek philosophers, especially by Aristotle,

who associated the causes producing earthquakes and volcanoes, islands and seismic sea waves, all of which were attributed to the accumulation of vapors in the earth. This natural order of thought as developed by the Greeks presents a striking contrast to the disconnected and anachronous views on these subjects still current in our own time, and admonishes us to give ample heed to the independent conceptions of the Greeks who were not so much swayed as some moderns are by contemporary opinion.

24. The theory recently current that great seismic disturbances of the earth's crust are due to unequal loading of different areas arising in erosion, denudation and deposits of sediment is, to say the least, unworthy of modern science, because such forces could produce no uplifts whatever, nor could they produce any serious continuous shaking, even if a slight movement of the ground should occur. It is the movement of molten rock under the earth's crust, in the process of adjustment of steam pressure, which forms mountains, shakes down cities and lays waste whole countries. The development of the highest mountain ranges about the deepest oceans shows that these great uplifts of the crust depend upon the sea and not at all on the shrinkage of the globe. The indications of nature indeed are as clear as the noonday sun, and all we have to do is to apply to these phenomena a little of the saving common sense which has distinguished mankind in the better ages of the human mind.

This summary of the results of these researches is necessarily incomplete, but probably sufficiently extended to afford an idea of the trend of the investigation. Among American geologists Dana approached most nearly to the true views of the physics of the earth's crust, and we shall therefore quote his statements as they were made over forty years ago. Some of his intuitions are quite remarkable.

VIEWS OF DANA.

In the first edition of his *Manual of Geology*, 1863, J. D. Dana treats of the general features of the earth and shows how the continents are walled in by mountains, erected about their borders, and finally adds (p. 29):

(*a*) "The continents thus exemplify the law laid down, and not merely as to high borders around a depressed interior, a principle stated by many geographers,— but also as to the highest border being on the side of the greatest ocean (first announced in American Jour. Sci. (2) xvii, vols. iii, iv, 1847, and xxii, 335, 1856). The continents then are all built on one model, and in their structure and origin have a relation to the oceans that is of fundamental importance." He also observes that the borders of continents are from five hundred to one thousand miles wide, and infers that "a continent cannot be less than a thousand miles, (twice five hundred), in width," otherwise it would not have the characteristic basin form with mountain barriers about a low interior.

(*b*) On page 731 he discusses the evolution of the earth's great outline reliefs, and of the successive phases in its progress, summarizing his conclusions as follows:

I. "The continents have mountains along their borders, while the interior is relatively low; and these border mountain chains often consist of two or three ranges elevated at different epochs."

II. "The highest mountain-border faces the largest ocean, and conversely."

III. "The continents have their volcanoes mainly on their borders, the interior being almost wholly without them, although they were largely covered with salt water from the Azoic age to the Tertiary. Also metamorphic rocks later than the Azoic are most prevalent near the borders."

IV. "Nearly all of the volcanoes of a continent are on the border which faces the largest ocean."

V. "The strata of the continental borders are for the most part plicated on a grand scale, while those of the interior are relatively but little disturbed."

VI. "The successive changes of level on coasts, even from the Azoic age to the Tertiary, have been in general parallel to the border mountain chains; as those of the eastern United States, parallel to the Appalachians, and those of the Pacific side, as far as now appears, parallel to the Rocky Mountains."

VIII. "The continents and oceans had their general outline or form defined in earliest time. This has been proved with regard to North America from the position and distribution of the first beds of the Lower Silurian,— those of the Potsdam epoch. The facts indicate that the continent of North America had its surface near tide-level, part above and part below it (p. 196), and this will probably be proved to be the conditions in primordial time of the other continents also. And, if the outlines of the continents were marked out, it follows that the outlines of the oceans were no less so."

The three other conclusions announced by Dana are of less interest, and need not be quoted here.

(c) The following deductions (p. 732) regarding the positions of the reliefs are of high interest:

"1. The situation of the great mountain chains, mainly near the borders of the continents, does not indicate whether the elevating pressure acted within the continental or oceanic part of the earth's crust. But the occurrence between the principal range and the sea coast of the larger part of the volcanoes (and, therefore, of the profound and widely-opened fractures) of these borders, of the most extensive metamorphic areas, and of the closest and most numerous plications of the strata, as so well shown in North America, are sufficient evidence that the force acted most strongly from the oceanic direction."

"2. The relation between the extent of the oceans and the height and volcanic action, etc., of their borders proves that the amount of force in action has some relation to the size and depth of the oceanic basin. The Pacific exhibits its greatness in the lofty mountains and volcanoes which begirt it."

"3. In such a movement, elevation in one part supposes necessarily subsidence in another; and, while the continental was the part of the crust which was elevated, the oceanic was the subsiding part."

In connection with the theory that the mountains are formed by the expulsion of lava from under the sea, though the operation of world-shaking earthquakes, these early views of Dana are of great interest. But in other respects he was led astray by the doctine of the secular refrigeration of the globe; for he says that "no other cause presents itself that can comprehend in its action the whole globe and all time." He thus speaks as if the entire globe were shrinking, whereas local changes only are occurring, and these always near the sea. Dana's views that "the pressure of the subsiding oceanic portion has acted against the resisting mass of the continents; and thus the border between them has become elevated, plicated, metamorphosed and embossed with volcanoes," is alike misleading and unjustifiable. To produce such an effect the settling of the ocean basin would have to be many miles, and we have shown that no such shrinkage has taken place since the crust was formed; on the contrary there is reason to think that the earth is expanding at a rate of from ten to one hundred times that of the contraction due to secular cooling. Moreover we have no more right to assume that the continent is squeezed by the settlement of the ocean, than that the ocean is squeezed by the settling of the continent.

(d) We have, however, recalled these views in order to do justice to the most original of the older American geologists, and also to let the student see where he departs from the true line of thought. Many years ago Rev. O. Fisher showed that shrinkage was wholly inadequate to account for the height of the mountains observed upon the earth, which are hundreds of times higher than the contraction theory will explain. In the paper on the cause of earthquakes it is shown that the contraction theory is also emphatically contradicted by the present distribution of mountains. And in the second paper, "On the Temperature, Secular Cooling and Contraction of the Earth, and on the Theory of Earthquakes held by the Ancients," it is shown that at present the earth is not contracting at all; so we are compelled to abandon the older theories entirely.

As heretofore developed, geology has presented the strange anomaly of offering no theories adequate to account for the uplift of mountains or the deposits of fossil beds thousands of feet above the sea. This is the more remarkable, since in the days of Humboldt, Lyell, and Darwin, the bodily elevation of the land was an accepted item of belief. But subsequently Lord Kelvin, Sir George Darwin and other eminent British physicists, showed from the investigation of tidal and other phenomena that the earth as a whole behaved as a solid, and under the influence of this line of thought geologists gave up the doctrine of the bodily elevation of the land, and restricted themselves to the collapse of portions of the crust under gravity. Such a line of thought, however, utterly fails to explain mountains and plateaus and islands, as well as shells and other organic remains at great height above the sea level. But it was felt that the argument of the physicists against the bodily yielding of the earth was unanswerable, and so it was, yet this does not exclude the existence of a layer just beneath the crust which in earthquakes behaves as fluid.

In my researches a theory is developed by which these two views may be reconciled, and it is, I think, clearly proved that in earthquakes there is movement of molten rock beneath the crust. It is this movement of molten rock beneath the earth's crust which produces most of the dislocations, crumpling, folding, and other phenomena studied in geology. If such a view is justifiable, it shows us how cautious we must be in drawing final conclusions, and how incomplete all the sciences still are today.

We must now refer to Daubrée's experiments, and the problem of explaining how the water gets beneath the earth's crust, to develop the steam power operative in earthquakes. Daubrée's experiments have shown that under pressure of its own superincumbent column, water may pass through cold and enter hot rocks, by capillary action, and increase the pressure within, notwithstanding the increase of steam pressure on the under side. In this way Daubrée explained volcanic eruptions, by which a column of molten lava is forced up into the vent of a volcano. Though Daubrée's results appear to have a good experimental basis, we may prove our fundamental proposition regarding the leakage of the oceans quite independently of these experiments.

Earthquakes are the processes by which mountains are produced, and observation shows that these forces act at a depth of some fifteen miles, where the pressure is so great that no vacancies exist. When the coast is upheaved by an earthquake it is clear that no real cavity is allowed to form beneath; in the same way we may conclude that when the sea bottom sinks after an earthquake no condensation of the matter of average density takes place beneath the bed of the sea. But matter is expelled from beneath the sea bottom and pushed under the land, so that the coast is upraised and the sea bottom sinks, to fill up the partial cavity formed beneath the sea by the expulsion of lava.

These phenomena are repeatedly observed in South America, the Aleutian Islands and elsewhere, and, so far as one can see, admit of but one interpretation. Hence we may conclude with certainty that the Andes have been formed by the expulsion of lava from beneath the bed of the adjacent ocean; this is the true meaning of the thundering of the earthquakes under the margin of the sea already witnessed for centuries, but not heretofore understood by men of science. This subterranean thunder is the outward expression of the mighty explosive forces by which the crust along the coast is uplifted into some of the mightiest mountains of the globe.

Since the earth is not contracting, nor experiencing any sensible changes due to secular cooling, it is evident that this expulsion of lava can only be accomplished by explosive vapor such as is seen to issue from neighboring volcanoes, which often break out into eruption simultaneously with an earthquake noticed to produce an elevation of the coast and a sinking of the sea bottom. This vapor therefore is nothing else than common steam.

Now the steam developing beneath the earth's crust and producing earthquakes and volcanic activity can be traced to but two possible sources: First, the original magma of the globe, which, in default of a better explanation, has been frequently invoked by the geologist; Second, the secular leakage of the ocean bottoms, effected through fifteen miles of solid rock like granite, which naturally appeals to the physicist. If the escaping steam, or any sensible part of it, came from the central magma of the globe, volcanoes and earthquakes necessarily would occur in the interior of the continents as well as along the coasts, on islands, and in the depths of the sea. For the continents are large areas, and altogether cover more than one-fourth of the total surface of the globe; yet the volcanoes and world-shaking earthquakes are confined to the neighborhood of the oceans or other large bodies of water.

It clearly follows therefore that the agitating vapor does not come from the central magma of the globe, but must come from the secular leakage of the ocean bottoms. This is unmistakably indicated by the most overwhelming evidence of nature, and hence it follows that the secular leakage of the ocean bottoms through fifteen miles of rock like granite is effected by the constant pressure of the water upon the bed of the sea. When we recall that the column of water resting on the sea bottom is often five miles deep, giving a steady pressure theoretically adequate for throwing a jet to that height, it is not at all surprising that the water should work down through fifteen miles of rock like granite.

Accordingly it follows also that Daubrée's experiments are applicable to layers of rock from fifteen to twenty miles thick, and our fundamental proposition regarding the secular leakage of the ocean bottoms is proved quite independently of Daubrée's experiments. In the case of our thinly encrusted planet so largely covered with water, the natural arrangement between the overlying oceans and the underlying molten globe constitutes a laboratory of the most imposing magnitude, infinitely transcending anything ever conceived by man, with gigantic experiments constantly going on.   All that is needed therefore is for the philosopher to interpret Nature's stupendous operations, which unfortunately only too often prove disastrous to human life, owing to our ignorance and disregard of natural laws.   The highest duty of the philosopher is to discover these laws and make them available to the public, so as to contribute as much as possible to the safety and repose of mankind.

It is often imagined by many that the captains of industry are the principal creators of national wealth and prosperity, and that discoveries of natural laws are of little value compared to material things.   Is it necessary to point out the inadequacy of this view?   Is not he who discovers how to safeguard and preserve the property of the State as essential to the public well-being as he who merely develops, without knowing how to build so as to preserve, the products of human labor?   Would it be extreme to hold that a real discoverer, a true philosopher, is as valuable to the State as any captain of industry?   His worldly possessions, it is true, may be small, but his discoveries are useful to all mankind of the present and future generations; yea, they are the one imperishable product of the age, a priceless heritage of civilization, and given *freely* to all the nations of the earth.

In view of what has been proved in the researches here sketched, there will in the future be no excuse for our cities on the coasts of deep seas being consumed by conflagrations after earthquakes; for it is shown that all places on the coasts of deep seas are liable to earthquake disturbances, and the people should be prepared for such emergencies by extra and independent systems of water works.   If San Francisco had possessed such knowledge before the late disaster, and had had the courage to live up to it, she would not have been laid waste by the fire, nor would the earthquake damages have proved very serious.   But human frailty is such that we can learn only by experience.   Let us hope that the lesson will not soon be forgotten, and that other cities on the coast will be prepared for possible emergencies.

In the same way there is little excuse for damage by seismic sea waves. If ships put promptly to sea on the first sign of the withdrawal of the water from the shore, they will usually be safe, and can ride securely over the waves due to the sinking of the sea bottom; whereas if they remain in the harbor they are almost sure to be stranded and perhaps destroyed, with enormous losses of life and property.

The researches of Science therefore have an eminently practical and humane value, in addition to their purely philosophic interest. The preservation and promotion of Science has therefore become one of the highest duties of the State; for the discovery of natural laws is really necessary to the protection of the people and the preservation of civilization.

CHAPTER XI.

1908.

HOW THE MOUNTAINS WERE MADE IN THE DEPTHS OF THE SEA.*

By T. J. J. SEE.

EARLY in 1906 the daily press published accounts of the sudden appearance in Alaskan waters of Metcalf Island, and the illustrated weeklies have since given photographs showing its eruption above the sea as a volcano. More recently, another island has been raised in the Aleutian chain; and every month or so we read in press dispatches of eruptions occurring somewhere in the sea, and of islands being lifted above the water.

The experienced navigator has often heard of or seen these submarine outbreaks, and regards the uplift of islands as a common occurrence — long familiar to the explorer of the oceans. It never occurs to him that these volcanic outbreaks are especially extraordinary. On the other hand, the learned scientist in the secluded life of the University, constantly occupied with books, is largely withdrawn not only from the world, but also from contact with actual nature, and overlooks or underestimates the significance of what is so often reported by the ocean voyager. The more active scientist explores the mountains on the land, but gives very little thought to those in the depths of the sea.

Thus the observations of the navigator have not been adequately considered by the explorer of the continent, and consequently the theories formed from the study of the land do not accord with the facts observed in the ocean. But as our knowledge of the ocean has increased, it has been remarked with surprise that the sea bottom is here and there upraised and folded into mountains, which sometimes project above the water as

---

* Reprinted from the *Pacific Monthly* for September, 1908, by permission of *Sunset — the Pacific Monthly*.

A VIEW OF PERRY PEAK IN JUNE, 1906.

This peak rose from the ocean depths in the winter of 1905-1906. It has since disappeared. Photo from Capt. F. M. Munger.

islands, and again are entirely hidden from our view by the great depths of the sea. The naturalist who has been occupied with the investigation of mountains on the land finds himself greatly perplexed to account for those in the oceans.

For a long time it was supposed that only isolated cones arose from the deep, and now and then appeared above the water as volcanic islands. This was in fact observed in the classic period by the Greek and Romans. Aristotle, Strabo and Pliny distinctly mention eruptions in the sea, and give accounts of how certain islands were raised above the water within historical times. In striking contrast to this natural attitude of the ancient writers, we find in the modern geologies no general theory of island formation. Considering the enormous advance in science during the past two thousand years, this appears to be a strange and almost unaccountable neglect on the part of the modern investigator.

When, however, the exact measurement of the ocean depths made within recent years showed not only peaks and cones scattered widely over the sea bottom, but also great ranges of mountains in the depths of the sea, the old view that islands arose only from isolated cones obviously could no longer be held. Geologists have long accepted the theory that the mountains were formed by the shrinkage of the earth, due to the progress of secular cooling, and they have explained the mountains on the land by the subsidence of the ocean basins, which, it was held, pushed up the edges of the continents. Yet if mountains exist also in the depths of the sea, this theory of oceanic subsidence would not well account for these submarine folds. Thus the discovery of mountain chains in the ocean excited the surprise without satisfying the curiosity of the naturalist.

By what process, then, are mountains formed in the sea, and are they formed on the land by the same cause? This is a question which we shall endeavor to answer in the course of this paper, and the result is so general as to be of interest to every reader of scientific literature.

Just south of the Aleutian Islands there is a deep trench in the sea, which has a depth of from 3,000 to over 4,000 fathoms — from 18,000 to over 24,000 feet. This depression is long and narrow, just like a trough, as if dug out by supreme intelligence; and right next to it on the north, the Aleutain Islands run parallel to this depression all along. The Aleutian Islands are in fact a mighty mountain range under water, with only a few peaks here and there projecting above the sea as islands. This great ridge is not only parallel to the deep trench just south of it, but also of almost exactly the same volume; so that if one had a shovel large enough to take off the island ridge and throw it in the trench, it would about fill it up.

Now if we go along in a level plain and come to a mound, with a depression by the side, of about the same volume, do we not immediately conclude that the mound came out of the hole in the ground, and that the mound-builders have been at work there? And if we find not only one mound, but many, each accompanied by an adjacent hole of corresponding volume, do we not infer that the several mounds came out of the respective holes, and that the whole group of mounds is the work of a colony of mound-builders? Such a group of mounds once existed where the city of St. Louis now stands, and for that reason the metropolis of the Mississippi Valley often is called the Mound City.

Again, suppose the mounds were arranged in a line, with the holes all on one side, and close together; a little shoveling would convert them into a continuous trench with a bank on one side, like an irrigation ditch. If we go into a level field and find such a trench and adjacent embankment of equal volume, so that the bank would fill up the depression, if shoveled in, we know that the ditch diggers have been at work, and that the bank was made of earth taken out of the ditch.

What we have here considered with regard to familiar sights on the land, we encounter also in the bed of the sea. There are islands with depressions or holes near them, of about equal volume; and there are ridges or mountain ranges with trenches near them of so nearly the same volume that the depressions could be filled up by shoveling off the elevations. Thus we are led to conclude that the elevations and the depressions are physically connected; and that the elevations resulted from matter taken from under the depressions, and transferred to its present position beneath the adjacent range.

Now in the case of these inequalities on our level fields, some process equivalent to surface shoveling was actually used. The islands and mountain ranges in the sea, however, were formed by a much mightier process; namely, by the expulsion of lava from beneath the earth's crust, which pushes it up in one place, and permits it to sink down in another, so that matter is transferred from one place to the other by the movement of lava streams beneath the cool, solid crust of the globe.

To understand how this takes place, let us consider the world-shaking earthquakes which so frequently occur in the Aleutian Islands. Major Dutton justly observes that this region is one of the chief breeding-grounds of world-shakers. And if we compare the distribution of earthquakes given in Milne's earthquake map of the world, with this region, we shall find that the trench and adjacent ridge run right through the center of the blackest part of the great earthquake belt surrounding the Pacific Ocean. This indicates that the earthquakes are concerned with the digging out of the trench to the south of these islands, and with the elevation of the islands themselves, a number of which have been raised above the water during the historical period. In fact three or more new volcanoes in this range have broken out since these islands were first explored by Europeans.

When a great earthquake occurs in the Aleutian Islands the shaking frequently is so violent that persons cannot stand upon their feet. In one well-known case further east, at Yakutat Bay, Alaska, September 10-15, 1899, a party of explorers felt the shaking so terribly that they could not stand on their feet and had to lie on the ground; and while they were thus prostrate, expecting the earth to open or an avalanche from the mountains to overwhelm

them, the adajcent sea was thrown into great eddies, and a huge
wave swept the shore, up-rooting the forests, and carrying the
helpless explorers some distance inland. By good fortune, however, they escaped without serious injury.

It may well be imagined that they were not altogether surprised to find that great avalanches of stone and ice had slid down
the mountains, and vast glaciers had slipped into the sea, carrying
everything before them. Nay, worse still! The solid land of the
coast for over a hundred miles had been bodily uplifted many feet,
the maximum ascertained elevation being forty-seven feet and four
inches. Barnacles, and other marine animals were now sticking
to the rocks far above the reach of the highest tides, and furnished
conclusive proof of the mighty uplift of the earth's crust.

This great earthquake was carefully investigated in 1905 by
Professor R. S. Tarr, of Cornell University, and Lawrence Martin,
of the National Geographical Society. Their investigation as
published in the *Bulletin* of the Geological Society of America,
May, 1906, included photographs showing the barnacles still
sticking to the rocks. Now from what is shown here, it follows
that when the sea coast is upraised by an earthquake, as often
happens, lava is expelled from under the sea and pushed under the
land. It is in this way that mountains are formed along the coasts
and in the depths of the sea. The parallelism of the mountains to
the sea coast is familiar to every student of elementary geography.

It often happens in the Aleutian Islands that a great earthquake is followed by a so-called "tidal wave," or as it is more
properly called, a seismic sea wave. In the most important class
of these waves it is noticed that after the earthquake the water
withdraws from the shore, by a gradual draining away, as in the
tides, only more rapidly. Ships anchored in the harbor are often
left stranded, and the bottom laid bare, even when the previous
depth of the water was seven fathoms. But in an hour's time or
less, the sea returns as a great wave, which, near the shore, becomes
a mighty vertical wall of water, and carries everything before it.
Ships are thus washed a long distance inland, and many of them

VIEW OF TWO SHIPS WASHED ASHORE AND WRECKED BY THE GREAT SEA WAVE FOLLOWING THE EARTHQUAKE AT ARICA, AUGUST 13, 1868.

From a photograph in the possession of Mrs. E. V. Cutts, of Mare Island, California.

lost by dashing against rocks during the dreadful inundation of the sea; and in the same way, cities lying near the sea level are overflowed. In some cases they are first shaken down by the earthquake, and then overwhelmed by the sea; so that Nature seems bent on their utter destruction — one calamity following swift upon another.

Now the cause of the withdrawal of the sea from the shore is the sinking of the sea bottom. The subsidence of the bed is indicated by the way in which the water drains away. Lava has been expelled from beneath the sea bottom till the overlying crust becomes unstable, and when it is again shaken in a great earthquake it often gives down. The water then flows in on all sides to fill up the depression in the sea level caused by the sudden drop of the sunken area; and after a little while the currents meet in the center of the depression, and by their mutual impact raise the depressed level into a ridge. The flowing of the currents towards the center of the depression draws the water away from the shore, so that the ships are left stranded on the bare bottom and perfectly helpless. And when the ridge upraised by the mutual impact of the currents at length collapses by the gradual settlement of the water under its own gravitation, a great wave is sent ashore to add to the horrors of the earthquake.

Many cases of the sinking of the sea bottom are known, and in some instances it is found that the drop amounted to hundreds of fathoms. It is by this process of undermining and sinking that the deep trench has been dug out near the Aleutian Islands. In fact, Nature gives a clear indication of her own mighty processes; for on the west coast of South America, in Japan, in the East Indies and elsewhere, the coast often is upraised by the same earthquake which causes the sinking of the sea bottom so clearly foretold by the withdrawal of the sea and its return as a great wave.

The uplifting of the sea coast indicates that something has been pushed under it, and the sinking of the adjacent sea bottom shows that it has been undermined by the expulsion of the lava which has been injected under the land. As the two areas are side by side, and both movements occur in earthquakes which disturb the intervening region most terribly (as if molten rock were moving beneath the crust) it follows that a mass of lava is expelled from under the sea and pushed under the neighboring coast. This unquestionably is the general process in the greatest earthquakes.

The continuation of this process over long periods of time gives rise to the expulsion of a vast quanity of lava from beneath the sea, and the crust along the shore becomes upheaved into a mighty ridge of mountains. In South America such uplifts of the coast, with accompanying seismic sea waves, have often been observed. This is the continuation of the process by which the Andes were formed.

The coast of Chile was raised by the earthquake of 1822. And in 1835, the movement was repeated on a still larger scale, in the earthquake witnessed by Darwin and Fitzroy, who were then on their famous voyage around the world. This disturbance raised the coast five or six feet for several hundred miles, and the city of Concepcion was totally destroyed.

On August 16, 1906, when Valparaiso was laid waste by one of the most terrible earthquakes of modern times, it is said that the coast was raised about ten feet. The earthquake of 1835 was calculated by Lyell to have raised the coast by an amount corresponding to the bulk of Mt. Aetna; in other words, according to our modern view, a bulk of lava equal to Mt. Aetna was pushed under the shore, and the sea bottom correspondingly undermined.

Not only are the displacements of matter beneath the crust large, but also in the same direction as those great movements of the past, by which the mountains have been so greatly uplifted, and the sea bottom so deeply sunk down.

For the beaches at Valparaiso were found by Darwin to have been uplifted 1,300 feet in recent geological time; and more recent travelers have found marine shells in the Andes at a height of at least 15,000 feet. Thus we connect the fossils at the greatest

RELIEF MAP OF CENTRAL CALIFORNIA.

Showing the more gradual slope of the Sierras towards the Pacific Ocean by which they were uplifted.

RELIEF MAP OF NORTH AMERICA.

Illustrating the New Theory that the Mountains are formed by the oceans, and thus run parallel to the sea coast. From Frye's *Complete Geography*, by permission of Ginn & Co., Publishers.

altitude with the uplift of the sea coast by earthquakes, and may affirm that most of our highest mountains were once beneath the sea, and have since been raised to such great heights by the continuation of the earthquake process. The small uplifts of the coast witnessed at the present time are but a part of the great expulsions of lava from beneath the sea towards the land, which resulted in development of mountains along the coasts and in the depths of the ocean.

In this manner the Aleutian Islands are being raised into a mighty mountain chain in the sea; eventually it will rise above the water and connect North America with Asia, so that the Arctic will be entirely cut off from the Pacific Ocean.

If now the question be asked why the earthquake and mountain-forming forces are so powerful in certain places, and so feeble in others, we reply that it is all due to the leakage under the hydrostatic pressure on the bottom resulting from the depth of the ocean. The deeper the ocean becomes the greater the pressure on the bottom, and the more water leaks through the crust, to form steam beneath. The explosive vapor slowly accumulates, and when it must have relief, the region shakes till a fault moves, and the crust readjusts itself so as to give more space beneath. Fault is the term used by geologists to denote a crack in the rocks of the earth's crust, which is made up of blocks like pavement, only very much larger.

It is observed that the earthquakes are always worst where the sea is deepest, because the leakage there is greatest. If one looks at a map of the ocean depths as laid down by the Coast-Survey measurements, he may tell from the trenches in the sea where the earthquakes are worst. These deep troughs always follow the earthquake belts, or rather the earthquakes follow these deep troughs, though some earthquakes occur remote from them. The vast majority of the greatest earthquakes, however, always occur near these dugout places in the sea bottom; as along the coast west of South America, near Guam, in the Friendly Islands of the Southern Pacific Ocean between Samoa and New Zealand, in the East Indies, near the Phillipines, the Japanese, Kurile, and Aleutian Islands.

It is well known that the worst earthquake country in the world is Japan, and just east of these islands the sea over an area of considerable extent is 4,600 fathoms deep. The hydrostatic pressure at the bottom of the sea is here great enough to throw a jet of water five and a half miles high. Is it any wonder that such a pressure should force the water slowly into the bowels of the earth?

The crust is made of solid rock, like granite, twenty miles thick, yet under such a pressure as that exerted by the deepest oceans, the water will slowly leak through, and form so much steam in the underlying lava that it will swell and finally shake, till it gets more space by pushing out at the edges.

The whole island of Nipon has thus been raised above the ocean. If Nipon were dug off and thrown into the Tuscarora Deep, it would just about fill up that immense depression. The earthquakes in Japan are due to the fact that the islands are still rising from the sea, and as the Tuscarora trench is deepening all the time, Japan will always be greatly afflicted by earthquakes and seismic sea waves.

The region of the Friendly Islands in the Southern Pacific Ocean, between Samoa and New Zealand, affords a good illustration of the formation of mountains in the open sea at some distance from a continent. Here two long, narrow connecting trenches are dug out to a depth of over 4,000 fathoms; and on the west, just parallel to the trenches, a mountain chain is lifting its crest above the water, a few of the highest peaks already projecting as islands.

It is observed that the range always is formed on the side of the trench opposite to the ocean, because the secular leakage of the ocean causes the expulsion of the lava to be effected in the direction of the land. The reason of this is that steam is formed under the ocean, but scarcely at all under the land; and hence it always works out towards the edges of the oceans, and thus walls in the sea by high mountains about their borders.

Over half a century ago the veteran American geologist, J. D. Dana, the famous professor at Yale College, noticed that the highest mountains lie opposite the deepest oceans, and conversely. He inferred that the relation of the extent and depth of the ocean to the height and grandeur of the mountains about its borders was of fundamental importance. Yet Dana did not perceive correctly the real cause of mountain-making, for all geologists have heretofore ascribed the formation of mountains to the shrinkage arising from the secular cooling of the earth.

Even now many persons will be surprised to learn that this old theory has no valid foundation in Nature, and will have to be entirely abandoned. But such is the case. It will have to be given up and thrown overboard, just like the more famous Ptolemaic system of astronomy, which was finally overthrown by Copernicus in 1543. Previous to that time Ptolemy's system had stood the test of fourteen centuries, since the epoch of the school of Alexandria, where the *Almagest* was composed in the reigns of Hadrian and Antoninus Pius, about 140 A.D.

In the same way, the contraction theory is venerable from age. It was vaguely hinted at by Newton, and in 1829 was given its final form by the famous French geologist, Elie de Beaumont. He held that the earth is cooling by the gradual dissipation of heat into space, and the nucleus shrinking away from the crust; so that at intervals the crust collapses to fill up the vacant space, and this causes the rocks to be crumpled and pushed up into mountain ranges formed along the lines of fracture.

If this theory were true the mountain chains ought to run in any direction with respect to the oceans; and they certainly would not always run parallel to the sea coast. In some cases at least the mountains would run diagonally across the continents; yet this never happens in practice, and we may be very sure that this antiquated theory has no foundation whatever in actual Nature.

The doctrine of the secular cooling of the globe has behind it the weight of ancient opinion, and still finds a place in most books which deal with the earth's development. But as a matter of fact secular cooling is of very little consequence, and the theory is correspondingly misapplied in many of the sciences today.

In my investigations on the *Temperature of the Earth* recently published by the American Philosophical Society at Philadelphia, it is shown that the cooling is confined almost exclusively to the crust of the globe, and that practically no shrinkage occurs from the escape of heat from the deep interior, because the amount of heat lost is altogether too small. Nor has such shrinkage been appreciable at any time since the crust was formed, in the original consolidation of the globe. Before the formation of a crust, when the primordial consolidation had not yet begun, there may indeed have been a considerable loss of heat from the incandescent surface, but since the outer layers became cooled and encrusted, and the oceans were formed from vapor previously floating in the atmosphere, the effects of cooling have been very slight indeed.

We may easily convince ourselves of the correctness of this view by recalling that no important changes now going on upon the earth can be clearly ascribed to the effects of secular cooling. The most important changes are those due to earthquakes, and earthquakes certainly are not due to that cause; for if they were, they would break out in the interior of the continents as well as along the coasts and in the depths of the sea.

Is not an inland region such as Kansas or Sahara cooling as much as an equal area of any sea coast? If cooling were the cause of the great earthquakes, why should they occur near the sea and not in high dry regions in the interior of the continents?

Moreover the Andes and the coast mountains in Alaska are constantly shaken, while those in Colorado, far from the sea, are never seriously disturbed. This shows that mountain-making depends in some way upon the sea; and we have seen that it arises from the leakage of the oceans, which develops steam beneath the crust. This swells and finally shakes and pushes out some of the saturated lava at the edges, so that the crust is uplifted into mountains along the borders of the continents and in the sea.

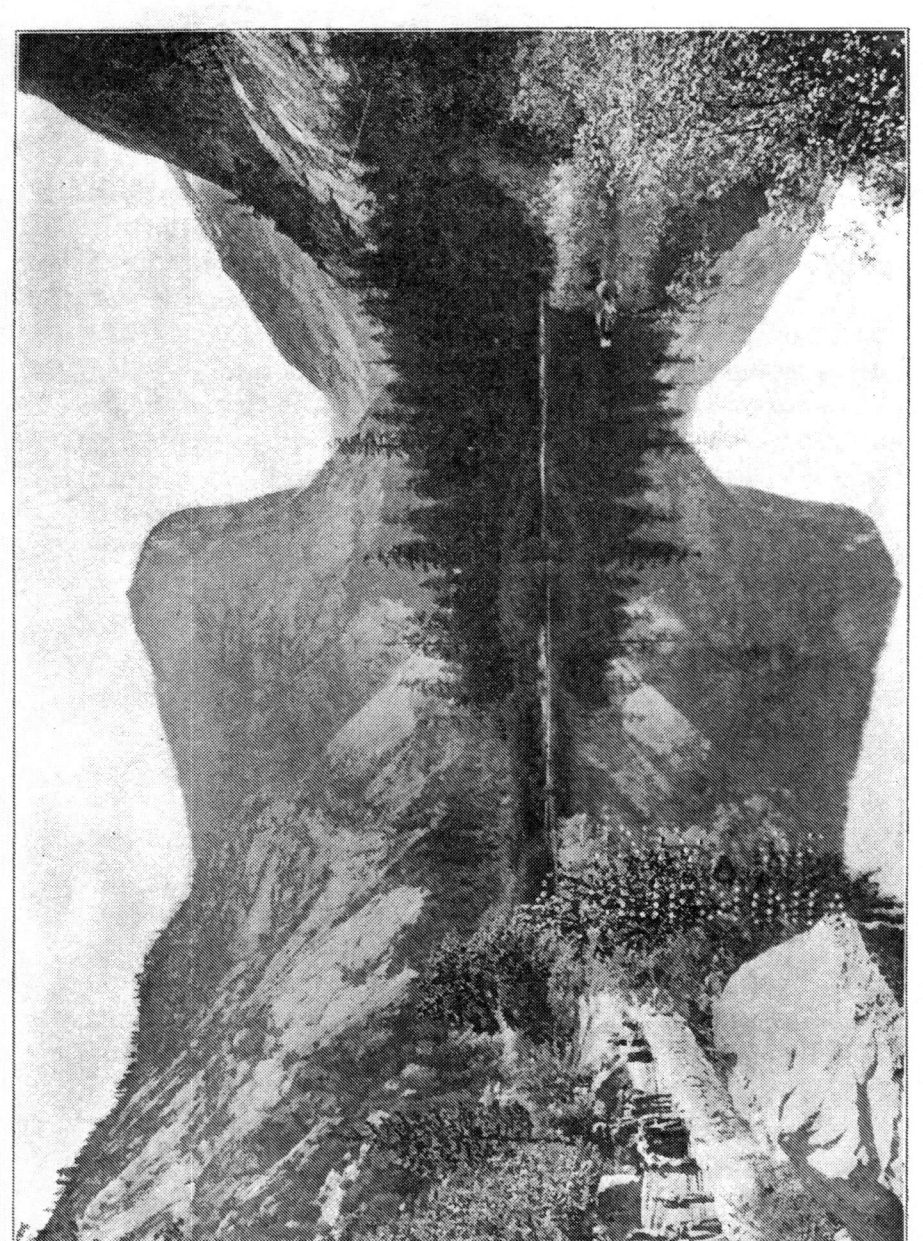

MIRROR LAKE AND HALF DOME.

Yosemite Valley, California.　Publications of Sierra Club, June, 1911.　Photograph by Pillsbury Picture Co.

Fossils now found far inland show that at one time the sea covered the high plateaus of our western states, and extended to the Rocky Mountains. The whole country west of Laramie, Wyoming, has been raised out of the sea in recent geological times; and earthquakes obviously have been the means of this great uplift, which has widened the continent by a thousand miles, and raised the plateaus about a mile above the sea.

In the same way the great plateaus in South America and in Asia have been uplifted by earthquakes. The plateau of Tibet is three miles above the sea, and bones of elephants and rhinoceroses now found there show that the uplift has occurred within recent geological time, because those animals could not live at that altitude. Accordingly they must have flourished there when Tibet was only about a mile above the sea, and the uplifting has since carried their bones to much greater elevation.

Perhaps the reader will agree that the process here outlined for certain mountain chains is the true one, but yet ask whether it is not possible that some have been formed by other causes, such as the shrinkage of the globe? He may notice that all mountains are not parallel to the sea coast, and thus imagine that such exceptional inland ranges were formed by a different cause. To this conjecture we may reply that Nature has one uniform process, and the formation in all cases is due to the same physical agency. And while we have not yet explored the earth's surface sufficiently to ascertain exactly how all the mountains were produced, we may be sure that the cause is always the same.

That some mountains could be formed by one process and some by another is inconceivable. We do not know the extent of the sea in past geological ages, and until this unwritten history is fully developed — it may take centuries to do it properly — we cannot make out the precise details by which all the mountains were formed. But we have proved how they are formed in the clearest cases, and as nearly all are parallel to the shore, as if due to the expulsion of lava from beneath the sea, there can be no possible doubt that we have found the true and universal cause of mountain formation in general.

The chief purpose of earthquakes is to raise land above the sea. These disturbances seem very destructive to animal and vegetable life, and especially to mankind; but without them the earth would still be entirely covered by the oceans, and none of the higher forms of life could have been developed on our planet.

Though the cosmical purpose of earthquakes was not understood by the ancients, the uplift of strata by these disturbances was distinctly taught by Strabo; and he cited the presence of shells far inland as proof of the former extent of the sea. These views have long been held by investigators, but in recent years Lord Kelvin and Sir G. H. Darwin have proved from their mathematical researches on the tides and other phenomena that the earth behaves as a solid, and hence does not have a liquid nucleus, as geologists had long been led to suppose. On this restricted view of the case, the uplift of the land above the sea could not be explained.

The geologists therefore gave up the theory that the interior of the earth is liquid, and the solid crust subject to uplifts, and adopted the view that the globe is solid throughout. This conclusion, however, is unjustifiable; for just beneath the crust is a layer which in earthquakes is shown to behave as a fluid. Molten rock actually moves beneath the solid crust in great earthquakes, and it is this enforced movement of the lava, some twenty miles beneath our feet, under accumulating steam pressure, that shakes down cities and often devastates whole countries.

When we have the oceans for an overlying tank of water, and the incandescent nucleus of our globe for a furnace, the natural arrangement is such that the leakage of the thin crust between the water and the underlying fire, is likely to give rise to some gigantic experiments. It is this secular leakage and nothing else which produces earthquakes, volcanoes, mountain formation, the uplift of islands and plateaus, seismic sea waves, and the feeble attraction of mountains long since noticed in geodesy. Six great classes of

MT. CHIMBORAZO, NEAR QUITO, ALTITUDE 20,498 FEET. (WHYMPER, 1880)
One of the most celebrated of the Andean Peaks. *Encyclopedia Americana.* From the Article, *Andes*, by special permission

MT. POPOCATEPETL, MEXICO.
A typical volcano, rising to an altitude of about 17,000 feet. Publications of the Sierra Club, June, 1911.

MT. HUASCARAN, IN CENTRAL PERU, ALTITUDE ABOUT 24,000 FEET.
Photograph and copyright by Miss Anna S. Peck, *National Geographical Magazine*, for June, 1909.
Used by special permission of Miss Peck.

MT. ACONCAGUA, IN CENTRAL CHILE.
The highest Volcano in the world, and long considered the summit of the Andes.   Altitude, 22,800 feet.

phenomena are thus connected and shown to depend on a single physical cause.

Volcanoes are only particular mountains, and it was noticed by the ancients that they are always developed in or near the sea. Thousands of eruptions occur in the sea bottom, but only occasionally do the new volcanoes reach the surface. More frequently the presence of fire under the sea is told by the boiling of the water, and by dead fish found floating on the surface. Even the Greeks and Romans noticed these submarine outbreaks, and their disastrous effects on marine animals.

Volcanoes on land always break out near the shore, in mountain ranges which are folded sharply upward — as in the Andes and the Aleutian Islands. Such sharp folds are always near the sea, and their dependence on it is also proved by the vast preponderance of water vapor which they emit. According to Sir Archibald Geikie, 999 in 1000 parts of all the vapor they emit is steam. The pumice which they blow out is only molten rock saturated with steam and other vapors, and afterwards dried up. And as pumice underlies every mountain, an earthquake which opens an orifice is sure to blow out considerable quantities of this light material. When pumice is ground up it makes ashes, and hence the vast clouds of dust blown out of volcanoes, which obscure the sun and are carried over the earth for hundreds and even thousands of miles.

As recently developed, geology has presented the singular anomaly of admitting the existence of shells and marine fossils thousands of feet above the sea, without any means of explaining how they got there; and at the same time denying the bodily elevation of the sea coasts by earthquakes, though formerly this doctrine of elevation was generally accepted. It is now easy to see how all these phenomena can be reconciled and explained by indicating the simplest of causes, the leakage of the ocean bottoms, which produces elevations and also depressions.

Not only do we prove the elevation of the sea coasts by earthquakes, which thus push lava under the land, from beneath the sea, but also that subsidences may happen somewhat less frequently. The sea bottom often sinks when lava is expelled from beneath it, so as to undermine the support from below; and in like manner any coast may subside temporarily if the subterranean movement of lava is such as to undermine the foundation. This has happened in numerous historical cases, of which we shall mention only a few.

In 1692, Jamaica was visited by a terrible earthquake, and afterwards about three-fourths of Port Royal sank into the sea, where the houses long afterwards could be seen beneath the waves.

The sinking was caused by a block of the earth's crust giving down during the earthquake, which had weakened the foundation.

In 1746, Callao, Peru, was terribly shaken by an earthquake, and the coast inundated by a seismic sea wave, said to have been eighty feet high. In this case the sea bottom sank some distance from the land, and it carried parts of the shore down with it. Old Callao was thus submerged beneath the waves, and the houses could be seen in the bottom of the new harbor.

Another good illustration of this undermining is afforded by the coast of Pamphylia, in Asia Minor. In the fourth century B.C., Alexander the Great marched his army along a road on the sea coast overhung by the Climax Mountains. Strabo says that on a stormy day, when the waves beat on the road, the soldiers waded to the middle of their bodies in water; at the present time the same road is covered by the water to a depth of over twelve feet, even when the weather is calm. Hence the whole coast must have subsided by about this amount. The shores of the Mediterranean present numerous cases of harbor works of the classic period, some above and some below the present level of the sea.

But the most celebrated case of subsidence is that of the Homeric City of Helike, which formerly stood on the southern shore of the Gulf of Corinth. In the year 373 B.C., the whole of Peloponnesus was shaken by a terrible earthquake. Helike and Bura were leveled to the ground, and great chasms opened in the

TYPICAL VIEW OF THE ANDES, NEAR ACONCAGUA, CENTRAL CHILE.

ground near the latter place; then the bed of the Gulf of Corinth gave down at least 100 feet, and carried Helike down with it. The inrush of the mighty sea wave destroyed ten Lacedemonian vessels lying in the harbor, and the sea rose so high about the Temple of Neptune that only the tops of the trees remained above the water, though for centuries afterwards the houses could still be seen beneath the waves. This happened when Plato was fifty-four, and at the head of the Academy in Athens, and Aristotle was a boy eleven years old. The sinking of Helike greatly perplexed the wisest of the Athenian sages, but in spite of all their learning and acuteness they were utterly unable to account for such a strange phenomenon.

In the light of the above theory it is easy to see that the earthquake had pushed lava from beneath the Gulf of Corinth, and thus caused the chasms to open near Bura. No doubt the mountains of Arcadia were badly shaken and somewhat uplifted; then the sea bottom gave down, and Helike disappeared beneath the waves. Such subsidences are less frequent than uplifts of the coasts, but they occur occasionally and sometimes cause great destruction.

Now that the cause of earthquakes and sea waves is perfectly clear, the people have a better means of protecting themselves against such calamities than formerly. No city on the coast of a deep sea is ever entirely safe from earthquakes and sea waves; but if good houses are built, and a place for refuge exists, in case the water retires from the shore after an earthquake, indicating that the sea bottom has sunk, the danger to the population is comparatively small. The only means of safety is to flee with the utmost speed to the high grounds, as the people in South America have learned to do by long and bitter experience. There is generally time enough for escape, before the wave returns; and even the ships in the harbor will be safe, if they promptly put to sea; for in the open sea, they can ride over the wave without injury, but if they lay in the harbor they are sure to be lost or washed inland.

Studies of the phenomena of the ocean and of the laws of the physical world by which the mountains are formed, owing to the secular leakage of their waters through the crust of the earth, may thus contribute greatly to the safety of mankind, as well as throw light on the mystery and grandeur connected with all the great secrets of Nature.

In this brief outline of the results embodied in four scientific memoirs recently published by the American Philosophical Society at Philadelphia, we have touched only upon those topics which seemed likely to be of most popular interest. The new theory has been adopted with enthusiasm in the highest circles of the scientific world; and hence the results here given may be considered as demonstrated. Since the death of Helmholtz, of Berlin, 1894, Professor Arrhenius, of Stockholm, has gradually taken the foremost place among the physicists of Continental Europe. He is one of those who have adopted the new theory from the first. Among others may be mentioned Professor Suess, of Vienna, the most eminent geologist in Europe, and the veteran physicists, Lord Kelvin and Sir Wm. Huggins, two of the most illustrious ex-presidents of the Royal Society.

CHAPTER XII.

1913.

FURTHER CONSIDERATIONS ON THE ORIGIN OF THE HIMALAYA MOUNTAINS AND THE PLATEAU OF TIBET.*

By T. J. J. SEE.

§1. *Introductory Remarks.*

THE four memoirs dealing with the cause of earthquakes, mountain formation, and kindred phenomena connected with the physics of the earth, which the writer had the honor to communicate to this Society in the years 1906-08, and have published in the *Proceedings*, have laid the foundations of a new theory of the physics of the earth's crust. The new theory already is widely adopted by the most eminent investigators, and the purpose of the present paper is merely to add a final confirmation of some interest.

During the past five years the writer's attention has been so fully occupied with the problems of Cosmogony that the problems relating to Geogony, or the formation of the earth, have been left largely in abeyance; and yet some new light has been shed on them, especially by the researches showing that the lunar craters are due to impact, and thus in no way similar to terrestrial volcanoes as was so long believed.

Quite recently it was thought worth while to re-examine the phenomena of the earth's crust, in the light of the New Science of Cosmogony resulting from the researches of the past five years. For in studying the problem of the origin of the Himalayas and the plateau of Tibet some important considerations were brought out that were not included in my former papers, and thus it seems

---

*Presented to the American Philosophical Society held at Philadelphia, on the occasion of the Annual General Meeting, April 17-19, 1913.

advisable to place them on record as confirming and extending my former investigations.

Moreover, the subject of the origin of the Himalayas is attracting attention abroad. Apparently without knowledge of my work Colonel Sidney G. Burrard, R. E., F. R. S., Surveyor-General of India, has been devoting considerable attention to the subject in 'Professional Paper No. 12, Survey of India,' a summary of which is given in *The Observatory* for November, 1912, p. 413:

"It may be remembered that several years ago Col. Burrard showed that there appears to be a subterranean mass of great density lying across India in mean latitude 23° north. He now shows that the observations indicate the existence of a line of low density between this subterranean mass and the Himalayas, and suggests that there was, or is, one long crack in the earth's subcrust extending from Sumatra round the Arrakan coast across Northern India, through the Persian Gulf to the Mediterranean, traces of which are seen in the parallel shores of the Gulf of Oman and the Persian Gulf. The crack has been filled with alluvial deposit across Northern India and in other places, but the Himalayas remain as the result of the rift in the earth, a great mass of matter having been pushed northward. It has been supposed by others that the Himalayan range was formed by the southward advance of the northern part of the Asiastic continent on to the Indo-African tableland."

The idea here developed by Colonel Burrard, including especially the light material under northern India, and the pushing of the Himalayas northward, is so very similar to that developed in my memoirs that it must be regarded as an independent confirmation of the theory that the mountains are formed by the sea. And as this conclusion applies to the greatest and most intricate range in the world, the external relations of which are not entirely simple, I deem it worthy of attention.

Finally, it may be noted that much interest has been awakened in this subject in England and other countries of Europe.

RELIEF MAP OF ASIA.

From Frye's *Complete Geography*, by permission of Ginn & Co., Publishers. Showing the development of the Himalayas and Plateau of Tibet by the Indian Ocean on the South, and other ranges of Mountains by the Pacific, along the Eastern shores of the Continent. Before India was raised from the ocean, the sea coast ran parallel to the Himalayas, as in the age of the Andes in South America.

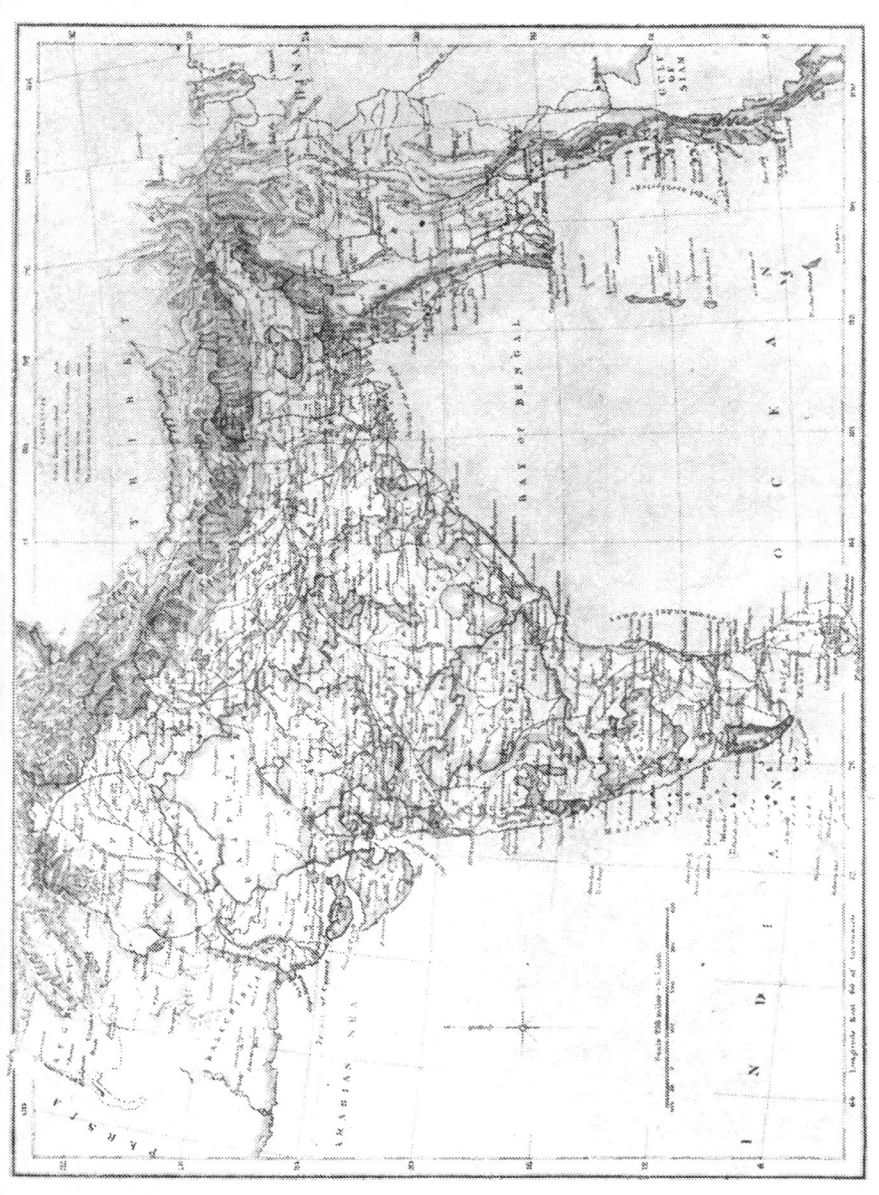

MAP OF INDIA.

From the *Encyclopedia Britannica*, ninth edition, showing the location of the Himalayas and Plateau of Tibet in relation to the neighboring parts of India.

The new theory already is widely taught in the schools of Great Britain and the Continent; and in his new work *The Growth of a Planet*, (The MacMillan Co., New York, 1911), the London geophysicist Mr. Edwin Sharpe Grew, M. A., concedes that the author's reasoning on the Aleutian Islands is unanswerable, and finally says:

"Dr. See has arranged his facts with great ingenuity, and the presentation of his case is the most powerful argument which has ever been advanced in favor of the view held since the days of Strabo, Aristotle or Pliny, that the expansive force of steam is the prime cause of volcanic and seismic disturbances."

In view of this general interest a few additional considerations on the origin of the Himalayas may be important. For after careful reflection I regard the Himalayas as the crucial test; and as the theory is triumphantly verified by a more complete study of this great range, it must hereafter be regarded as firmly and permanently established.

§2. *The Volumes of the Plateaus of the Rocky Mountains, of the Andes, and of the Himalayas.*

In the four Memoirs included in the *Proceedings* of this Society for 1906–08, the new theory of mountain formation is treated with considerable detail, but some numerical relations between the plateaus above mentioned are worthy of more attention than they have yet received.

The Pacific plateau of North America is of variable width, being less than 500 miles wide in Mexico, and perhaps 600 miles wide in Canada, but from 1,000 to 1,500 miles wide in the United States. Perhaps 750 miles wide would be a good average estimate of the whole plateau. And the height may be taken as approximately 5,000 feet, or a mile above the sea. These average figures will satisfactorily represent the Pacific plateau in North America. It is noticed also in many places that where the plateau is broadest it is of less average height; but where it is narrower the height is somewhat increased.

In the Andes the same principles prevail. The plateau is highest in the region of Lake Titicaca, where the elevation is over 12,600 feet, or 2.5 miles. The width here does not exceed 300 miles. Further north, near Quito, it narrows up, and is not over half this width; but in Columbia it again spreads out to a width of 300 or 400 miles, but is only about 6,000 or 8,000 feet in height, scarcely more than half that along the more southern portion of the Andes.

It is noticeable that the height decreases from 12,600 feet near Lake Titicaca, to 11,000 feet in central Peru, and perhaps 10,000 feet at Quito; while south of Titicaca the height does not decrease appreciably till central Chile is reached, after which it falls steadily till the continent sinks beneath the sea at Cape Horn.

Now it is remarkable that if we take a typical section of the highest and broadest part of the Andean plateau, 2.5 miles high by 300 miles wide, the numerical product of width by height in miles is 750. And the Rocky Mountain plateau, one mile high and 750 miles wide, gives the same product, 750 square miles.

To be sure this product can be varied considerably by taking different sections of the plateaus of North and South America, but all in all this average estimate appears to be a fair one. For in the article *Andes*, in the *Encyclopedia Britannica*, 9th edition, Sir Archibald Geikie estimates the bulk of the Andes as of the average width of 100 miles, and the height 13,000 feet. The present estimate gives greater width but somewhat less height.

On the whole, I am inclined to think that the average sectional area in the Andes is somewhat less than that in the Rocky Mountain plateau; for between Colorado and the Pacific coast the width is about 1,500 miles, and the average height about a mile. The plateau is much narrower in Canada, and very much narrower in Mexico, practically disappearing entirely in Central America and Panama. Thus at one point in the United States the sectional contents may be twice that in the Andes; yet the average sectional volume for the Pacific plateau of North America is not much greater than the larger sectional volumes for the plateau of the Andes.

The significance of this equality in the sections of the two plateaus lies in the fact that both are the products of the common Pacific Ocean, one in the northern, the other in the southern continent. The new theory does not require that the volumes should be exactly equal, but it implies that they should be comparable, and such is the fact in a very striking degree.

Let us now consider the plateau of Tibet, in comparison with that of the Andes. The height of western Tibet is about 15,000 feet, while eastern Tibet has an elevation of only 11,000 feet. The breadth also varies from some 200 miles on the west to 500 miles at the eastern extremity (General Strachey, Article *Himalayas, Encyclopedia Britannica*, 9th edition).

Accordingly, if we take the wider part of western Tibet as having a sectional height of three miles and a breadth of 250 miles, the product in miles is 750, exactly the same as in the Andes and the Rocky Mountains. Further east in Tibet the width may be 500 miles, and the height about two miles, which gives a sectional product of 1,000. This is larger than the average Andean product adopted above, and more like that of the Rocky Mountain plateau west of Colorado.

But the circumstance that the sectional volumes of three great plateaus in the three leading continents of the globe should all be so nearly equal is fully as impressive a fact as the related fact that all of these plateaus should overlook the same great ocean by which they were elevated.

Altogether the similarity in the volumes of sections of these three greatest plateaus is so striking as to make it difficult to deny that it constitutes practically a mathematical demonstration that these plateaus were uplifted by the Pacific Ocean. The relationships here brought out as to the volumes of these plateaus, in addition to the situations about the Pacific Ocean, could not well be accounted for by chance, even if we did not know the cause of mountain formation. But as the cause of mountain formation is fully understood, the cause which has built the plateaus is also clearly shown, and it is impossible to consider any other explanation than that here outlined.

§3. *General Law that where a Continuous Plateau increases in width, it decreases in elevation.*

This law doubtless results from the process of uplifting by which the mountains and plateaus have been raised above the sea. For example, in case of the continuous plateau crowned with mountain crests which surrounds the Pacific Ocean from Cape Horn to Alaska, and then extends down the south eastern shores of Asia, runs westward through India, and down the east shore of Africa to the Cape of Good Hope, it is observed in each of the four continents traversed that where the plateau is highest it usually narrows in width, and *vice versa*.

Thus we have seen that the plateau of the Andes is high in Chile, Bolivia, Peru and Ecuador, but in Columbia falls to about half its former level, but expands to about double width. This expansion of the width of the plateau in Columbia is characteristic of plateau formation in general. There are slight exceptions to the rule, but the conformity to it is much more noticeable. For example, at Titicaca the width is about 250 miles, but some distance north of this region the Andean plateau seems to narrow up till the width scarcely exceeds 150 miles, in Ecuador; but it then spreads out again as the range enters Columbia.

It is not easy to explain this narrowing of the range, unless the great width and great height at Titicaca are due to the indentation of the coast at this point, giving uplifting forces from both directions, at the same time. This explanation seems to be well founded, and is confirmed by the corresponding effect north of central India, where the plateau of Tibet reaches its maximum elevation.

Accordingly, we probably should conclude, that the width of the Andean plateau is normally less than at Lake Titicaca, and the width there is due to a combination of forces from the two lines of coast, meeting at an angle of about 135°. It is therefore a fact in South America that wherever the plateau is widest, it decreases in elevation, as in Columbia.

In this problem of uplift, however, something depends on the depth and width of the adjacent elevating ocean, and thus a certain amount of variety should result. Since the adjacent sea is not of uniform effectiveness, we should expect minor deviations from the law; but obviously they should not be too pronounced.

In North America, the same general law holds true. Wherever the plateau is narrow, as in central Mexico, the elevation is great; but where it is wide, the elevation generally is lower. There are of course some exceptions to the rule, but it generally holds true.

For example, along the Rocky Mountain range the highest part of the plateau probably is in Colorado, where the whole Pacific plateau is widest; but this only indicates that the forces which raised such high mountains as Pike's Peak, also raised a high plateau in the general region, independent of the width of the plateau afterwards elevated from the sea. And so on generally.

The rule that the plateau decreases in height when it increases in width, must be understood to apply to a region of not too great width. For when the width is very great, we have rather a series of plateaus added together side by side than a single one; and the final result is a composite effect, one *plateau section* fitting onto another, and the whole series of sections running together as an unbroken embankment of variable height.

In view of these considerations, a plateau so wide as that between Colorado and California is really a series of plateaus, each of unusual width at this point, and the whole effect therefore a very broad compound plateau. The entire Pacific plateau is the cumulative work of the ocean, done in successive sections; and as the ocean is deepest opposite California, the uplift naturally has been greatest in this part, which also developed the Sierra

Nevada Mountains, and at a still earlier stage the Wasatch range in Utah.

The history of the building of the Pacific plateau from Colorado to California is too long to be described here, but these hints on the method by which it was elevated give some idea of the growth of the continent westward from the ancient border which was east of the present Rocky Mountain range.

§4. *The Cause of the great height of the plateaus of western Tibet and Titicaca.*

Since writing the Memoirs of 1906–08, I have had occasion to re-examine the relationship of the great mountains to the plateaus, and of the plateaus to the sea, with the result of confirming in the most conclusive manner the uplift of the plateaus by the ocean. It is found that the plateau of western Tibet has almost exactly the relationship to the ancient sea valley formerly covering northern India, that the plateau of Titicaca now has to the border of the Pacific Ocean.

If we examine a good map of northern India, we shall find not only that the Indus and Ganges now flow in the ancient sea valley formerly depressed below the waves, and now elevated less than 1,000 feet above the ocean; but also that this valley made a sharp bend in north central India. It has the form of the Greek letter lambda, with the Ganges leg of the lambda by far the longest, and the included angle about 105°.

If the lava expelled from beneath this ancient sea valley came from two directions, at such an angle, the forces of uplift naturally would accumulate at the head of the sea valley. For they would come from the southeast and also from the southwest, as well as from the south; and the result of compounding these forces, would be magnified forces of unusual intensity, directed to the elevation of the Himalayas of north central India. This is exactly what has taken place; and hence we see why the plateau of Tibet is so high in the western part of that great "roof of the world."

If now we turn to the region of Lake Titicaca, in South America, we find an exactly similar relative situation. The coasts from the south and northwest meet at an angle of some 135°; and the forces producing the uplift have come from the two directions, and also from the west. The result has been a convergence of the forces tending to produce an uplift; but as the angle of 135° is less acute than in northern India, where the angle is 105°, it is not remarkable that the plateau of Titicaca is less elevated than that of western Tibet, where the forces converged more powerfully and were so compounded as to produce the maximum elevation.

It certainly is not accidental that these two highest plateaus of the world stand in *similar centers of converging forces directed from the ocean;* and that the higher plateau of western Tibet has the forces converging at the smaller angle of 105°, and therefore compounding more effectively to produce a greater power of uplift, for equal energy directed from the side of the sea.

And as the observed phenomena confirm the theory in every detail, one finds it very difficult to believe that any other cause has shaped these stupendous uplifts of the earth's crust.

It is also easy to see why the height of the plateau of Tibet is less towards the east, where the elevation is only 11,000 feet. For in the eastern part only a side pressure was available for the uplift, and the forces of elevation did not converge towards a point, as in western Tibet and near Lake Titicaca, in Bolivia.

§5. *Some phenomena connected with the great earthquake at Arica, August 13, 1868.*

One of the most important means of judging of earthquake phenomena is the evidence afforded by eye-witnesses; and this becomes especially valuable when we know the nature of earthquake processes, because it then becomes possible to see in the descriptions given by eye-witnesses new meaning.

Accordingly, we add a brief account of the terrible earthquake at Arica, August 13, 1868, which was a continuation of the movements directly concerned with the uplift of the plateau of Titicaca. For it was a survival of the ancient movements which brought about this elevation, and as the region is still near the sea, it is of special interest, because it bears on the elevation of the plateaus of the Himalayas, now further inland.

In his "Light Science for Leisure Hours," p. 199, the late Professor R. A. Proctor describes the havoc wrought by the earthquake at the neighboring town of Arequipa as follows:

"At five minutes past five (P.M.) an earthquake shock was experienced, which, though severe, seems to have worked very little mischief.   Half a minute later, however, a terrible noise was heard beneath the earth; a second shock more violent than the first was felt; and then began a swaying motion, gradually increasing in intensity.   In the course of the first minute this motion had become so violent that the inhabitants ran in terror out of their houses into the streets and squares.   In the next two minutes the swaying movement had so increased that the more lightly built houses were cast to the ground, and the flying people could scarcely keep their feet. 'And now,' says Von Tschudi, 'there followed during two or three minutes a terrible scene.   The swaying motion which had hitherto prevailed changed into fierce vertical upheaval.   The subterranean roaring increased in the most terrifying manner; then were heard the heart-piercing shrieks of the wretched people, the bursting of walls, the crashing fall of houses and churches, while over all rolled thick clouds of a yellowish-black dust, which, had they been poured forth many minutes longer, would have suffocated thousands.'   Although the shocks had lasted but a few minutes, the whole town was destroyed. Not one building remained uninjured, and there were few which did not lie in shapeless heaps of ruins."

This description was drawn for the phenomena observed at Arequipa, but that it would serve equally well for Arica is sufficiently indicated by the accompanying photographs of the town as it was before and after the earthquake.   A more terrible record of desolation could hardly be imagined.

THE CITY OF ARICA, PERU, AS IT APPEARED BEFORE AND AFTER THE EARTHQUAKE
AND SEA WAVE OF AUGUST 13, 1868.

From photographs in the possession of Mrs. E. V. Cutts, of Mare Island, California.

THE SHIP IN THE FOREGROUND IS THE U. S. S. WATEREE.

It was washed half a mile inland by the great sea wave at Arica, Peru, August 13, 1868. From a photograph in the possession of Mrs. E. V. Cutts, Mare Island.

THE VOLCANO EL MISTI, FROM AREQUIPA, PERU,

Altitude about 19,000 feet.

(From the *Annals of Harvard College Observatory*, Vol. XXXIX, Part I, Plate I).

With this brief but striking description of the earthquake, we may now turn to the seismic sea wave at Arica, and here I shall again quote Proctor's account, which is based on the elaborate technical memoir prepared by Professor F. Von Hochstetter in the *Sitzungsberichte* of the Vienna Academy of Sciences for 1868, Vol. LVIII, Abth. II.   Proctor's account runs thus:

"At Arica the sea wave produced even more destructive effects than had been caused by the earthquake.   About twenty minutes after the first earth-shock, (*i.e.* 5:25 P.M.) the sea was seen to retire, as if about to leave the shores wholly dry; but presently its waters returned with tremendous force.   A mighty wave, whose length seemed immeasurable, was seen advancing like a dark wall upon the unfortunate town, a large part of which was overwhelmed by it.   Two ships, the Peruvian corvette 'America' and the United States 'double-ender' 'Wateree,' were carried nearly half a mile to the north of Arica, beyond the railroad which runs to Tacna, and there left stranded high and dry.   This enormous wave was considered by the English vice-consul at Arica to have been fully fifty feet in height.

"At Chala, three such waves swept in after the first shocks of earthquake.   They overflowed nearly the whole of the town, the sea passing more than half a mile beyond its usual limits.

"At Islay and Iquique similar phenomena were manifested. At the former town the sea flowed in no less than five times, and each time with greater force.   Afterwards the motion gradually diminished, but even an hour and a half after the commencement of this strange disturbance, the waves still ran forty feet above the ordinary level.   At Iquique, the people beheld the inrushing wave whilst it was still a great way off.   A dark blue mass of water, some fifty feet in height, was seen sweeping in upon the town with inconceivable rapidity.   An island lying before the harbour was completely submerged by the great wave, which still came rushing on, black with the mud and slime it had swept from the sea bottom.   Those who witnessed its progress from the upper balconies of their houses, and presently saw its black mass rushing close beneath their feet, looked on their safety as a miracle. Many buildings were indeed washed away, and in the low lying parts of town there was a terrible loss of life. After passing far inland the wave slowly returned seawards, and strangely enough, the sea, which elsewhere heaved and tossed for hours after the first great wave had swept over it, here came soon to rest.

"At Callao a yet more singular instance was afforded of the effect which circumstances may have upon the motion of the sea after a great earthquake has disturbed it. In former earthquakes Callao has suffered terribly from the effects of the great sea wave. In fact, on two occasions the whole town has been destroyed, and nearly all its inhabitants have been drowned, through the inrush of precisely such waves as flowed into the ports of Arica and Chala. But upon this occasion the center of subterranean disturbance must have been so situated that either the wave was diverted from Callao, or more probably two waves reached Callao from different sources and at different times, so that the two undulations partly counteracted each other. Certain it is that although the water retreated strangely from the coast near Callao, insomuch that a wide tract of the sea-bottom was uncovered, there was no inrushing wave comparable with those described above. The sea afterwards rose and fell in an irregular manner, a circumstance confirming the supposition that the disturbance was caused by two distinct oscillations. Six hours after the occurrence of the earthshock, the double oscillations seem for awhile to have worked themselves into unison, for at this time three considerable waves rolled in upon the town. But clearly these waves must not be compared with those which in other instances had made their appearance within half an hour of the earth-throes. There is little reason to doubt that if the separate oscillations had reinforced each other earlier, Callao would have been completely destroyed. As it was, a considerable amount of mischief was effected; but the motion of the sea presently became irregular again, and so continued until the morning of August 14, when it began to ebb with some regularity. But during the 14th there were occasional renewals of the irregular motion, and several days elapsed before the regular ebb and flow of the sea were resumed."

In this excellent account of the great sea wave at Arica, August 13, 1868, Proctor makes no allusion to the U.S.S. *Fredonia*, which was lying at anchor with the *Wateree*; and we add therefore that the *Fredonia* is reported to have been capsized as the wave advanced, and nothing was ever again heard of her, all the officers and crew having been lost with the wreck of the vessel.

The *Wateree* was but little injured, and afterwards served as a hotel. The picture of the stranded *Wateree* here reproduced was made by an officer who visited the scene sometime after the disaster. This valuable historic photograph has been preserved by Mrs. E. V. Cutts of Mare Island, to whom the author is indebted for this impressive illustration of the effects of this great sea wave. The previous illustrations show the city of Arica before this earthquake, and the mere wreckage which remained after the inundation of the sea.

In an earlier passage than that above cited, Proctor quotes the description of an eye-witness, which tells of the movements of the ships:

"The agent of the Pacific Steam Navigation Company, whose house had been destroyed by the earth-shock, saw the great sea wave while he was flying towards the hills. He writes: 'While passing towards the hills, with the earth shaking, a great cry went up to heaven. The sea had retired. On clearing the town, I looked back and saw that the vessels were being carried irresistibly seawards. In a few minutes the sea stopped, and then arose a mighty wave fifty feet high, and came in with a fearful rush, carrying everything before it in terrible majesty. The whole of the shipping came back, speeding towards inevitable doom. In a few minutes all was completed — every vessel was either on shore or bottom upwards.'"

§6. *Pratt's reasoning on the density of the matter under the ocean, plains and mountains, and its application to India and the Himalayas.*

Pratt's reasoning in regard to the density of the matter in and beneath the crust of the earth, and its bearing on the new theory of earthquakes is described in my paper on "The Cause of Earthquakes, Mountain Formation and Kindred Phenomena Connected with the Physics of the Earth," published in the *Proceedings* of this Society for 1906, pp. 344–346. His main conclusion is stated thus:

"This (deflection of the plumb line) shows that the effect of variations of density in the crust must be very great in order to bring about this near compensation. In fact the density of the crust beneath the mountains must be less than that below the plains, and still less than that below the ocean-bed." (Pratt, *Figure of the Earth*, 3d edition, Art. 137, pp. 134–135).

Again:

"The conclusion at which we have arrived in Article 137, that the parts of the crust below the more elevated regions are of less density, and the parts beneath the depressed regions in the ocean are of greater density than the average portions of the surface, seems to bear additional testimony to the fluid theory. For it shows, that nothwithstanding the varied surface, seen at present in mountains and oceans, the amount of matter in a vertical prism drawn down at various places to any given spheroidal stratum is the same, although its length varies from place to place as the earth's contour varies." (idem, p. 162).

This subject of the density of the matter hidden from our view beneath the crust of the earth has also been discussed by the late Professor Henri Poincaré, in an address on *French Geodesy*, translated by Professor George Bruce Halstead, and published in the *Popular Science Monthly* for February, 1913. The eminent French geometer reasons as follows:

"But these deep-lying rocks we cannot reach exercise from afar their attraction which operates upon the pendulum and

RELIEF MAP OF EUROPE.

From Frye's *Complete Geography*, by permission of Ginn & Co., Publishers. Showing the mountains uplifted by the Mediterranean on the South, and by the Atlantic on the North. An impressive confirmation of the New Theory, by the reliefs of the oldest continent of the globe.

FIG. b. WATER HEMISPHERE, WHICH HAS THE WORLD RIDGE AROUND IT.

(FROM SEE'S *Researches*, Vol II. 1910)

FIG. a. MAP SHOWING THE WORLD RIDGE (from FAYE'S *Complete Geography*, by permission of GINN & Co., Publishers). It will be noticed that the high mountains and great plateaus everywhere face the outside, which is towards the water hemisphere. This map therefore bears impressive testimony to the truth of the new theory, and the world ridge stands as an everlasting witness to the secular action of the ocean in uplifting the land hemisphere of the globe.

deforms the terrestrial spheroid. Geodesy can therefore weigh them from afar, so to speak, and tell us of their distribution. Thus will it make us really see those regions which Jules Verne only showed us in imagination.

"This is not an empty illusion. M. Faye, comparing all the measurements, has reached a result well calculated to surprise us. Under the oceans, in the depths, are rocks of very great density; under the continents, on the contrary, are empty spaces.

"New observations will modify perhaps the details of these conclusions.

"In any case, our venerated dean has shown us where to search and what the geodesist may teach the geologist, desirous of knowing the interior constitution of the earth, and even the thinker wishing to speculate upon the past and the origin of this planet."

From this extract it will be seen that the most eminent French authorities recognize the conclusions first formulated by Pratt over half a century ago. It only remains to consider the application of Pratt's theorem to the Himalayas and the plateau of Tibet.

If, as Pratt says, "the density of the crust beneath the mountains must be less than that below the plains, and still less than that below the ocean bed," it is very difficult to see how this could have come about except by the greater uplift of the mountains, by the injection of more light material beneath, while a less amount of such material has been injected under the plains, and scarcely any has remained under the ocean bed, because it tends to work out by the path of least resistance. This is the only explanation which satisfies the observed phenomena, and conforms to the known fact that the mountains and plateaus are uplifted by the expulsion of matter from beneath the sea, in world-shaking earthquakes. Thus the known facts of geodesy as respects the Himalayas are fully explained. And the explanation rests on principles established by a variety of mutually confirmatory observations.

§7. *Defects in the Doctrine of Isostacy as commonly stated.*

The doctrine of Isostacy as commonly stated is vitiated by a serious if not fatal error; and it is necessary to overcome this defect if the doctrine is to hold its place in modern thought.   In *Science* of February 10, 1911, Professor J. F. Hayford presents a paper based on the valuable data he obtained in the work of the U.S. Coast and Geodetic Survey deduced from seven hundred and sixty-five series of astronomical observations at eighty-nine stations in the United States.   The causes assigned, however, are so inadequate that it seems worth while to point out the defects in his reasoning, which is as follows:

"Columns A and B have been assumed to contain equal masses. There is complete isostatic compensation.   The pressures at the bases of the two columns are equal, and at any less depth, X, the pressure is greater in A than in B.   Now assume that in the normal course of events a large amount of material is being eroded from the high surface of column A and deposited on the low surface of column B.   After this erosion has been in progress for some time the isostatic compensation will no longer be perfect.   The pressure at the base of B will be greater than at the base of A.   The pressure very near the top of B will still be less than at the same level in A so long as the top of A remains higher than the top of B. There will be some intermediate level at which the pressure in the two columns is the same.   Call this level of temporary equality of pressure in the two columns the neutral level.   As the process of erosion and deposition progresses the neutral level will gradually progress upward from its original position at the base of the columns.   Eventually if no interchange of mass took place between the columns except at the surface, and no vertical displacement occurred in either column, the neutral level would reach the surface when the process of erosion and deposition became complete and the upper surfaces of the two columns were at the same level. During the process of erosion and deposition the excess of pressure in A at any level above the neutral level will continually decrease.

Similarly, at any level below the neutral level the excess of pressure in B will continually increase as the erosion progresses and the neutral level will rise. Thus there will be established a continually increasing tendency for the material below the neutral level in B to be squeezed over into A. If the stresses tending to produce this undertow from the lower part of B to A become greater than the material can stand, the flow will take place as indicated by the arrow in the figure. If the material flows without change of volume, as if it were incompressible, the upper part of A and its surface will be raised, the upper part of B and its surface will be lowered, the neutral level will sink and an approximation to the original conditions with complete isostatic compensation will be re-established.

"This is the general case of isostatic readjustment by the action of gravitation alone. Gravitation tends to produce a deep undertow from the regions where deposition is taking place to the regions where erosion is in progress, in the direction opposite to that of the surface transfer of material.

"Let us suppose that the isostatic compensation at a given stage in the earth's history is practically complete for a continent, that the process of erosion from the greater part of the continent and deposition around its margins is in progress, and that the process of readjustment by a deep undertow is in progress."

The fatal defect in this reasoning consists in the fact that it begs the question, and does not in any way explain the elevation of the margin of a continent, but only how it may maintain its present form by a process of readjustment. This is like a river rising higher than its source, a man trying to lift himself by pulling on his boot-straps, or the logician reasoning in a circle. For in order to explain the development of the inequalities of the earth's crust, we must not only explain the adjustment and balancing between adjacent parts, but also *how the original uplift came about*, to give the observed contrast in surface levels.

Now on the premises used by Hayford, it is possible to explain how a given inequality of surface levels, when once existing, *can be maintained;* but it is not possible to account for the *origin of the inequalities of level. Isostacy as thus depicted is not an active creative agency, but simply a negative process for maintaining existing inequalities.* Under the doctrine as above stated, the height of a mountain or plateau could never increase, for that would require the exertion of positive elevating forces, not mere balancing for maintaining inequalities of levels already existing.

Accordingly, this formulation of the doctrines of Isostacy is defective, and inadequate to account for the phenomena of the earth's crust.

The true doctrine should include not only the *balancing process* described by Hayford, but also those *elevating forces directed from the sea,* by which the mountains are elevated as narrow walls about the borders of continents, on the great plateaus which spread out as wider embankments beneath them. Without these positive uplifting forces, no continent could ever have a mountainous border thrown up about it.

No doubt the elevation is produced under approximately isostatic conditions. Mountains can be forced up only to a certain height, the transfer of lighter material under the higher parts thus giving nearly equal mass in all equal prisms drawn to the center of the earth. The path of least resistance is towards regions of elevation, and the underlying material expands as the surface level is forced up. If this were not so the greater weight under the elevated region would cause it to subside to the common level. In this way, and in this way only, can progressive elevation be produced.

The weakness of the old method of reasoning is further illustrated by Hayford's remarks:

"Under a region of deposition two effects of opposite sign tend to occur. The effect of increased pressure tends to produce chemical changes accompanied by decrease of volume and so to produce a sinking of the surface. The blanket of deposited mate-

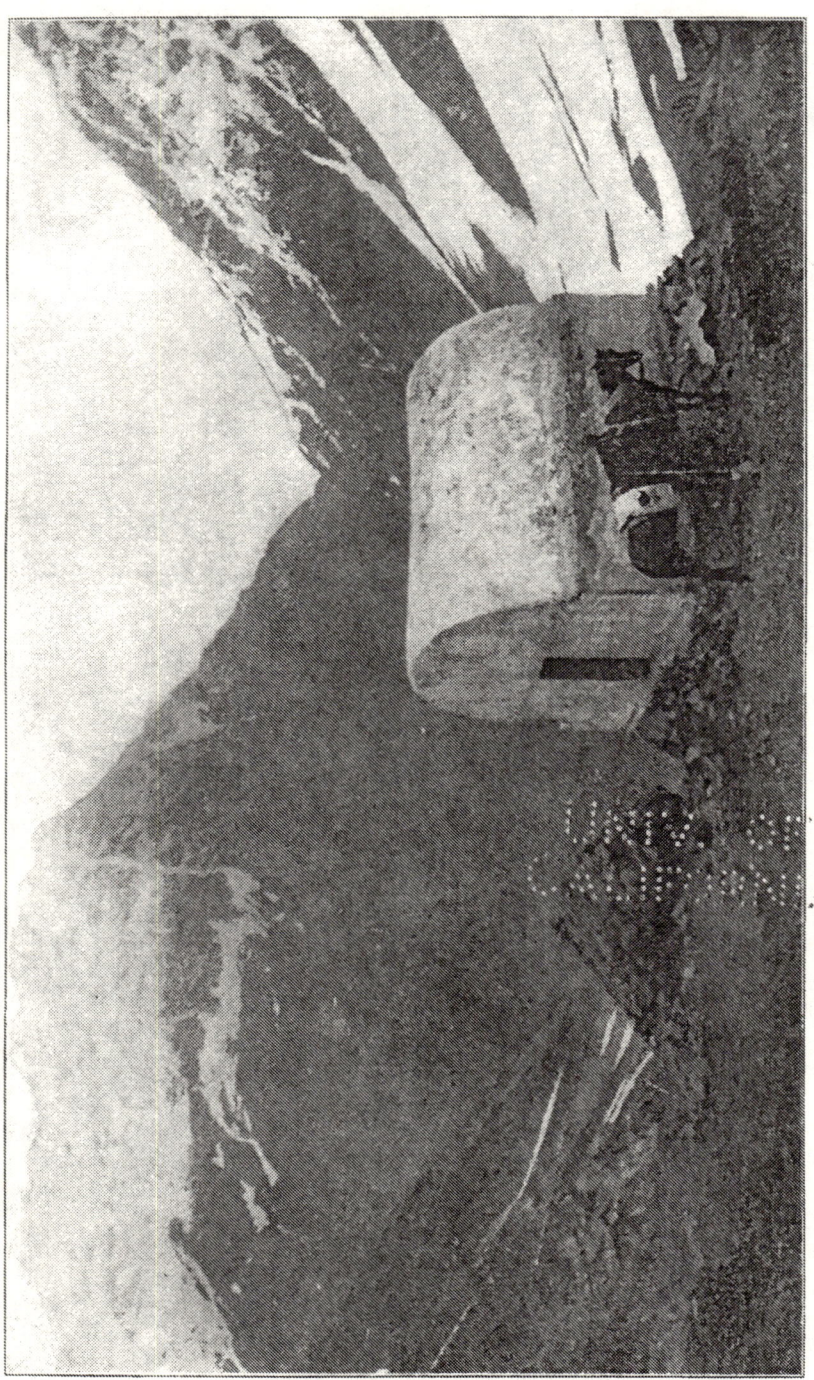

PASSAGE IN THE ANDES, BETWEEN CHILE AND ARGENTINA.

Showing a Stone House built for the shelter of travelers, against violent storms which are frequent at these great altitudes.
Photograph by Harriet Chalmers Adams, *National Geographical Magazine* for May, 1910.

VIEW OF THE ALPS, FROM THE SUMMIT OF MATTERHORN.

Showing the terrible upheavals involved in the uplift of the Alps. Photograph by G. P. Abraham, *National Geographical Magazine* for June, 1909.

rial tends to raise the temperature in each part of the material covered, to increase the volume of this material, and thereby to raise the surface. The temperature effect may serve in time to arrest the subsidence caused by increased pressure or even to raise the surface and change the region of deposition into one of erosion.

"The changes of temperature just described are due directly to erosion and deposition. If as an effect of erosion and deposition an undertow is started tending to re-establish the isostatic condition, this undertow, a flow of material presumably solid, necessarily develops considerable heat by internal friction. The increase of temperature so produced tends to cause an increase of volume. It may favor new chemical changes, including changes from the solid to the liquid state, which may be accompanied by a change of volume. The undertow tends to be strongest not under the region of rapid deposition, but under the comparatively neutral region between the two in which neither erosion nor deposition is much in excess of the other, see Figure 2. Hence the undertow by increasing the temperature and causing a change of density may be directly effective in changing the elevation of the neutral region between two regions of deposition and erosion.

"Horizontal compressive stresses in the material near the surface above the undertow are necessarily caused by the undertow. For the undertow necessarily tends to carry the surface along with it and so pushes this surface material against that in the region of erosion, see Figure 2. These stresses tend to produce a crumpling, crushing and bending of the surface strata accompanied by increase of elevation of the surface. The increase of elevation of the surface so produced will tend to be greatest in the neutral region or near the edge of the region of erosion, not under the region of rapid erosion nor under the region of rapid deposition."

The criticism against this reasoning is the same as that used above — namely, it will explain only balancing, but not the uplifting of great mountain walls along the sea coast. Nothing but the transfer of lava from beneath the sea, and the expansion of it under the mountains will explain the observed mountain walls along the borders of continents; and this requires positive forces of elevation, not mere negative processes. The advocates of Isostacy, as heretofore taught, have left that doctrine with such a serious defect that this correction is necessary to give it a rational basis.

§8. *The uplifting of the Himalayas, Arrakan and Afghanistan Ranges explains the great Asiatic earthquake belt. Confirmation of Colonel Burrard's impressions that the Himalayas have been pushed northward, but not by a change in the rotation period of the earth.*

We have seen that the region now occupied by the rivers Indus and Ganges was formerly a sea valley; and that after the Himalayas were elevated to a great height, the valley itself was slowly raised above the ocean.

If proof is asked that the valleys of the Indus and Ganges were formerly below the sea, it is furnished by the well established fact that such valleys as the San Joaquin and Sacramento in California were below the sea when the Sierras were being elevated. What has happened in California has also happened in India; and the same process of elevation will eventually give a fertile habitable valley in the belt just south of the Aleutian Islands now covered by a sea nearly five miles deep.

This proof that the valleys of the Indus and Ganges once were several miles beneath the sea level is absolute. For it is definitely known how the mountain ranges and adjacent valleys are crumpled, and finally raised above the sea. And what has happened for mountain ranges in general, has happened also for the Himalayas and the valleys adjacent thereto.

In order to round out the view here traced, it only remains to add that the Arrakan coast of farther India contains two chief mountain chains, one of which is the backbone of the Malay Peninsula; and the other is the range terminating at Cape Negrais, but continuing under the sea in a string of islands, and reappearing further south as Sumatra and Java. The Andaman Islands and several volcanoes in the sea appear between Cape Negrais and

MT. KENGCHENJUNGA, NEAR MT. EVEREST, AND SECOND HIGHEST PEAK OF THE HIMALAYAS.

Altitude, 28,150 feet.   Photograph by Vittorio Sella, *National Geographical Magazine* for June, 1909.

MT. EVEREST, THE HIGHEST PEAK OF THE HIMALAYAS AND OF THE WORLD.

Altitude 29,002 feet above sea level. Photograph by Vittorio Sella, from Chunjerma Pass (Nepal), 80 miles distant, *National Geographical Magazine* for June, 1909.

THE RUWENZORI.

In Equatorial East Africa, rising to an altitude of 18,600 feet. This snow capped range in the hottest part of Africa was explored by the Duke of the Abbruzzi in 1906. Photograph by Vittorio Sella, from the south, *National Geographical Magazine*, for June, 1909.

Sumatra. And both Java and Sumatra are noted for their terrific volcanic violence. This volcanic chain is analogous to that of the Aleutian Islands, except that the middle part is submerged, and the two ends raised above the waves.

The line of thought here developed enables us to understand the volcanic activities of farther India, and also the terrible belt of earthquakes in Assam and the adjacent regions south of the Himalayas. Part of the ancient sea valley is above the water as low land, and part still in the ocean, and covered by the sea to a considerable depth.

West of India, we have the complicated mountain ranges and earthquake belts of Afghanistan and Persia. It would be difficult if not impossible to understand the phenomena they present if studied alone; but if studied in connection with the developments of India and farther India above discussed, it is easy to see that Afghanistan and Persia were built up in like manner, and at no very distant epoch were beneath the sea.

In his article on the *Himalayas, Encyclopedia Britannica*, 9th edition, the late General Strachey has strongly emphasized the view that the mountains and table lands of Afghanistan and Persia are intelligible only in connection with those of India. "It is after the middle tertiary epoch that the principal elevation of these mountains took place, and about the same time also took place the movements which raised the tablelands of Afghanistan and Persia, and gave southern Asia its existing outlines."

He also points out the fact that at no very distant geological epoch the ocean extended from the Arabian Sea through the Persian Gulf to the Caspian and Mediterranean. The continuation of the earthquake belt through this region of western Asia is therefore quite intelligible, and the existence of active volcanoes near the Caspian a survival of present and former relations to the ocean.

The annual rainfall south of the Himalayas amounts to about thirty-six feet, and this is so enormous as to be almost as effective as a shallow sea in keeping alive earthquake processes.

It is established by observation, for example, that the very active volcano Sangai, in the terrible rain belt at the head of the Amazon, in Ecuador, has its activity about doubled during the worst period of the rainy season, owing to the effects of surface water. If in South America the volcanic forces can be visibly augumented by copious surface water, it is easy to understand that the terrible rains of India may also operate to keep alive the earthquake processes almost as well as an overlying sea.

The earthquake belt south of the Himalayas is thus perfectly explained. And the extension of this line of disturbance through to the Caspian presents no difficulty, when account is taken of the recent situation of the sea over a large part of this region of western Asia.

In conclusion it only remains to add that Colonel Burrard's argument, cited in section 1 above, that the Himalayas resulted from the pushing of a great mass of matter northward, undoubtedly is correct. This fact appears to be as well established as the rising and setting of the sun, and further discussion of the subject is superfluous.

The cause of this northward movement is also fully established, but it is not that imagined by Colonel Burrard. In the *Observatory* for May and June, 1912, will be found a discussion by Colonel Burrard of considerable interest, but founded on the premise that the earth's speed of rotation is variable and has undergone considerable changes within the period covered by geological history.

The writer's *Researches on the Evolution of the Stellar Systems*, Volume II, 1910, show that the views formerly held by Lord Kelvin and Sir George Darwin are now quite inadmissible; and that the earth's rotation has not changed sensibly since the earliest geological time. Thus Colonel Burrard's premise that the retardation of the earth's rotation might cause a flow of matter towards the poles is wholly inadmissible.

Besides, there are other means of showing that such was not the origin of the Himalayas. These great mountains of India, for example, should no more be due to a change in the earths' rotation, than should the Andes, which run almost exactly north and south, and by their course along the meridian, exclude an explanation founded on a change in the speed of the earth's rotation.

And as the Andes are well known to have been formed by the sea in the way we have described, it is certain that the same cause uplifted the Himalayas and the plateau of Tibet.

From these considerations it will be seen that the modern sciences of Geogony and Cosomogony are closely related, and that neither can be perfectly developed without the aid of the other. Just as it is impossible to develop a satisfactory theory of the formation of the earth without data drawn from the modern Science of Cosmogony; so also Cosmogony itself has been much improved by a Science of Geogony which gives a correct theory of terrestrial mountain formation. For that has aided in establishing the origin of the lunar craters, and the early growth of the earth itself by impact — the existing ranges of mountains having been subsequently formed by the sea and thus made parallel to the coasts.

On the other hand, without the theory that the mountains generally are formed by the ocean, which is so clearly established for the typical range of the Andes, running exactly north and south, our ideas of the origin of the Himalayas might have remained obscure for ages.

It is scarcely necessary to point out that these results illustrate somewhat impressively the value of a *comprehensive vision* in the study of the Sciences. Without this power for comparing together the most remote objects there can be no progress in discovery of the highest order.

Starlight on Loutre, Montgomery City, Missouri,
    March 27, 1913.

CHAPTER XIII.

1911.

THE EVOLUTION OF THE STARRY HEAVENS.*

By T. J. J. SEE.

WE are assembled to consider the great Law of Nature which governs the Evolution of Worlds, and to celebrate the Founding of a New Science of the Starry Heavens. Prior to the establishment of the Science of Cosmogony, from researches made here in California during the past few years, the most recent Astronomical Science developed by a modern investigator was *Astrophysics*, which was founded by the late Sir William Huggins half a century ago. From this circumstance it is not without inspiration to recall the lively interest taken by this illustrious pioneer in the development of the New Science of *Cosmogony*. For just as in early manhood he foresaw with prophetic vision the great possibilities of *Astrophysics*, so also in the last years of a long life consecrated to the advancement of truth, this venerable philosopher was one of the first to welcome the founding of a New Science of Cosmical Evolution. We may pause to recall the early words of Sir William Huggins, which were the more appreciated because they were uttered before the New Science had become established in the scientific world.

Writing from London, under date of August 11, 1908, he says:—"I hasten to thank you for your letter giving me early information of your bold and startling new theory of spiral nebulae. It takes one's breath away to endeavor to realize the going round of these long drawn out wisps, I suppose, billions of billions of

---

* Address to the California Academy of Sciences, delivered August 7, 1911. Reprinted from *Popular Astronomy* for November-December, 1911.

ΘΙΙΣΗΗ, Ο ΓΕΩΜΕΤΡΗΣ

ΕΚ ΤΗΣ ΒΙΒΛΙΟΘΗΚΗΣ

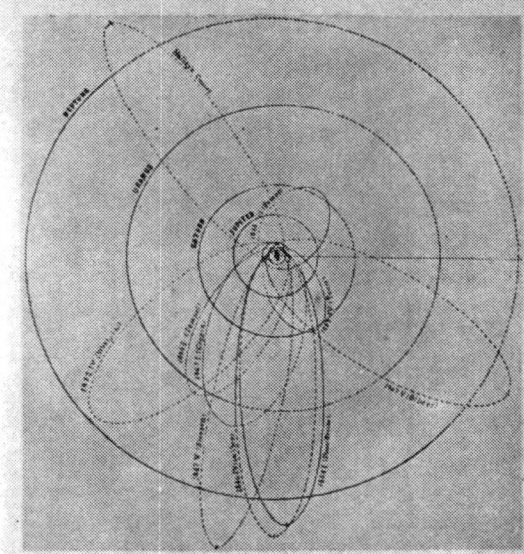

Ο ΘΕΟΣ ΑΕΙ ΓΕΩΜΕΤΡΕΙ

A BOOK-PLATE REPRESENTING ONE OF THE GREATEST LAWS OF NATURE.
Presented to Professor See by Citizens of California, 1911, with the appropriate inscription:
"THE DEITY ALWAYS GEOMETRIZES," which naturally is dear to the Mathematician.

miles long! At the first blush one would hardly expect them to make headway in any resisting medium. But your theory gets out of the astonishing difficulty of how they exist, if *at rest*, in any state approaching equilibrium. If, as you say it does, the thing works out, we seem to have reached something like certainty in a subject which hitherto has been in more senses than one a nebulous one. I am greatly interested and shall look forward to the fuller working out of your ideas. Laplace's theory is no doubt vulnerable."

In a note of June 6, 1909, Sir William added: "It is indeed an exciting time when one's old notions are disappearing under the light of new knowledge. One almost regrets the time when one could sleep comfortably in Laplace's bosom."

On September 12, 1909, Sir William wrote: "I have received, and desire now to thank you for, separate copies of your important papers on the Capture of Satellites, and of the Moon, which appeared in the *Astronomische Nachrichten*. From the point of *sentiment* it is, perhaps, disappointing to learn that our old Moon is not an earth-son, but some gypsy body, and that all the planets and satellites of our system are not children and grand-children of the sun, but 'undesirable aliens' from nobody knows where! But fact and truth come before sentiment, and your views claim the earnest consideration of all astronomers."

Another celebrated philosopher who early welcomed these new advances and therefore is not to be forgotten by us to-night, is the lamented Schiaparelli, the most illustrious Italian astronomer since the days of Galileo. He heartily rejoiced to be able to recognize in the recent discoveries the aurora which heralds the coming day of a New Science of Cosmogony, and pointed out that heretofore astronomers had been occupied mainly with ascertaining the present state of the heavens.

On the occasion of this anniversary, three years after the first private announcements were made to Sir William Huggins, ex-president of the Royal Society, and acknowledged by him in the letters above quoted, we find the New Science of Cosmogony already widely recognized by the most eminent astronomers and geometers. To all who have extended this generous welcome to new truth struggling for a foothold in the world, it is needless to say that we return most humble and hearty thanks, but to none more appropriately than the illustrious Poincaré, the foremost natural philosopher and geometer of our age.

Writing to me from Paris under date of July 6, 1911, this incomparable mathematician says: "I have made use of your book (*Researches*, Vol. II) in my course this year, although I had not expected to do so, since I did not receive the volume till near the close of the last lesson; I then insisted, with profit, on the capture of planets by a resisting medium.

"My course is being published and I shall send it to you as soon as it appears, that is to say, in the month of November. You will see there the remarks and the difficulties which your theories have suggested to me.

Your very devoted colleague,

POINCARÉ."

Among the other investigators who have joined in this notable advance, special mention should be made of the work of our eminent colleague Professor E. W. Brown, of Yale University, for an important extension of our knowledge of the Capture of Satellites (*Monthly Notices of Royal Astronomical Society*, March, 1911); and of the recent researches of Professor Elis Strömgren, of the Royal Observatory of Copenhagen, demonstrating the elliptical character of the orbits of all comets, thus showing that they are attached to the solar system, and do not move in parabolic or hyperbolic orbits, as was long believed. This work of Strömgren has removed the last important difficulty in establishing the Science of Cosmogony. Indeed his researches on comets seem likely to constitute the most notable advance in our theory of these mysterious objects since the days of Tycho, Kepler and Newton.

POINCARÉ.

The eminent French mathematician and natural philosopher, and one of the greatest of
modern astronomers.

ΙΠΠΑΡΧΟΣ

ΑΝΗΡ ΦΙΛΟΠΟΝΟΣ ΚΑΙ ΦΙΛΑΛΗΘΗΣ

HIPPARCHUS.

The founder of the Science of Astronomy, and the most famous of the Greek astronomers. This genuine portrait of Hipparchus is based on an antique cameo found by Admiral Smyth, the British amateur astronomer, during a cruise in the Mediterranean about the year 1813, most likely at Athens or Alexandria. An outline of it is given in Chambers' Astronomy, Vol. III. As here presented it has been carefully enlarged by Mr. A. E. Axlund, and the deficient parts filled out by Professor See, who added the base, with inscription from Ptolemy, who praises Hipparchus as a "labor-loving and truth-loving man."

I. CIRCUMSTANCES ATTENDING THE DEVELOPMENT OF THE NEW SCIENCE OF COSMOGONY.

From these considerations it is evident that we have recently witnessed the development of a new science of the starry heavens. As will be seen hereafter it throws a clear light upon the astronomy of the invisible,* and illuminates the remotest regions of space almost as brightly as those well-lighted portions in the neighborhood of the sun, where the planets move. In fact it has been justly remarked that our new science lights up the firmament not unlike a new star which suddenly appears in the sky; and its development seems to have been almost as unexpected. We are still dazzled by the splendor of the light which has been suddenly thrown on the invisible processes of creation. For the processes of cosmical evolution are so slow that they extend over vast ages, and in general cannot be directly *observed*, but must be *inferred*, from the *order* now found to pervade the sidereal universe.

Like Astronomy itself, Cosmogony in a primitive way dates back to the age of the Greeks, having been allegorically treated by the poets and afterwards more adequately developed by such natural philosophers as Anaximander, Democritus and Anaxagoras; so that it is at once the oldest and the newest of the sciences. But it is only within the last twelve years that we have secured the necessary data of observation, on the nebulae, chiefly by Keeler and Perrine at Lick Observatory, and introduced rigorous mathematical criteria which give us the permanent basis of a true physical science. Accordingly whilst *Astronomy proper* was placed on a secure foundation by the researches of such ancient geometers as Apollonius, Aristarchus and Archimedes, combined with the observational data of Timocharis, Hipparchus and Ptolemy, *Cosmogony* proved to be much more difficult to reduce to a satisfactory basis of observation and demonstration, and has

---

* Systems of planets, asteroids, satellites and comets are wholly invisible at the distance of the fixed stars, yet they are now proved to exist about all these suns.

become a Science only since the beginning of the twentieth century.

It is justly remarked that a high order of knowledge of the stars and their systems and of the chaotic nebulae from which they arose was necessary before it was possible to attempt to develop a real science of world formation. Thus for upwards of 2,000 years Cosmogony remained little more than an unsatisfactory collection of opinions; and even quite recently one eminent mathematician, who still adheres to the old way of thinking, has likened Cosmogony to Astrology, holding that the secrets of the origin of the universe are forever beyond the powers of the human mind. These views, of course, are erroneous, and yet they give us some idea of the difficulties which have been overcome. It is a remarkable fact that our philosophical difficulties have consisted chiefly in false premises. These obstacles ought to have been forseen and avoided, but there were peculiar circumstances which long deceived the most eminent mathematicians — including Laplace, Sir John Herschel, Lord Kelvin, Newcomb, Darwin, Tisserand, and Poincaré. We shall presently trace the development of the New Science of Cosmogony with enough detail to render the results intelligible, but we shall first consider the conditions requisite for the creation of a new mathematical science.

II. CONDITIONS REQUISITE FOR THE FOUNDING OF EXACT SCIENCES.

As already pointed out, Cosmogony deals with the laws of the formation of the heavenly bodies; and the perfection of this new physical science must be regarded as the ultimate object of all astronomical research. However special our individual investigations may be, this is the one ultimate purpose which they may be supposed to serve. And until the laws of cosmical evolution can be at least roughly outlined all our astronomical efforts are as aimless for the discovery of the highest laws of Nature as are the unguided steps of the blind leading the blind. No wonder that astronomers should value researches which will give us light on the laws of Cosmogony, heretofore veiled in the darkness of perpetual night. Such discoveries are like the heavenly manna for feeding the famished wanderer in the wilderness searching for the way to the promised land.

The pioneer in Science must always be both an explorer and an apostle. His path must necessarily be lonely and desolate, and beset by the most unexpected difficulties. It takes as courageous a soul to lead the way to new fields of knowledge as it does to blaze the way to a new civilization, such as the pioneers of our country founded in early days of this Republic. No wonder that those who came after the hard and rough work is done have always said "Blessed be the memory of the pioneers."

Let me justify this opinion of the difficulties of the highest mathematical science by the great authority of Plato, who has been justly regarded as the most luminous intellect of the ancient times. This greatest of the Greek sages declared that "an astronomer must be the wisest of men; his mind must be duly disciplined in youth; especially is mathematical study necessary; both an acquiantance with the doctrine of number, and also with the other branch of mathematics, which, closely connected as it is with the heavens, we very absurdly call *Geometry*, the measurement of the earth." (Epinomis, p. 988–900).

With Plato's estimate of the intellectual qualification of an astronomer before us, will anyone believe that a modern astronomer can have any real standing who is not a mathematician? If sound mathematical knowledge was necessary in the simple age of the Greeks, how much more necessary is it now, with problems vastly more complex and difficult than any treated by the ancients? Obviously Astronomy is not possible without the exact methods of mathematics, and this criterion is a safe one in fixing the standard of any physical science.

Not only must the astronomer be the wisest and intellectually the most penetrating of men, but in order to be a discoverer of the first order, he must be just in his habits of mind and wholly devoted to truth. In a celebrated saying preserved by Plutarch, (Quest. Conv., VIII, 2) Plato declares that "the Deity always geometrizes"—ὁ θεός αεί γεωμέτρει.* Since the astronomer there-fore labors to discover the laws and processes established by the Deity from the foundation of the world, it is evident that this highest order of truth can be perceived only by those who are philosophically equable and altogether devoted to the search for the correct principles of science. The kingdom of ideas thus dis-closed to the faithful philosopher passeth not away, but endureth from generation to generation, as ageless as the heavens!

III. Six Principal Epochs in the Science of the Heavens.

The importance of any development in astronomical science depends on the light it throws on the physical causes which under-lie the phenomena of the universe. Laplace justly says that Tycho Brahé, great observer though he was, had little intuition into causes, and history therefore does not rate Tycho in the same class with Kepler and Newton, who established the laws of the heavenly motions. By this criterion that the importance of a discovery depends on the light it throws on causes, we find that there have been six principal epochs in the history of Astronomy.

1. *The Epoch of the Greeks,* who studied the apparent mo-tions of the planets, and deduced the fact that their paths are nearly exact circles; whence it was supposed that the orbits are circular, because the Deity had chosen this perfect geometrical figure for the paths of the heavenly bodies. This comprised the work of Plato and Aristotle, Eudoxus and Apollonius, Aristarchus and Archimedes, Hipparachus and Ptolemy.

2. *The Epoch of Copernicus,* who established the heliocentric theory of the world in 1543, and showed that Aristarchus of Samos was right in holding that the stars are at a nearly infinite distance from our sun, and thus should suffer no sensible displacement from the annual motion of the earth in its orbit.

---

* The plate with this inscription, used as a frontispiece to this address, is really a book-plate kindly presented to me by California friends who take great interest in the recent discoveries in Cosmogony. The portrait is one of Plato, and, above, Kaulbach's painting of Homer and the Greeks,— representing the atmosphere in which Plato lived. The other figures represent the spiral nebula 74 Piscium and the finished solar system.

3. *The Epoch of Kepler and Galileo*, the one the discoverer of the laws of the planetary motions, the other the inventor of the telescope and discoverer of the laws of falling bodies, by which terrestrial and celestial motions could be compared and critically investigated. These great discoveries paved the way for the science of the heavenly motions as developed by Newton.

4. *The Epoch of Newton*, who established the law of universal gravitation and reduced all observed phenomena to approximate conformity with this great law of nature.

5. *The Epoch of Lagrange and Laplace and Herschel.* The first two great geometers verified and extended the Newtonian law, and also established the essential stability of the solar system; while Herschel explored the sidereal universe and thus afforded an observational basis for an imperfect beginning of Cosmogony in the old nebular hypothesis. The problem of the stability of the solar system now appears in a new light, for we find that only planets with stable motions have survived, while a vast number of small bodies moving in unstable orbits have been swallowed up and destroyed to lay the foundations of the larger masses of our system. The orbits which survive are thus free from mutual entanglement, and arranged as if to endure almost forever.

6. *The Epoch now growing out of the Development of a Science of Cosmogony.* This was made possible partly by the application of the spectroscope to the heavenly bodies, which was begun by Sir Wm. Huggins in 1864, and afterwards perfected by the development of Astronomical Photography, and partly by the solution of the restricted problem of three bodies. This two-fold advance led to a great increase in our knowledge of the nebulae and of their mode of development into Cosmical Systems, under laws which are demonstrated to be consistent with the established principles of the mechanics of the heavens.

The present epoch is the one towards which all the previous epochs have pointed, and for which the great discoveries of the past have laid the foundations. The epoch of Cosmogony has been especially advanced by the researches and discoveries of American astronomers, beginning with the photographic work of Keeler in 1899; so that this science of the centuries seems likely to be peculiarly an American science. It has been considerably advanced also by eminent European investigators, among whom Darwin, Poincaré, Arrhenius and Strömgren seem to have taken the leading part.

In order to bring out the most significant facts, we shall consider in succession a number of topics. It is not necessary to dwell on Laplace's old nebular hypothesis, because it is now universally abandoned by astronomers, but we may recall very briefly the line of argument developed in Babinet's criterion, by which the detachment theory was finally overthrown, and the new theory of capture, or of addition from without, was introduced to take its place.

Such a complete transformation of this great subject necessarily involves new causes heretofore quite overlooked; among which we should mention the resisting medium and the operation of repulsive forces in nature. The resisting medium has exercised vast influence in building up central masses and reducing the size and eccentricity of orbits, producing incidentally the capture of satellites; while the repulsive forces have operated to disperse matter in the form of fine dust from the stars, to produce nebulae, which finally condense into all manner of planetary and stellar systems. Even the comets as well as variable and temporary stars, thus find a simple explanation in accordance with the general laws of the heavens.

IV.   BABINET'S CRITERION SHOWS THAT LAPLACE'S COSMOGONY RESTS ON A FALSE PREMISE.

In the *Comptes Rendus* of the Paris Academy of Sciences for March 18, 1861, Babinet introduced an important criterion showing that Laplace's cosmogony was erroneous, by proving from the mechanical principle of the conservation of areas, that when the sun is expanded to fill the orbits of the planets, as imagined by Laplace, the rotation is much too slow to develop a centrifugal force adequate to detach the planets. The following table gives the principal data from Babinet's criterion as now applied to the planets and satellites of the solar system:

I. TABLE SHOWING THE APPLICATION OF BABINET'S CRITERION TO THE PLANETS AND SATELLITES WHEN THE SUN AND PLANETS ARE EXPANDED TO FILL THE ORBITS OF THE BODIES REVOLVING ABOUT THEM.

Solar System.

Planet.	R_0 The Sun's Observed Time of Rotation.	P_0 Observed Period of Planet.	R_c Time of Sun's Rotation Calculated by Babinet's Criterion.
Mercury	25.3 days =0.069267 yrs.	0.24085 yrs.	479 yrs.
Venus	....	0.61237 "	1673 "
The Earth	....	1.00000 "	3192 "
Mars	....	1.88085 "	7424 "
Ceres	....	4.60345 "	24487 "
Jupiter	....	11.86 "	86560 "
Saturn	....	29.46 "	290962 "
Uranus	....	84.02 "	1176765 "
Neptune	....	164.78 "	2888533 "

Sub-systems.

Planet.	Satellite.	R_c Adopted Rotation of Planet.	P_0 Observed Period of Satellite.	R_0 Time of Planet's Rotation Calculated by Babinet's Criterion.
The Earth	The moon	1 day	27.32166 days	3632.45 days
Mars ...	Phobos	24.62297 hrs.	7.6542 hours	190.62 hours
....	Deimos	....	30.2983 "	1193.53 "
Jupiter .	V	9.928 hrs.	11.9563 hours	64.456 hours
....	I	......	1.7698605 days	14.60 days
....	II	......	3.5540942 "	35.900 "
....	III	......	7.1663872 "	93.933 "
....	IV	......	16.7535524 "	290.63 "
....	VI	......	250.618 "	10768.8 "
....	VII	......	265.0 "	11602.4 "
....	VIII	......	930.73 "	61997.2 "
Saturn..	Inner edge of ring	10.641 hrs.	0.236 days	0.6228 days
....	Outer edge of ring	......	0.6456 "	2.383 "
....	Mimas	......	0.94242 "	4.2902 "
....	Enceladus	......	1.37022 "	7.0615 "
....	Tethys	......	1.887796 "	10.822 "
....	Dione	......	2.736913 "	17.751 "
....	Rhea	......	4.517500 "	34.620 "
....	Titan	......	15.945417 "	186.05 "
....	Hyperion	......	21.277396 "	273.06 "
....	Iapetus	......	79.329375 "	1580.1 "
....	Phoebe	......	546.5 "	20712. "
Uranus.	Ariel	10.1112 hrs. (Cf. A.N., 3992)	2.520383 days	33.714 days
....	Umbriel	......	4.144181 days	65.435 days
....	Titania	......	8.705897 "	176.05 "
....	Oberon	......	13.463269 "	314.83 "
Neptune	Satellite	12.84817 hrs. (Cf. A.N., 3992)	5.87690 days	141.8 days

II. TABLE OF DATA RELATING TO THE SOLAR SYSTEM.

Planet.	Centrifugal Force, calculated from data of Babinet's criterion, present orbital centrifugal force being unity.	Density of Central Body, when expanded to fill orbit, that of atmospheric air at sea level being unity.
Mercury	0.000000253	0.001776
Venus	0.000000134	0.0002723
The Earth	0.000000098	0.0001029
Mars	0.000000064	0.00002913
Ceres	0.000000035	....
Jupiter	0.000000019	0.000000732
Saturn	0.000000010	0.000000118
Uranus	0.0000000051	0.0000000146
Neptune	0.0000000032	0.0000000038

III. TABLE OF DATA RELATING TO THE SATELLITE SYSTEMS.

Planet.	Satellite.	Centrifugal Force, calculated from data of Babinet's criterion, present orbital centrifugal force being unity.	Density of Central Body, when expanded to fill orbit, that of atmospheric air at sea level being unity.
The Earth	The Moon	0.00005657	0.01965
Mars	Phobos	0.001612	1151.
	Deimos	0.000644	73.05
Jupiter	V	0.034408	58.93
	I	0.014694	4.66
	II	0.009277	1.15
	III	0.005820	0.285
	IV	0.003323	0.0523
	VI	0.0005416	0.000232
	VII	0.0005217	0.000208
	VIII	0.0002254	0.0000169
Saturn	Inner Ring	0.1435	
	Mimas	0.048254	16.45
	Enceladus	0.037651	7.61
	Tethys	0.030436	4.11
	Dione	0.023772	1.96
	Rhea	0.017017	0.717
	Titan	0.0073449	0.0576
	Hyperion	0.0060716	0.0324
	Iapetus	0.0025205	0.00232
	Phoebe	0.0006962	0.000049
Uranus	Ariel	0.0055888	2.40
	Umbriel	0.0040111	0.88
	Titania	0.0024454	0.200
	Oberon	0.0018287	0.082
Neptune	Satellite	0.0017177	0.43

It should be noticed that the centrifugal force varies as the square of the velocity divided by the radius. Thus in the case of the earth, actual revolution in the orbit occupies one year, whereas the hypothetical nebulous sun expanded to fill the earth's orbit requires 3,192 years for a rotation; and the rotational centrifugal force therefore is only $1 : (3,192)^2$ of what is required to detach the earth, or less than a ten millionth part. In the case of Neptune, the calculated time of rotation for the expanded central nebula by Babinet's criterion, is 2,888,000 years, whereas Neptune actually revolves in 165 years. The calculated time of rotation is thus 17,500 longer than the observed time of revolution; and the rotational centrifugal force is therefore only $1: (17,500)^2$ or $1:306,-250,000$ of the centrifugal force required to detach Neptune.

In view of these facts we know that the planets never were detached from the sun by acceleration of rotation as held by Laplace and long believed by astronomers; but on the contrary that they were formed independently, at a great distance, and have since approached the sun as their orbits have been made smaller and rounder and rounder under the secular action of a resisting medium.

In regard to the satellites, the case most favorable to the detachment theory is offered by the inner ring of Saturn, but even here the rotating planet, when expanded to fill the ring, gives only one-seventh of the centrifugal force required for detachment. So that the theory of detachment is wholly given up, not only for the planets, but also for all the satellites of the solar system. Moreover, the retrograde satellites of Jupiter, Saturn and Neptune are easily explained by the modern capture theory, while they cannot be harmonized with the old nebular hypothesis of Laplace, which is therefore quite abandoned by all recent investigators.*

---

* These statements are *positive*, because Babinet's criterion, based on the conservation of areas, is incontestable, having in the rotation of bodies the same dynamical rigor that the law of gravitation has for the orbital motions of the planets. Curiously enough prominent astronomers occasionally overlook the decisive import of these elementary mechanical principles. Thus in POPULAR ASTRONOMY, for October, 1911, p. 467, Professor E. B. Frost, Director of the Yerkes Observatory, is led to the sad conclusion that "no adequate substitute has been proposed" for the abandoned theory of Laplace. He adds that these views are shared by friends whose opinions he values, showing that they are quite unaware of the notable progress recently made, and that obscurity regarding the significance of this dynamical principle still is widespread, although carefully treated by me three years ago when I first called attention to Babinet's neglected work of 1861, and more fully developed in my *Researches*, Vol. II, a copy of which was presented to Professor Frost in October, 1910.

There are at least three good reasons why the capture of satellites is inevitable: (1) The planetary rotations are not rapid enough to throw the bodies off, even if none of them revolved in the contrary direction, as observed in the case of the outer satellites of the systems of Jupiter and Saturn. (2) The density of the expanded central globes would in all cases be too small to exert any sensible hydrostatic pressure outward, so that unless the angular rotation gave adequate centrifugal force, the deficiency could not be supplied by hydrostatic pressure from the center. (3) It is found that if set in revolution with the velocity assigned by Babinet's criterion the satellite in every case would fall into the planet before half a revolution was accomplished, (cf. Proc. Am. Phil. Soc., Vol. XLIX, No. 197, Nov., 1910, p. 356). It therefore follows incontestably that the satellites can have been set revolving in their orbits only by capture, or addition from without, which is clearly indicated also by the retrograde motion of the outer satellites of Jupiter and Saturn.

V. How the Satellites were Captured.

In 1836 the celebrated German mathematician Jacobi communicated to the Paris Academy of Sciences an integral of the problem of three bodies in the restricted case where the system is made up of a sun attended by a planet revolving in a circular orbit; and the third body a particle of insensible mass. This is the case which is of special interest in Cosmogony, and here it has found its widest application. In 1877 the work of Jacobi was much extended by Dr. G. W. Hill in his researches on the Lunar Theory, which have been the starting point of the profound researches of Poincaré, Darwin and others on periodic orbits, and related topics in celestial mechanics.

Dr. Hill showed that in the restricted problem of three bodies, implied in Jacobi's integral, there is a partition of the whole space into three parts,— one about each of the large bodies, the sun and planet, and a larger domain enclosing both bodies — within which the power of control over the particle is vested in the two bodies individually and collectively, respectively. The closed surface about the earth includes the orbit of the moon, and the orbits of the other satellites in like manner are within the closed surfaces about their several planets; and Dr. Hill remarks that this arrangement is necessary to secure stability. (Hill's Collected Mathematical Works, Vol. I, p. 330). If a satellite is once within this region, with the surface of zero velocity closed about it, it cannot escape, but will always remain attached to the planet, and its radius vector will have a superior limit. How the moon and other satellites came within these closed regions Dr. Hill did not inquire; and subsequent investigators appear to have supposed that as these bodies cannot now escape from their planets, so also they cannot have come in from a remote distance, but must have originated where they now are. This is the view put forth by Moulton in his discussion of Professor W. H. Pickering's suggestion that Phoebe had been captured by Saturn (Astrophysical Journal, October, 1905, p. 178); but such reasoning is easily shown to be erroneous by the following considerations:—

Jacobi's integral, as originally given by him, is based on the differential equations for unrestricted motion in empty space, and no account is taken of the additional terms which must be added to the differential equations of the motion of the sun, planet, and particle, when the motion is very slightly conditioned by the introduction of a nebular resisting medium, such as existed in the early history of our system, and is now observed to be widely diffused throughout Nature. Jacobi's original integral, therefore, requires the addition of a secular term to represent the actual movement of a sun, planet, and particle; and the complete expression for any particle whose coordinates are x_i y_i z_i, becomes:

$$x_i^2 + y_i^2 + \frac{2(1-\mu)}{\sqrt{(x_i-x_1)^2+y_i^2+z_i^2}} + \frac{2\mu}{\sqrt{(x_i-x_2)^2+y_i^2+z_i^2}} = C_i + a_i t_i \ldots (1)$$

The secular term a_i t_i makes the constant C_i increase with the time.

Now the surfaces of zero relative velocity, which define the closed spaces about the planets, have larger values of C_i the nearer we approach to the sun or planet. This is easily seen in the accompanying plate from Darwin's celebrated memoir on Periodic Orbits (Acta Mathematica, Vol. XXI). When the particle or satellite revolves against resistance, therefore, the second member

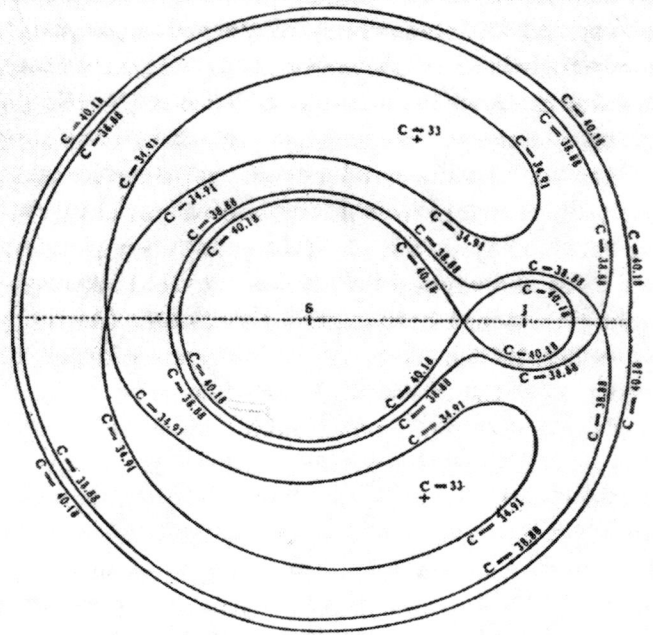

CURVES OF ZERO VELOCITY (DARWIN)

This diagram illustrates the hour-glass shaped space through which the particle may move and drop down nearer the sun or planet, till it becomes captured by one of the larger bodies.

of (1) increases, and there is a secular shrinkage of the surface of zero relative velocity. Accordingly the particle drops down nearer and nearer these centers, and the surface finally becomes closed, leaving it no longer free to move about both bodies in the hour-glass shaped space, as formerly, but restricted to the sphere of influence controlled by the sun or planet individually, as the case may be. The particle which once revolved about both the sun and planet can no longer do so, but becomes an inferior planet (satellite of the sun) or a satellite of the planet.

This is how the satellites of the solar system were captured. At first they moved principally under the attraction of the sun, and could pass from the sun's to the planet's domain, through the neck of the hour-glass shaped space connecting the two spheres of influence. When the neck is narrow, Darwin says that a particle which passes from the sun's to the planet's control may revolve about it hundreds of times before quitting the planet's sphere to return again to the sun's control. And if resistance is meanwhile encountered, so that the neck of the surface of zero velocity becomes closed, it is clear that the particle never will quit the sphere of the planet's control, but will abide there permanently as a satellite.

Thus it incontestably follows that the satellites of Jupiter, Saturn, and other planets formerly moved about the sun, and since they were captured have had their orbits reduced in size and rounded up under the secular action of the resisting medium formerly pervading our solar system. Satellites may cross over the line SJ before coming completely under the planet's control, in which case they will move retrograde. In such cases the neck connecting the two spaces is extremely narrow. But as the neck usually is not so narrow as to produce crossing satellites, most of them naturally move direct, in accordance with observation. This is the reason also why the planets have direct rotations on their axes. The planets have in no case been inverted, as some have recently supposed, in order to account for the retrograde motion of the satellites of Jupiter and Saturn.

VI. CAPTURE THEORY OF SATELLITES INDEPENDENTLY CONFIRMED BY BROWN AND POINCARÉ.

The above discussion is substantially that given by the writer in the *Publications of the Astronomical Society of the Pacific* for August, 1909. The subject has since been treated more in detail and from a slightly different point of view by Professor E. W.

Brown, in the *Monthly Notices* of the Royal Astronomical Society for March, 1911, p. 453. Brown considers the oscillations of an asteroid about the triangular points, where Lagrange showed that there are particular solutions of the problem of three bodies, and a small body may revolve in stability when the asteroid is subjected to small disturbances, as under the action of a resisting medium. Brown shows that it will revolve in periodic orbits about the triangular point, but the constant C of the Jacobian integral will steadily increase and the periodic orbits increase in size; and finally it will reach a critical stage corresponding to the equilibrium point in opposition to Jupiter, where Lagrange showed that another particular solution of the problem of three bodies exists. Under disturbances all these solutions are unstable, and for values of C well beyond this critical value, Brown adds that the orbits "consist (1) of an inner planetary orbit making complete revolutions round the sun in the positive sense; (2) of an outer planetary orbit making complete revolutions round the sun in the negative sense relative to the moving axes; (3) of a satellite revolving round Jupiter in the positive sense." In other words, an asteroid passing through these equilibrium points with suitable velocity corresponding to the critical value of C, may pass under the control of Jupiter and become a satellite of that planet, as I demonstrated in 1909 (A.N. 4341–42).

Finally it remains to add, as already pointed out, that the capture of satellites has been treated also by Poincaré in his course at the Sorbonne during the present year, which is being published and will appear in November. Astronomers and mathematicians naturally will be interested in the forthcoming work of this great master of celestial mechanics. In a recent letter he tells me that he insists on the capture of planets as satellites under the action of a resisting medium.

It is worthy of remark that as far back as 1906 Professor Elis Strömgren, now of Copenhagen, while occupied with the motion of three bodies made a very similar investigation of the problem of cusps and loops, and obtained some remarkable results (*Astron.*

Nachr. No. 4155) which are now found to confirm the capture of satellites.

From this brief outline it will be seen that the capture theory of satellites is now established and very generally accepted by the leading authorities in this difficult branch of mathematical astronomy.

VII. THE ORIGIN OF THE RETROGRADE REVOLUTIONS OF THE SATELLITES AND OF THE DIRECT ROTATIONS OF THE PLANETS ON THEIR AXES.

In my work of 1909, quoted above, it was shown how the retrograde motion of the satellite could arise, by the body crossing over the line $S\,J$ in passing through the neck of the hour-glass space before it came under the control of the planet. It may arise also in other ways. We have seen above that in passing through the equilibrium point, in opposition to Jupiter, the satellite usually will move direct, because there is a space of finite extent in this region corresponding to the critical value of the Jacobian integral, and unless the disturbance is considerable, the gradual transition will give a direct revolution; but if the disturbance be larger, at this critical stage, the satellite may be driven beyond the center of the equilibrium point and set revolving in a retrograde direction. This result is very similar to the case (2) above quoted from Brown's paper, where he concludes that the asteroid may make complete revolutions around the sun in the negative sense relative to the moving axes.

We need not dwell at greater length on the motions of satellites. It is obvious that they may move either direct or retrograde, as first pointed out by me in 1909. But if most of the satellites have direct motion, those which are retrograde will be likely to be destroyed, unless they are so situated as to escape serious collision. It is remarkable that the retrograde satellites of Jupiter and Saturn are on the outside of their systems, where they could easily survive; and this no doubt is the secret of their escape from destruction. Probably they were captured quite late in the history of the solar system, when the resisting medium was relatively ineffective, as shown by the rather large surviving eccentricities of their orbits.

And now just as the satellites usually have direct orbital revolutions, so also do the meteorites and other small masses of cosmical dust circulating in the vortices about the planets, of which the satellites alone are large enough and bright enough to be visible in our telescopes. When swarms of this dust collide with the planet, therefore, the tendency is to give the globe a direct rotation on its axis, because the number of particles having direct revolutions greatly predominates over those having retrograde revolution. This is the secret of the direct rotations of the planets on their axes; and whenever the down-pour of dust is appreciable the axial rotations are being accelerated. It is not strange therefore that the sun, Jupiter and Saturn have equatorial accelerations, which long proved bewildering to astronomers.

VIII. The Obliquities of the Planets.

The problem of the obliquities of the planets long presented great difficulty to the astronomer, and was not solved till 1908, when it was shown by the present writer that it is determined by the capture and absorption of small bodies revolving about the sun in planes nearly coinciding with the orbits of the planets. The countless collisions of these small bodies with a planet like the earth are illustrated by the meteors vaporized in our atmosphere to the number of over a billion daily. In a century this dust would make a layer a millimeter thick all over the globe. The same down-pour of cosmical dust occurs on the other planets, and often times the masses are larger than those now swept up by the earth, as we see by the embedded satellites which produced the lunar craters.

As they revolve about the sun in orbits, which on the average are not much inclined to the orbit of the earth, the tendency is to tilt the earth's axis into a position at right angles to the plane of the ecliptic. The obliquity thus tends to vanish, as illustrated by Jupiter, the greatest of the planets, which has thus acquired a very small obliquity of some 3°, from the capture and absorption of comets, asteroids and satellites. The almost zero obliquity of Jupiter shows the normal development of the process. As a test of the theory it was shown by actual calculation that Saturn would have the present obliquity of some 28° nearly destroyed if the mass of that planet were trebled, to become equal to that of Jupiter, by the same process of the capture and absorption of small bodies moving near the plane of the planet's orbit. The increase of the obliquities from Jupiter to Saturn and Uranus therefore is natural, and in accordance with established theory. Within Jupiter's orbit the obliquities decrease from Mars (24.5°) to the earth (23.5°) and Venus (12° or 15°); and the rotation periods also decrease from $24^h 37^m 22^s$ in the case of Mars, to $23^h 56^m 4^s$ (sidereal day) for the earth, and $23^h 21^m$ for Venus. The order thus existing among the terrestrial planets shows that they have been formed by a very regular cause which has produced harmonious effects.

When the nuclei of the planets were first formed far from the sun, they may have rotated in almost any planes, determined by the collisions previously experienced; but as they drew nearer the sun the rotations became direct and more and more harmonious, as now observed. Beyond a doubt this is the true explanation of the obliquities of the planets of our solar system; and similar laws operate to establish corresponding obliquities for the planets revolving about the fixed stars generally. Accordingly it follows that the planets attending the fixed stars have seasons and alternation of day and night, such as we are familiar with, and therefore they are habitable by living beings like those observed on the earth.

IX. THE CAPTURE OF THE MOON BY THE EARTH.

The case of the terrestrial moon is of special interest, because it is relatively by far the largest of all our satellites, and was formerly supposed by Lord Kelvin and Sir George Darwin to have had an exceptional origin. But it was shown by me in 1909 (A.N.,

4343) that the moon was formed like the other satellites, and is in fact a planet which the earth captured from space, just as the other satellites were captured by their several planets. We shall not here go into the details of the moon's origin, beyond pointing out the reasons why a terrestrial origin for the moon is impossible. (1) The rupture of the earth's figure of equilibrium, which Darwin assumed to account for the origin of the moon, postulates a primitive rotation in less than three hours, or nine times faster than at present. From the causes which produce planetary rotations, as set forth above, we know that no such rapid rotation could have existed in the case of the earth. (2) Even if such rapid rotation had existed, the matter detached from the earth would have taken the form of a swarm of small bodies, and these meteorites never could have united into one mass, as now observed in our actual moon. (3) The satellites of the other planets are recognized to be captured bodies, and the same process naturally will have operated in giving the earth a satellite, even if it is of exceptionally large mass. It should be especially noted that the large mass presents no difficulty to the capture theory. The anomaly lies rather in the small size of the earth, since several of the satellites of Jupiter and Saturn are fully as large as the moon, while those of Uranus and Neptune are not enormously smaller. (4) In Darwin's celebrated graphical method for tracing the moon back to the earth, it is found to be impossible to bring the two globes close together, because at nearest approach a space of over 4,000 miles intervenes between the surfaces, which cannot be bridged over. This contradiction to the terrestrial theory indicates that it is vitiated by an error, and must be unconditionally given up.

For these four weighty reasons we conclude that our moon can be nothing else than a planet which came to us from the heavenly spaces. It follows also that the earth always did rotate in about the same time as at present, and has never suffered retardation from about three hours as Darwin inferred. This simplifies very considerably many problems of Geology, and brings the Cosmogony

THE MOON, TEN DAYS OLD, PHOTOGRAPHED BY LOEWRY AND PUISEUX AT
THE PARIS OBSERVATORY, FEBRUARY 23, 1896.
Naked Eye View. (From See's *Researches*, Vol. II, 1910, Plate XI.)

of the earth and moon into harmony with that found in the rest of the solar system, and in the sidereal universe.

X. THE ORIGIN OF THE LUNAR CRATERS AND MARIA.

Ever since Galileo's discovery of the mountains on the moon, it has been a problem for astronomers to explain the craters and other phenomena on the lunar surface. Notwithstanding the fact that the lunar craters are totally different from those on the earth, it has been believed until very recently that they had a volcanic origin. It turns out, however, that the lunar craters are due to impact of smaller bodies against the lunar surface; and this explains the sunken character of the craters, which are all below the normal level of the lunar surface; the small volume of the walls in comparison with that of the crater basins; the steepness of the inner wall, while the outer one has a more gradual slope; the central peaks which are residues of the satellites that produced the craters; the superposition of one crater over another, and many other phenomena which show that impact, and not volcanic action, has produced the mountains on the surface of the moon. In the same way it is shown that the *Maria* are due to conflagrations which have melted down to a dead level considerable areas of the lunar surface, only the more prominent walls here and there surviving as "ghost craters."

It is a very remarkable fact that can scarcely escape the notice of the sagacious historian of the future that prior to my work on Earthquakes and Mountain Formation (Proc. Am. Philos. Soc., Philadelphia, 1906–8), terrestrial mountains were erroneously explained by the secular cooling and contraction of the earth, whereas they are really formed by the leakage of the oceans and the expulsion of lava under the land, and the mountain ridges therefore run as great walls along the border of the ocean, as in the typical case of the Andes in South America. The current explanation of terrestrial mountain formation was thus entirely erroneous. The new theory that our mountains are formed by the sea has, however, already been very generally accepted. On the other hand, the lunar craters were supposed to be of volcanic origin, whereas they really are due to impact. Thus, wonderful as it may seem, the causes assigned in both cases were erroneous.

Besides the evidence of general character above cited the theory as to the origin of the lunar craters by impact now rests on an absolute proof of mathematical kind as follows. It is shown by the researches of Lehman-Filhé's (A.N. 3479–80) and Strömgren (A.N. 3897) that increase of the central mass of the planet by the downfall of cosmical dust will decrease the mean distance of the satellite, but not the eccentricity of its orbit. It is shown in my *Researches*, Vol. II, 1910, that the eccentricity can be diminished only by the action of a resisting medium such as operated in the capture of the satellites. As the eccentricities of the satellite orbits usually are evanescent, showing that they have been destroyed by the action of a resisting medium, we should expect the moon's surface to bear witness to this process of cosmical bombardment, by which the orbits of the satellites have been rounded up. Thus indentations analogous to the lunar craters ought to exist, and as they are all of one type, their origin must be assigned to the impact of smaller satellites against the lunar surface. Our proof of the origin of the lunar craters is therefore essentially an absolute proof which admits of no dispute.

If it be asked why indentations similar to the lunar craters were not produced on the earth, our answer is that such terrestrial craters due to impact did exist before Geological History began, but they have since been quite obliterated by the effects of the oceans and atmosphere, while modern terrestrial mountains of a totally different type have since been developed along the borders of our seas by the leakage of the oceans. These manifold errors afford us an impressive warning as to the worthlessness of traditional opinion, because so much of our reasoning in physical science heretofore has been based on false premises.

Finally it may be remarked that the satellites of Jupiter and Saturn are variable, as if covered by maria like our own moon, so that the conflagrations which melted areas and produced maria on our satellite have also occured elsewhere, in accordance with the requirements of this simple theory.

XI. Original Extent of the Solar System and the Existence of Planets beyond Neptune.

Babinet's criterion shows beyond doubt that the nuclei of the planets were formed at a great distance from the sun and have since had their orbits decreased in size, largely by the increase of the sun's mass, and rounded up into almost perfect circles, by the action of a resisting medium. As the planets were not thrown off from the sun, this is the only possible way in which they can have been set revolving in such singularly circular orbits. Moreover since it is proved in my *Researches*, Vol. II. and confirmed by the investigations of Strömgren, that the comets are surviving wisps of nebulosity coming to us from the outer shell of our ancient nebula, there is thus developed an independent line of argument showing that the solar nebula was originally of vast extent with a radius of from 10,000 to 50,000 radii of the earth's orbit.

The proof found in Babinet's criterion that the nuclei of the planets originated at a great distance from the sun and have since approached the center is thus confirmed by the elliptical theory of comet orbits; and thus a connection is established between the planets now near the sun and the comets still receding to great distances. In fact the planets were built up in the nebula by the gathering in of cosmical dust, such as we observe in meteor showers raining down on us from disintegrated comets; and thus all the matter now in the planets once was in the solar nebula in the form of comets. By the destruction of countless comets, the planets have been built up to their present dimensions, while at the same time they have neared the sun and been made to revolve in orbits which are so nearly circular, that the Greek philosophers believed that the Deity had chosen the circle for the paths of the planets, because the ancient geometers regarded the circle as a perfect figure.

From these considerations it is evident that our planetary system extends much beyond Neptune, and several of the unseen planets revolving in this remote region of space may yet be discovered by observation. The orbital motion, however, will be very slow, and if the search is attempted by photography the exposures will have to be long and perhaps extended to successive days. Neptune's orbit is so round that we can no more think of our system terminating at this limit than we can imagine the satellites of Jupiter confined within the narrow limits of the old satellites discovered by Galileo.

XII. NATURE OF OUR SYSTEM OF COMETS—ELLIPTICAL ORBITS PREDICTED BY NEWTON—RESEARCHES OF STRÖMGREN.

We have already alluded to the conclusion reached by the writer in 1909 that the orbits of all comets are elliptical, because they are the residue of the ancient nebula which formed our system and thus continue to come to us from the vast outer shell which still survives after the interior of the nebula has been destroyed in forming the central sun and planetary system. By the researches of Strömgren this is now definitely proved to be the true origin of our system of comets.

Historically the problem of the significance of the comets presented great difficulty. In 1687 Newton remarked in the *Principia* that the comets revolve in very elongated orbits, which are really ellipses, but so eccentric as to resemble parabolas in the region near the sun; and are diffused indifferently over the celestial sphere, so that they are not confined to the Zodiac, like the planets. He adds that while the law of gravitation will account for the motions of these bodies, it will not explain how they came to be started in such widely dispersed orbits. The formation of our system from a nebula made up of elements expelled from the stars of the Milky Way and thus gathered together from all directions in space is the only possible explanation of the system of comets. It thus points to the general operation of repulsive forces in Nature,

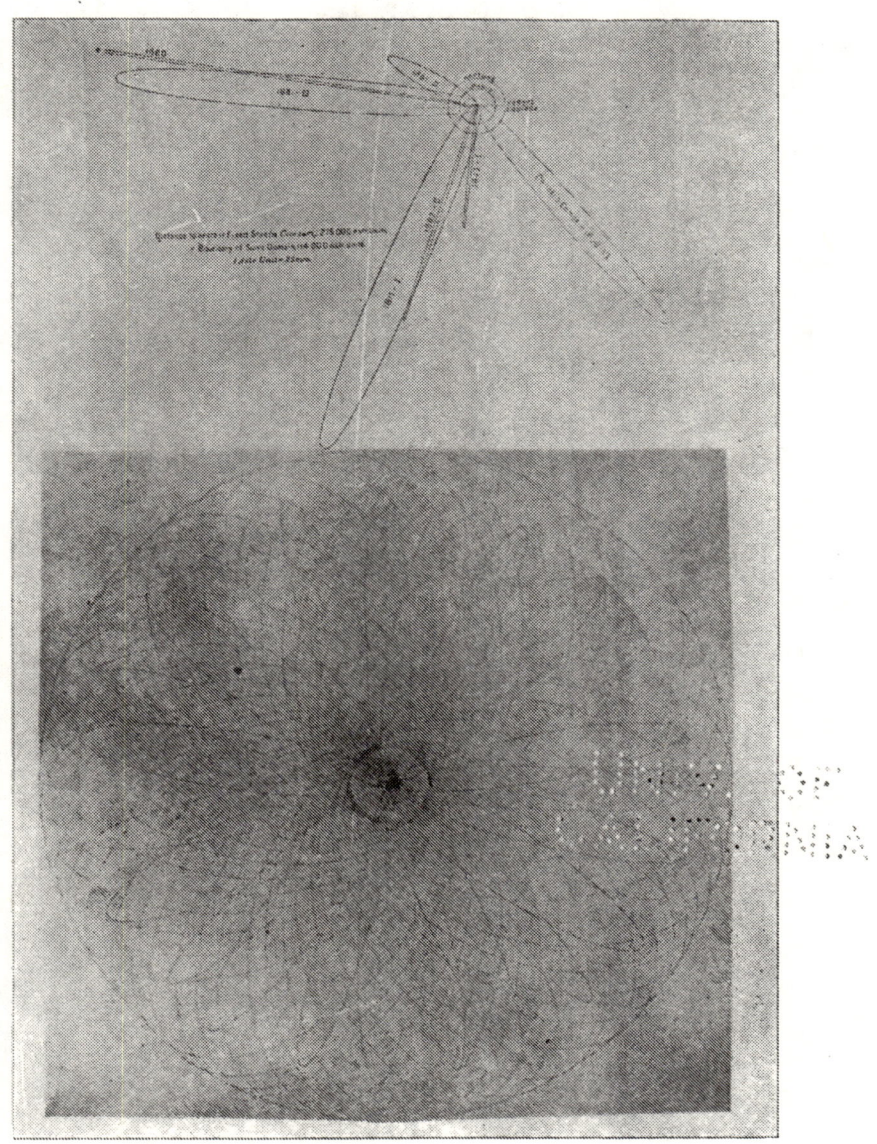

ILLUSTRATIONS OF THE NEW THEORY OF COMETS DEVELOPED BY
T. J. J. SEE.

The lower figure illustrates the vast system of small bodies circulating about the Sun and constituting the outer shell of the primordial nebula. The upper figure from Lowell's "Solar System," shows the orbits of a few actual comets which have appeared in the short interval since Newton's famous comet of 1680.

and constitutes an impressive illustration of the formation of nebulae gathered from a system right at hand.

This theory of the origin of our system of comets has been confirmed by the researches of Leuschner (1906) and Fayet (1906) and more especially of Strömgren (*Vierteljahrsschrift*, October, 1910), who subjected the supposed hyperbolic comets to a critical test, and found every one of them to be elliptic; so that we have to abandon the view long held that some of these bodies move in parabolas and hyperbolas. After two centuries of wandering in the wilderness we thus return to Newton's view of 1687. And the reason for the elliptical orbits of comets is to be found in the nature of the system of comets, wisps of nebulosity coming from the outer shell, as the surviving residue of the ancient nebula which formed our solar system.

XIII. UNIVERSALITY OF REPULSIVE FORCES IN NATURE ESTABLISHED BY HERSCHEL'S ARGUMENT REGARDING THE OPERATION OF CENTRAL POWERS IN THE CLUSTERS AND NEBULÆ.

In the Philosophical Transactions of the Royal Society for 1789, 1811, and 1814 Sir William Herschel has developed a powerful and celebrated argument for the operation of central powers in the formation of star clusters and nebulæ. The star clusters tend to globular figures and increase in density toward their centers; and the same tendency is shown to operate in the nebulæ, many of which seem to be made up of concentric spherical shells of uniform brightness, but accumulating towards the center in such a way as to show a gradual increase of density with maximum in the nucleus, which often is occupied by a nebulous star. There are thousands of these objects, all following the same law, and on the uniformity of the tendency Herschel founds his irresistible argument for the operation of central powers in shaping and moulding the figures of sidereal systems.

Herschel's discussion is so convincing that we need not dwell on it beyond adding that if now we exactly *reverse his argument* we obtain at once a most comprehensive proof of the universal operation of repulsive forces in Nature. For if central powers produce the observed symmetrical condensations, it is obvious that the matter now condensed was formerly diffused somewhat equably about these centers, and could have acquired this arrangement in space only by accumulation from all directions: and therefore at an earlier period the matter was expelled from stars lying in all directions in the general stratum of the Milky Way. Accordingly we thus obtain a most satisfactory proof of the operations of repulsive forces throughout Nature. The familiar proofs of repulsive forces supplied by the solar corona and by the tails of comets pointing from the sun, are thus supported by others drawn from the system of comets about our sun and from the star clusters and nebulæ in every part of the sidereal heavens.

XIV. Arrangement of the Nebulæ in Canopies on Either Side of the Milky Way due to the Action of Repulsive Forces.

If repulsive forces are everywhere at work expelling dust from the stars for the formation of nebulæ, it is evident that as it is repelled by the stars it will tend to gather especially in vacant regions or spaces remote from the stars, and should accumulate with maximum density near the poles of the Milky Way. Thus have arisen the great canopies of nebulæ on either side of the Galaxy. As the dust now forming into nebulæ slowly develops into stars, they drift back into the central starry stratum of the Milky Way, while other new nebulæ take their places; so that the *arrangement of contrariety*, with nebulæ on either side of the starry stratum, is maintained by a process of slow circulation. The observed arrangement of the nebulæ and stars in the sidereal universe is thus the outcome of the grouping of the stars in one great stratum, which may itself be the effect of the mutual attractions of the whole mass and of repulsive forces operating over vast time.

ISOGRAPHIC PROJECTION OF THE NORTHERN CELESTIAL HEMISPHERE.

The nebulæ are represented by dots, the clusters by crosses.
(From See's *Researches*, Vol. II, 1910.)

For over two centuries after the establishment of the law of universal gravitation by Newton in 1687, philosophers took account of attraction only, and ignored the effects of repulsive forces, so that the natural philosophy of the heavens was essentially incomplete, being but half developed. In more recent times account has been taken of repulsive forces and their paramount part in dispersing matter for the formation of sidereal systems, and the result is the full treatment of the two great tendencies in nature, with a more symmetrical development of the grand science of natural philisophy.

XV. THE UNIFORMITY IN THE DISTRIBUTION OF THE CHEMICAL ELEMENTS DISCOVERED BY HUGGINS IN 1864 ALSO IMPLIES THE OPERATION OF REPULSIVE FORCES IN NATURE.

The beautiful discovery of Sir William Huggins, in 1864, that the chemical elements are essentially the same wherever a star twinkles, may be said also to point to repulsive forces in Nature. For if these were not incessantly at work, to keep the elements well stirred, by a process of mixing, it is probable that transmutations going on in certain places might develop at length great inequalities in the distribution of the elements, and the universe would not present the aspect of essential uniformity so clearly disclosed by observation. These results reveal to us some of the greatest laws of Nature, and give us the true cause for the wonderful order found to pervade the starry heavens,

When we consider the hazy, dust-like aspect of the nebulæ it is strange that we should not earlier have read the riddle of these remarkabie objects as produced by the gathering together of dispersed dust; for the existence of these cosmical clouds in the universe is as clear an indication that matter is dispersed from the stars by the action of repulsive forces as the aqueous clouds in our atmosphere are of the renewal of terrestrial evaporation. Any philosophic observer studying the nebulæ through the telescope ought to have been able to recognize that these hazy cloud-like masses are essentially the evaporation-products of the stars, and that they must be incessantly renewed by the repulsive forces at work from these centers of condensation and radiation.

But false ideas of Cosmogony were everywhere prevalent, and instead of looking upon the nebulæ as renewed by the expulsion of dust from the stars, the current view was that the nebulæ represented world stuff not yet used up since the creation. Now in the arguments of the great Herschel, before cited, he shows that some of the sidereal systems have been millions of ages in forming, and as others have been of very different duration, it is possible to prove mathematically that the formation of all parts of the universe did not begin at any one epoch, however remote, but is a process of constant renewal, under the cyclic process here described, the condensation of the nebulæ forming stars and planetary systems and the expulsion of dust from the stars forming the nebulæ.

The philosophical difficulty now overcome by the introduction of repulsive forces for scattering the dust from the stars and thus producing nebulæ, and finally setting the bodies, into which the nebulæ condense, in orbital motion, as if by the action of projectile forces, is one which has been recognized since the time of Anaxagoras (500–427 B.C.) He taught that the sun, moon, and stars had been torn away from the (supposed) common center of the earth by the violence of the cosmic revolution, just as Kant and Laplace long afterwards supposed the planets to have been thrown off by the rotation of the solar nebula. Anaxagoras' difficulty of accounting for the tangential or projectile forces which set the heavenly bodies in motion is stated in the notable work on *Greek Thinkers*, by Professor Theodore Gomperz of the University of Vienna as follows:

"There was only a single point in his theory of the formation of the firmament and the universe in which he deserted his mechanical and physical principles to assume an outside intervention. That first shock which set in motion the process of the universe that had hitherto been in repose reminds us in a most striking

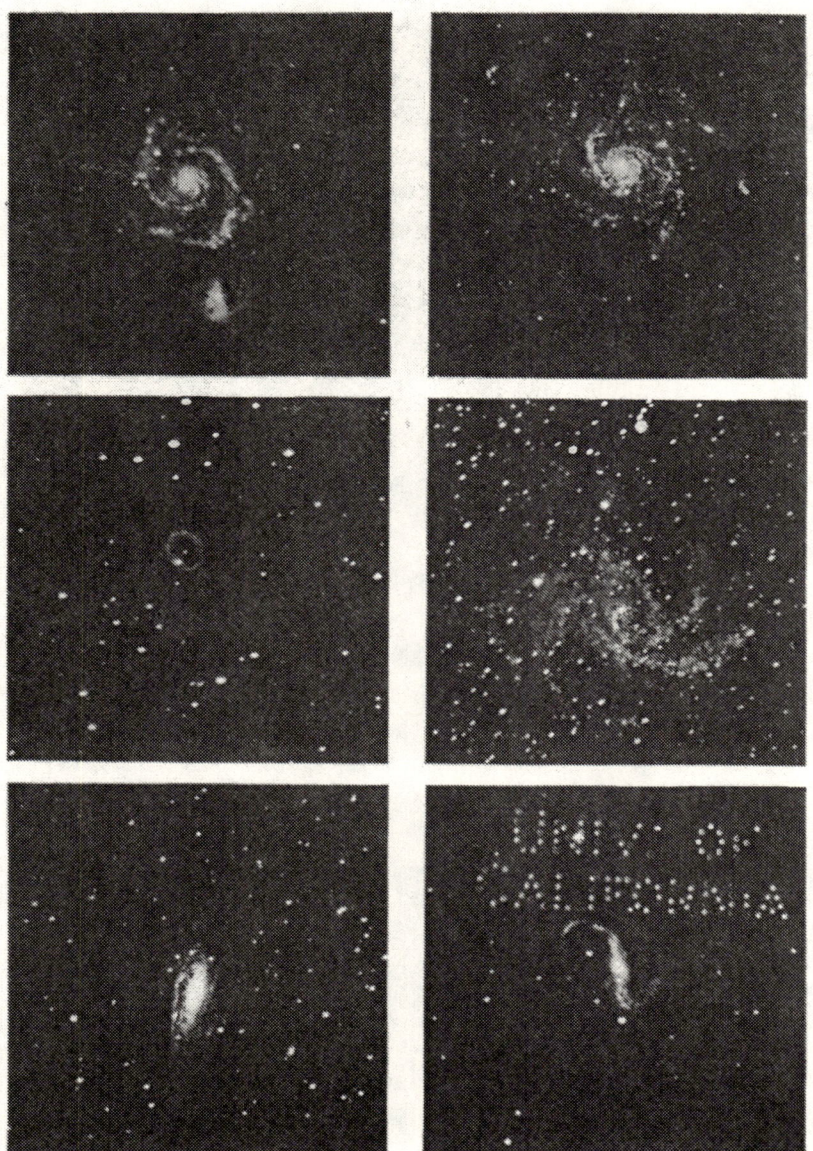

Plate E

SPIRAL NEBULAE PHOTOGRAPHED AT LICK OBSERVATORY:

M 51, CANUM VENATICORUM;   M 101, URSAE MAJORIS;

H. IV 13, CYGNI;   H. IV 76, CEPHEI;

H. I 53, PEGASI;   H. I 55, PEGASI.

(From See's *Researches*, Vol. II, 1910).

    This plate shows impressively that the attendant bodies are not thrown off, as was long imagined, but necessarily added on from without, because in several cases there are no central bodies at all, or scarcely any; but the matter is plainly gathering in from without, and working down towards the center.

fashion of the first impulse which the Deity is supposed by some modern astronomers to have given to the stars. Or rather it would be more correct to say that both ideas are practically identical. They were intended to fill up the same lacuna in our knowledge: they spring from the same desire to introduce in the mechanism of heaven a second force of unknown origin to take its place by the side of gravity." (*Greek Thinkers*, p. 217, translated by Magnus, 1901).

The explanation of *projectile forces* (such as those which set the planets revolving) now adopted, rests on the original dispersion of dust by the stars, and its inevitable collection into a nebula of unsymmetrical figure, which gradually settles and coils up, thus producing a whirling vortex about the center of the nebula, which becomes the sun, while the surviving planets circulating about it have their orbits reduced in size and rounded up into almost perfect circles by the action of the resisting medium. This is a vast improvement in our theories of the mechanics of the heavens, and as it follows directly from well established laws of motion, the traditional difficulty in the mechanical theory of the universe completely disappears, and we see that the revolutions of the stars is a necessary consequence and a proof of the interaction of attractive and repulsive forces in nature.

XVI. SPIRAL, ANNULAR, ELLIPTICAL, PLANETARY AND IRREGULAR NEBULÆ.

As nebulæ arise from the collection together of particles of dust expelled from the stars, it naturally follows that the clouds thus developed will seldom be of perfectly regular figure, but will often consist of two or more streams settling down and coiling up under the effects of their mutual gravitation. The settling of a stream of unsymmetrical figure towards its center of gravity thus produces a *spiral nebula.* In rare cases the streams may coil about in such a way as to produce an *annular* or *ring nebula like that in Lyra. Ring nebulae* are therefore special cases of the more general type of *spiral nebulæ*. If the whirlpool is of somewhat even density, and viewed obliquely, it appears to be an *elliptical nebula*. When the elements come together somewhat symmetrically from all directions, and the density is somewhat uniform, we have a *planetary nebula* — a type which seems to be quite numerous. Most of the nebulæ, however, are of irregular figure, as ought naturally to happen from the way they are formed. In time they tend to settle down and assume more symmetrical form, but the process is excessively slow, owing to the feebleness of the attractive forces, and the rarity of the mass of cosmical dust, which usually allows the light of stars to pass through it, even when thousands of times the diameter of the solar system.

For a long time after the age of Herschel and Laplace it was usually assumed that the nebulæ are *figures of equilibrium* maintained by high temperature and hydrostatic pressure, but of late years these views have been quite abandoned. The nebula are much too rare for the exertion of any hydrostatic pressure. This is proved from actual calculation in the solar system, by the fact that if the sun be expanded to Neptune's orbit, as held in the abandoned theory of Laplace, the density of the resulting nebula is two hundred and sixty million times less than that of atmospheric air at sea level, or thousands of times less than that of the most perfect vacuum attainable.

A planetary nebula is therefore analogous to the infinite system of comets revolving in all directions about the sun, except that the comets are dense enough to render the whole nebula faintly visible, which probably is not true of *our system of comets* as seen from the other fixed stars. The vast extent and incredible rarity of our system of comets and meteoric trains make them the best known illustrations of what the average nebula really is.

Some nebulæ contain certain self luminous gases, probably shining at very low temperature by luminescence or electric excitation, but most of the elements are non-luminous and give no spectral indications of their presence.

XVII. THE PRINCIPAL CAUSE OF VARIABLE STARS TO BE SOUGHT IN THE ACTION OF A RESISTING MEDIUM.

It is shown in my *Researches on the Evolution of the Stellar Systems*, Vol. II, 1910, that, although quite unseen, planetary systems really exist about the fixed stars which appear to be single under the most refined observations of our greatest telescopes. Our instruments reveal to us chiefly the bright companions at some distance (visual double stars), or massive companions revolving rapidly and in such close proximity as to become visible only by the periodic shift of the spectral lines (spectroscopic binary stars). In both classes of these objects the masses must be considerable, while the planets attending the fixed stars revolve quite unseen and forever beyond the reach of our most powerful instruments.

We know that planets attend the fixed stars for two reasons: (1) They attend our sun, which is definitely known to have developed from a nebula. (2) The mode of formation which was operative when the planets began as small nuclei in the distance and neared the center of the system under the attraction of gravitation will necessarily have operated in the same way about the other stars, which arose from nebulæ under the very same laws. Therefore the fixed stars generally have systems of planets, asteroids, satellites, and comets; and the double stars are simply those systems in which the smaller bodies have been so united as to produce large companions.

Now as all the stars have companions, and the resisting medium exists everywhere, though with varying density, it follows that those companions which plunge through considerable resistance at perihelion will experience a variation in brightness. The blazing up of the light will be comparatively rapid, the fall in brightness more gradual, depending on the slower process of cooling. These are the variable stars, of which more than a thousand are known.

Some clusters are quite filled with variable stars, and it is observed that their periods are very constant. This shows that these clusters are still supplied with ample nebulosity, and that variation of such great regularity can depend on nothing but orbital motion for its regulating cause.   Where the variation is irregular, one should suspect the presence of several disturbing bodies the compound effects of which do not give regular periodicity.   In other cases there are phenomena of eclipses to be dwelt with, as in the Algol and Beta Lyræ variables, but we need not dwell on these details.

The important thing for us to observe is that the great cause which has rounded up the orbits of our planets, enabled the planets to capture their satellites, and given rise to the lunar craters, by the destruction of millions of small bodies, is operative throughout the universe; and it is therefore no wonder that many of the stars are variable.

XVIII. New Stars due to Collisions with Attendant Bodies.

As all the fixed stars are attended by systems of planets and comets, it will inevitably happen that collisions of disastrous character between some of these bodies and their central suns will occasionally occur.*   My investigation of this question proves that the Novæ follow the Milky Way in just the proportion that should occur if the outbursts depend simply on the thickness of the stars on the back ground of the sky, so that wherever the stars are numerous there the Novæ will appear.

It was formerly supposed by some that the stars actually come into collision with one another; but it is now realized that such disasters are too rare to become noticeable, whereas collisions with attendant planets or comets within the system must be infinitely more frequent.   Above all, as the Novæ are of short duration, this fact points to conflagrations such as might follow from

---

* In this way probably arise the so-called *stellar nebulæ*, which are correctly distinguished from the *planetary nebulæ*.   The former follow the Milky Way like the *Novæ*, and undoubtedly these two classes of objects are connected, though this apparently has not been suspected heretofore.

the collision of a small mass, but not of one sun with another. Accordingly it has come to be accepted that the new stars are due to collisions with minor masses of the type of planets or very large comets.

The theory that a comet might fall into a star which had wasted in splendor was held by Newton, and thus our modern view is merely an extension of that put forth by the immortal author of the *Principia* in 1687.

XIX. CONNECTON ESTABLISHED BETWEEN ALL CLASSES OF HEAVENLY BODIES.

The most significant result of the New Science of Cosmogony as now developed is that these laws unite all the different classes of the heavenly bodies into one continuous and unbroken whole. Every star is a sun, attended by an infinite system of comets, and by companions, whether the system has the form of a double star or the more general type of a planetary system made up of numerous small bodies. Whenever a system has a dominant body like Jupiter, it has also a system of asteroids gathered within its orbit, and a group of short period comets, such as our own Jupiter has captured. The comets are destroyed, and the dust of their disintegration serves to build up the masses of the planets.

In the transition of the asteroids over Jupiter's orbit, some are captured and become satellites, which usually have a direct revolution, but a lesser number may move retrograde, as actually observed in the solar system. The collisions of captured particles with the planets give these globes a direct rotation on their axes, and establish obliquities like those observed in the planets revolving about our sun. The meteors, comets, asteroids, satellites and smaller planets are consumed in building up the larger bodies of the system. If a large companion revolves in an eccentric orbit, most of the planetary bodies may be swallowed up in one of the two large masses and thus lead to the development of a double star. Should the stars be far apart there may arise a closer companion giving a triple or quadruple star, or one of the components of a double star may become a spectroscopic binary. When a nebula of vast extent is formed and develops by condensation at many centers we have a cluster, with companions attending the individual stars, and by revolving in the nebular resisting medium giving us *cluster variables*, often with wonderful regularity of period.

Collisions of large comets or planets with suns which have wasted in splendor supply new or temporary stars, which blaze forth wherever the stars are crowded on the background of the sky, and therefore principally along the course of the Milky Way. The dust expelled from the stars to form nebulæ may take any of the observed forms, and thus we have *spiral, annular, elliptical, planetary* and *irregular nebulæ*. Astronomers now recognize the following classes of cosmical bodies: 1, single stars: 2, double stars, including both visual and spectroscopic binaries; 3, multiple stars; 4, clusters of stars; 5, star-clouds in the Milky Way; 6, the Milky Way itself, as a clustering stream of smaller systems traversing the circuit of the heavens and here and there culminating in a perfect blaze from the intensity of the accumulated starlight; 7, variable stars; 8, temporary stars; 9, planetary systems; 10, systems of satellites; 11, systems of asteroids; 12, systems of comets; 13, spiral nebulæ; 14, annular nebulæ; 15, elliptical nebulæ; 16, planetary nebulæ; 17, irregular nebulæ; 18, diffuse nebulosity, often covering whole constellations; 19, canopies of nebulæ accumulating with maximum density near the poles of the Milky Way; 20, two or more streams among the stars, indicating that the observed order of the universe is slowly changing with the flight of ages.

It is obvious that a Science of Cosmogony which is founded on a true basis should connect these different classes of bodies one with another, and thus establish an unbroken continuity in the observed order of Nature.

In the new edition of the *Encyclopedia Britannica*, under the article *Stars*, it is pointed out by Mr. A. S. Eddington of the Royal

Observatory, Greenwich, that a fundamental contradiction arises in our conceptions of cosmical evolution when, on the one hand, we try to pass from systems of binary stars and planets, supposed to be thrown off from the central nebula by the fluid fission process of Poincaré and Darwin to the star clusters, on the other, which are supposed to be due to the aggregation of matter towards centers, as imagined by Herschel. If Mr. Eddington had read my papers of 1909 carefully, and above all the second volume of my *Researches*, 1910, he would have seen that this long-standing contradiction is now permanently removed, because I have proved that the uniform Law of Nature is one of aggregation of matter towards the large centers of attraction, while the only throwing off that ever takes place is that of small particles expelled by the action of repulsive forces. Mr. Eddington's article doubtless was prepared several years ago, but the failure to bring it up to date in this and many other cases shows that the *Britannica* is antiquated before it leaves the press, and it is not remarkable therefore that it has so largely disappointed the scientific world.

From the foregoing theory it thus appears that we have a simple and consistent explanation of all classes of the heavenly bodies in their mutual relationship and distribution in space. The harmony and order thus introduced into apparently confused and extremely varied phenomena is the best proof that the laws now recognized are the true Laws of Nature.

XX. PHILOSOPHICAL SIGNIFICANCE OF PLATO'S CELEBRATE SAYING THAT THE DEITY ALWAYS GEOMETRIZES.

One of the most beautiful of these laws, as disclosed by the New Science of Cosmogony, appeals especially to the geometer. And as it has left a profound impress upon the geometry of the heavens, we may conclude these remarks by a brief explanation of it. We have seen that the nebulæ are formed by the gathering together of fine dust expelled from the stars, and that it eventually condenses into larger bodies. This unsymmetrical figure of a nebula often causes it to settle, under its own gravitation, and develop into a spiral resembling the spiral of Archimedes. The sun of the system develops at the center, while planets are formed in the distance and made to approach the sun in orbits becoming smaller and smaller and rounder and rounder, owing to the secular effects of the nebular resisting medium. And the final outcome is a planetary system of the beauty and order found about our sun, the planets being attended by captured satellites and endowed with axial rotation and small obliquity, often surrounded by atmospheres and oceans, with all the conditions favorable for habitability.

This development represents one of the greatest and most general laws of nature. Now if drawing ellipses and slowly transforming them into circles for the orbits of planets, and thus establishing orderly systems out of the chaos of a spiral nebula may be considered geometrizing, then Plato certainly was right when he declared that the Deity always geometrizes — $\delta\ \theta\acute{\epsilon}o\varsigma\ \grave{\alpha}\grave{\epsilon}\iota\ \gamma\epsilon\omega\mu\acute{\epsilon}\tau\rho\epsilon\iota.$

A sublimer truth than this probably never will be disclosed to mortals. When we behold the starry heavens on a cloudless night we may well recall the geometrizing of the Deity which is always going on for establishing the beauty and order of the Cosmos.

U.S. Naval Observatory,
Mare Island, California,
    August 7, 1911.

CHAPTER XIV.

1911.

DETERMINATION OF THE DEPTH OF THE MILKY WAY.*

By T. J. J. SEE.

(Read January 5, 1912.)

INTRODUCTORY REMARKS.

THE problem of determining the depth of the Milky Way, as accurately as possible, is one which has now engaged my attention for over twenty years, and I will therefore take this occasion to bring together the results at which I have arrived, partly because they are of high general interest, and partly because the progress thus made will prove instructive as to the methods which must be adopted for the measurement of the distances of the most remote objects of the sidereal universe. Here we have to deal with distances so immense that the method of annual parallaxes, commonly used for the stars comparatively near the sun, utterly fails; and recourse must be had to other methods which will serve for the greatest distances to which our modern giant telescopes can penetrate.

Alpha Centauri, the nearest of the fixed stars, was also the first to be sucessfully measured for parallax, by Thomas Henderson, of the Cape of Good Hope, in 1831; but the work was not reduced till January, 1839, and meanwhile Bessel had measured the parallax of 61 Cygni in 1838 and promptly published the result of his triumph. Of late years astronomers have given greatly increased attention to the question of the distances of the stars and systematic campaigns of the most laborious kind have been carried on by Gill; Elkin and Chase, of Yale; Kapteyn, of Groningen; and Schlesinger, at the Yerkes Observatory, Chicago. Some

---

*Reprinted from *Proceedings American Philosophical Society*, Vol. li., 1912.

three hundred and fifty stars have now been studied by the standard method of parallaxes, and for most of these objects, perhaps about two hundred in number, fairly satisfactory data have been deduced; but the method can be extended only to stars within less than one hundred light-years of our sun, and is therefore very limited in its applicability, owing to the small diameter of the earth's orbit, and the insensible effects of the annual displacements resulting from the orbital motion of our planet.   As nature herself has fixed the limits of this method, astronomers have naturally cast about for other methods of greater generality and have finally developed processes of surprising power, of which an account will be given in the present paper.

§1.   OUTLINE OF THE METHODS ADOPTED.

Among previous investigators who have occupied themselves with the difficult problem of the profundity of the Milky Way the first place will be universally assigned to the incomparable Sir William Herschel, who extended his researches over many years, and reached results which were for a time accepted, but have been rejected for three quarters of a century, and yet are now proved to be essentially correct.   It is very remarkable and exceedingly unfortunate that Herschel's conclusions have been generally rejected by his son, Sir John Herschel, and other astronomers during the past seventy-five years.   But before discussing the circumstances which led to this outcome I shall recall the modern attempts at the solution of the problem of determining distances in the Milky Way.

After the spectroscope came into use, and Huggins had applied Doeppler's principle to the motion in the line of sight (1868) it was pointed out by Fox Talbot in 1871 (Brit. Assoc. Report, 1871, p. 34, Pt. II.) that the possibility existed of determining the absolute dimensions of the orbit of a pair of binary stars which had a known angular dimension in the sky, and thus parallaxes might be found of systems very remote from the earth.   In 1890, while a post-graduate student at the University of Berlin, I developed this method still further, and showed how it could be used also to test the accuracy of the law of universal gravitation in the stellar systems.   The spectroscopic method then outlined was brought to more general form in 1895, and it at once occurred to me to point out its use for measuring the distance of clusters in the Milky Way (A.N. 3,323), as more certain than Herschel's method of star gauges.

Our age is one of rapid improvement in all scientific processes and during the past sixteen years naturally much progress has been made in double-star astronomy, as well as in our knowledge of nebulæ and clusters.   On looking more closely into the spectroscopic method, which in 1895 had been shown to be applicable to objects 1,000 light-years from the sun, and might thus include all suitable double-stars within this sphere, I became convinced that while it is a great theoretical advance over the old method of parallaxes, it still is quite inadequate for finding the distances of the most remote objects in the sidereal universe.   Accordingly in 1909 I returned to the improvement of Herschel's method as the most promising, for the determination of the distances of *the most remote objects*.   Here are the grounds for this decision:

1.   It was noticed, as remarked by Burnham, that revolving double stars are rare, if not unknown, in clusters, and among the star-clouds of the Milky Way — not because such systems are not present in these masses of stars, but because they cannot be separated, owing to the great distances at which these masses of stars are removed from us.

2.   When double stars cannot be clearly separated in the telescope they cannot be used for parallax by the spectroscopic method; and thus the spectroscopic method, while having a wider range of application than the method of parallaxes, in something like the ratio of the size of the double star orbit to that of the orbit of the earth, is yet applicable only to stars within about 1,000 light-years of our sun.

3.   It will be shown below that the most remote stars are separated from us by a distance of at least 1,000,000 light-years,

and as this space is a thousand times that to which the spectroscopic method may be applied, it follows that there is no way of fathoming these immense distances except by the improvement of the method of Herschel.

And just as in my "Researches on the Evolution of the Stellar Systems," Vol. II, 1910, p. 638, I had been able to adduce substantial grounds for returning to the vast distances calculated by Herschel, so also during the past year I have been able to add to the proof there brought forward, and will proceed to develop it in the present paper.

§2.   HERSCHEL'S METHOD DEPENDING ON THE SPACE PENETRATING POWER OF TELESCOPES.

In his celebrated star gauges Herschel employed a twenty-foot reflector of eighteen inches aperture, and calculated the space-penetrating power of such an instrument from the ratio of the aperture of the telescope to that of the pupil of the eye.   The comparative distance to which a star would have to be removed in order that it may appear of the same brightness through the telescope as it did before to the naked eye may thus be calculated. Herschel found the power of this twenty-foot reflector to be seventy-five; so that a star of sixth magnitude removed to seventy-five times its present distance would therefore still be visible, as a star, in the instrument.

Admitting such a sixth magnitude star to give only a hundredth part of the light of the standard first magnitude star, it will follow that the standard star could be seen as a sixth magnitude star at ten times its present distance; and if we then multiply by the space penetrating power, we get 750 as the distance to which the standard star could be removed and still excite in the eye, when viewed through the telescope, the same impression as a star of sixth magnitude does to the naked eye.   Thus if Alpha Centauri be distant 4.5 light-years, it would be visible in Herschel's telescope at a distance of 3,375 light-years.   This is about the distance ascribed to the remoter stars of the Milky Way by Newcomb and many other modern writers; but of course it is much too small, for the following reasons:

(*a*)   Newcomb and other astronomers cite the possibility of some of the stars being as much as 1,000,000 times brighter than the average solar star, and in that case the star might be seen at $\sqrt{1,000,000} = 1,000$ times that distance, or 3,375,000 light-years, with an instrument having a space penetrating power no greater than that employed by Herschel, provided that no light is extinguished in its passage through space.

(*b*)   If the telescope be more powerful than Herschel's 20-foot reflector, the light gathered will be increased in the ratio of $x^2/(18)^2$, where $x = $ diameter of mirror; and for the 60-inch reflector at Pasadena, $x = 60$, over nine times as much light could be gathered, or stars seen over three times as far away. Thus if the stars have only about 10,000 times the luminosity of the sun, they could still be seen with the Pasadena reflector at a distance of over a million light-years. For $3,375\,\mathrm{l.\text{-}y.} \times 3 \times 100 = 1,012,500$ light-years.

(*c*)   The sensitiveness and accumulative effects of the photographic plate, will enable us to extend our sounding line still further out into space by some three magnitudes, or four times the distance; and thus with a modern 60-inch reflector we could photograph stars at a distance of about four million light-years, if they have 10,000 times the standard solar luminosity, and no light is lost in space. How much light is really lost in space will be considered later, but it may be stated here that it probably is decidedly less than was concluded by Struve.

§3.   INDEPENDENT CALCULATION OF THE DISTANCE OF THE REMOTEST STARS OF THE HELIUM TYPE.

From the data given in *Lick Observatory Bulletin* No. 195, we find that 225 helium stars employed by Campbell in his line of sight work have an average visual magnitude of 4.14. Of the four variables given in this *Bulletin*, we have used the maximum brightness in three cases, because they are of the algol type. In the case of u Herculis, we have used the mean magnitude, because the type of variable does not appear to be as yet well established.

Here then we have 225 helium stars at an average distance of about 540 light-years. For in *Lick Observatory Bulletin* No. 195, p. 121, Campbell finds the 180 class B, or helium, stars to have an average distance of 543 light-years, while in *Publications of the Astronomical Society of the Pacific* for June-August, 1911, p. 159, Professor Curtis gives 534 light-years as the average distance of 312 helium stars. The former distance for 180 stars being greater than the latter distance for 312 stars, we may take 540 light-years as the distance of the 225 helium stars here under discussion, the average magnitude of which is 4.14.

If the average magnitude were decreased to 21.14, by removal to 2,512 times their present distance, which would reduce the average brightness by 17 magnitudes, the distance of the stars would be multiplied by 2,512, and become 1,356,480 light-years. This is for the helium stars as they are, without any hypothesis as to brightness, or as to the extinction of light in space, which will be considered later.

The question will naturally be asked whether helium stars really exist at these great distances. We may unhesitatingly affirm that they do, because of the well-known whiteness of the small stars of the Milky Way. It is true that Pickering has investigated the distribution of the helium stars in the *Harvard Annals*, Vol. 56, No. II., and Campbell quotes these data in *Lick Observatory Bulletin* No. 195 as showing that the helium stars are all bright objects. Pickering believed his tabulations to indicate "that of the bright stars, one out of four belongs to this class (B), while of the stars of the sixth magnitude there is only one out of twenty; and that few if any would be found fainter than the seventh or eighth magnitude." The implication here is that no helium stars exist at very great distances corrresponding to small magnitudes; but of course such a view is untenable.

It probably is true that the group of helium stars at a distance of some 540 light-years from our sun, and thus comparatively near us, does cease after a certain faintness and distance has been reached; but is equally certain that other clusters or clouds of helium stars recur at greater distances, among the millions of small white stars constituting the Milky Way. For as Herschel long ago noticed the Galaxy is everywhere observed to traverse the circuit of the heavens in a *clustering stream;* and our view of it from the region of the sun is not essentially different from the view that could be obtained from other points in this starry stratum. Add to this consideration the fact of the well-known whiteness of the small stars in the Milky Way, and we are authorized to conclude that an indefinite number of clusters or groups of helium stars will be found in the Milky Way, and thus such stars will certainly exist at the greatest depths to which our giant telescopes can penetrate.

We must therefore be on our guard against the superficial view, that because the helium stars near the sun fade away as the sixth magnitude is approached, other groups of stars of this type do not occur at greater distances. The typical whiteness of the millions of small stars which make up the Milky Way, and the clustering character of that magnificent collection of stars, alike forbid any such inference.

Herschel had the correct view of the constitution of the Galaxy a century ago. Unfortunately his works have been very inaccessible, and are so little used that many erroneous conceptions have been given currency by more superficial investigators. It is impossible to commend too highly the movement now on foot in England to reissue the collected works of Sir William Herschel. In all that pertains to the sidereal universe as a whole he is easily the greatest of all modern astronomers, and will always remain unrivaled.

§4. EXPLANATION OF THE METHODS EMPLOYED BY CAMPBELL FOR FINDING THE AVERAGE DISTANCE OF THE GROUP OF NAKED EYE HELIUM STARS.

This is essentially a combination of the line of sight motion as found at Lick Observatory, with the proper motions resulting from observations with the meridian circle, by many observers, as worked up by Boss of the Dudley Observatory, Albany, New York. By the recent study of several thousand of the brighter stars included in his Prelimimary General Catalogue, Professor Boss has deduced their proper motions with a high degree of accuracy. Campbell found from 180 of these stars resembling our sun in spectral type that their average cross proper motion in the sky, from the values derived by Boss, was about 0.11 second of arc per annum, while at the same time their average speed in the line of sight shown by the spectrograph at Lick Observatory was 8.9 miles per second, or two hundred and eighty million miles a year. Having the average motion in the line of sight, in absolute units, and the average cross proper motion in seconds of arc, it is easy to find how far away a base line of 280 million miles would have to be to subtend an angle of 0.11 of a second of arc. It turns out to be ninety-two light-years.

In this way it is possible to get the average distances of large groups of stars. Here are some of the results found by Campbell.

Type	No.	Average Yearly Cross-motion	Average Radial Velocity in Miles per Second	Average Relative Parallax	Average Distance in Light-years
$B - B_5$	312	0.0078	3.9	0.0061	534
$B_8 - B_9$	90	0.0182	4.2	0.0129	253
A	172	0.0368	6.5	0.0166	196
F	180	0.1075	8.9	0.0354	92
G	118	0.0748	9.9	0.0223	146
K	346	0.0516	10.4	0.0146	223
M	71	0.0384	10.6	0.0106	308

This table contains the most important results of the Campbell-Boss method of obtaining average distances for large groups of stars. It need scarcely be remarked that its significance can hardly be overrated. But whilst the *average values* given are quite trustworthy, the method is of course inapplicable to the *individual stars*; and if their distances are to be found, recourse would have to be had to the standard method of parallaxes, or to the spectroscopic method in the case of visual binaries.

§5. SOME OF THE DISTANCES OF THE REMOTEST STARS AS HERETOFORE CALCULATED BY ASTRONOMERS.

1. Sir William Herschel, *Phil. Trans.*, 1802, p. 498, "almost 2,000,000 light-years."
2. Sir John Herschel, "Outlines," edition of 1869, p. 583, "upwards of 2,000 light-years."
3. Guillemin, "The Heavens," trans. by Lockyer, 1867, p. 433, "upwards of 20,000 light-years."
4. Bartlett, "Spherical Astronomy," 1874, p. 149, "upwards of 2,437.5 light-years."
5. Newcomb, "Popular Astronomy," edition of 1878, p. 481, "about 14,000 light-years" (for the Herschel stars).
6. Clerke, "System of the Stars," 1890, p. 314, "less than 36,000 light-years."
7. Ranyard, "Old and New Astronomy," 1892, p. 748, "less than 70,000 light-years."
8. Young, "General Astronomy," edition of 1904, p. 563, "10,000 to 20,000 light-years."
9. Newcomb, "The Stars," 1908, p. 319, "at least 3,000 light-years."
10. See, "Researches," Vol. II, 1910, p. 638, "4,500,000 light-years."

From this table it will be seen that there was a great falling off in the distances following the epoch of Sir William Herschel; and that the present writer was the first to recognize the fallacy of the recent estimates of distance, and to restore the large values used by that unrivaled astronomer one hundred and ten years ago. Here we have a good illustration of the retrogradation of opinion in astronomy, under the cultivation of inferior genius. Sir John Herschel's preference for such small distances over the large values used by his father is indeed remarkable and very regrettable. Evidently the small value used by Newcomb is simply an echo of the reduction in distance made by Sir John Herschel. The absurdity of these small values — not over five times that of the helium stars of 4.14 magnitude investigated at Lick Observatory — ought to impress us with the small importance to be attached to any opinion merely because it is currently accepted. Thus we have a clear case of misleading tradition transmitted from the second Herschel, and the amazing spectacle of the whole world using values about a thousand times too small, for the greater part of a century, in times which were supposed to be very enlightened. Strange indeed that the correct work of the great Sir William

Herschel should have been neglected all this time! Will it seem credible to future ages that such a remarkable retrogradation of opinion could have occurred and persisted during the nineteenth and twentieth centuries? If so, it must be attributed to the narrowing effects of extreme specialization, which, with the advance of science, has been difficult to avoid in our time, and yet is utterly disastrous to the growth of true natural philosophy as the study of nature in the widest sense.

§6. OTHER METHODS FOR CONFIRMING THE GREAT DEPTH OF THE MILKY WAY.

(a) The girdle of helium stars about our sun, according to the Lick determination, has a mean distance of 540 light-years, or a mean diameter of 1,080 light-years. If this be one-twentieth of the average thickness of the Milky Way stratum, as one may infer from the appearance of certain clusters in the constellation Sagittarius, which are near enough to be studied intelligently, then we have 21,600 light-years for the average thickness of the Milky Way.

Now when we traverse the Milky Way from Centaurus to Cepheus, over an arc of 180° in length, the central band appears to the naked eye to have a width of 3° or 4°, as was long ago remarked also by Herschel and Struve. This is an extension along the circle of the Galaxy of about 60 times its thickness. If then the thickness be 21,600 light-years, the double depth of the stratum in both directions becomes about two-thirds of $21,600 \times 60 = 864,000$ light-years. And if only the faint or distant telescopic stars be considered, the width of their belt of distribution is narrower, and the depth would be found several times greater yet. Wherefore it seems certain that the profundity of the Milky Way, considerably exceeds a million light-years, and may be several times that depth.

(b) Accordingly if we make the very moderate hypothesis that the width of 3° or 4°, which was also noticed by Herschel and Struve, represents chiefly the nearer portion of the Galaxy; and that the remoter portion has a width not exceeding 1°, we should conclude that the depth may be found by multiplying the thickness or apparent angular width of 21,600 light-years by the number of degrees in the radius, 57.3.   This gives for the depth 1,237,-680 light-years, and this value might be considerably increased by adjustments in the data which are not improbable.

(c) In addition to these general arguments, founded on the principles of geometry, we might introduce another based on actual measurement.   The Lick helium stars, of average brightness 4.14 mag., were found to have an average distance of 540 light-years. If they were brought near enough to us to appear of 1st magnitude, this distance would have to be divided by $4 = \sqrt{(2.512)^3}$, and thus we find for the first magnitude helium stars a distance of 135 light-years.

Now in calculating the plan of the construction of the heavens from the apparent breadth of the Milky Way, Herschel arrived at the conclusion that the thickness of the stratum is about 80 times greater than the diameter of the sphere including the first magnitude stars represented by Sirius (*Phil. Trans.*, 1785, p. 254).   And if the average distance of these stars be taken as 135 light-years, the mean diameter of the shell in which they are included will be 270 light-years.   This would give exactly 21,600 light-years for the thickness of the stratum of the Milky Way, as before.

It is true that Herschel classed all first magnitude stars in one group, and took no account of the fact that the helium stars are the more remote and the more brilliant; yet regarding the Galaxy as a stratum of stars chiefly of the helium type, which certainly is true of all the more distant portions of that magnificent collection of stars, we may consider the reasoning of this great astronomer as still valid.   And the argument in regard to the depth of the Milky Way is thus the same as that given above under (a) and (b).

§7.   THE EFFECTS OF THE EXTINCTION OF LIGHT IN SPACE.

This problem has been treated with some detail in the 23d chapter of my "Researches," Vol. II., 1910, but we shall here examine the subject with greater care, especially as to the most probable average value of the coefficient of extinction. The light was shown by Struve to be defined by the equation

$$\xi = \frac{I}{x^2}(0.990651)^{x-1}, \tag{1}$$

where x is the distance of the star, in units of $\triangle = \sqrt{(2.512)^n}$ and n is the difference in magnitude. At very great distances nearly all the light is cut off, and it therefore becomes a question of high importance to determine as accurately as possible the proper value for the coefficient of extinction.

Struve's value, used in the above formula, seems to be too small, and I have therefore calculated a new table, to show the effect of increasing the coefficient. In justification of this course it should be recalled that Sir William Herschel ignored extinction entirely; but while this procedure obviously is defective, it is pretty clear, from the aspects of the Milky Way as now made known by modern research, that Struve's coefficient is decidedly too small. The following table shows the effects of varying the coefficient, upon stars 17 magnitudes fainter, corresponding to a distance 2,512 times larger, where $x-1=2,511$.

TABLE FOR VARYING COEFFICIENT OF EXTINCTION.

λ=Ceoff. of Extinction.	λ^{x-1}.	Fractional Part of Light Transmitted, in Spite of Extinction,
0.990651	0.000,000,000,05709	$\frac{1}{17514\ 000\ 000}$ (Struve's value)
0.995	0.000,003,4072	$\frac{1}{293\ 490}$
0.996	0.000,042,571	$\frac{1}{23490}$
0.997	0.000,52923	$\frac{1}{1889.5}$
0.998	0.006,5567	$\frac{1}{152.51}$
0.999	0.081,091	$\frac{1}{12.332}$ (See's value)
0.9995	0.284,846	$\frac{1}{3.5107}$
1.00000	1.000,00	1.00000 (Herschel's value)

From the study of this table, we perceive that at the distance $x = 2,512$, corresponding to an enfeeblement of 17 magnitudes, from mere increase of distance alone, the extinction of light varies from almost total loss, with Struve's co-efficient, to no loss whatever, on Herschel's tacit hypothesis of zero extinction. This latter view, however, certainly is extreme, and probably all modern astronomers agree that there is extinction of light due to cosmical dust in space. A hazy background of dust is shown on the photographs of the Milky Way and other portions of the sky, and proved to pervade the solar system by the universal prevalence of meteors.

Since, however, both comets and nebulæ are found to be extremely tenuous bodies, and observed to transmit the light of stars with but excessively slight enfeeblement, it is obvious that the general extinction will be much smaller still, but yet appreciable. I have therefore adopted a co-efficient of 0.999, about one-hundredth larger than Struve's, as best harmonizing all known phenomena. This value, it is true, is much nearer to Herschel's than to Struve's co-efficient, yet it admits an extinction of light which becomes appreciable at great distances, while for moderate distances it is nearly insensible; and I believe this to correspond closely with all the known facts of the sidereal universe.

An enfeeblement to one-twelfth at a distance appropriate to stars 17 magnitudes fainter, could easily be compensated for by a corresponding abnormal brilliancy of the remotest stars, which on several grounds seems to be highly probable. Thus our procedure involves no extravagant assumptions as to the great brightness of the most distant stars, or as to large extinction of light, while on the other hand it avoids Herschel's tacit hypothesis of zero extinction, which certainly is unjustifiable.*

---

* In an important paper read to the Bavarian Academy of Sciences, June 10, 1911, p. 459, Professor H. von Seeliger likewise reaches the conclusion that the absorption is very small, amounting to 0.34 of a magnitude at 780 times the distance of Sirius, which Seeliger takes for the border of the sidereal system.

§8.   A GRAPHICAL METHOD FOR DETERMINING THE DEPTH OF
THE GALAXY, BASED ON THE STUDY OF CLUSTERS.

1.   Make a diagram of ten or twenty concentric circles, separated by equal intervals, each corresponding to one hundred thousand light-years.   In this scheme no clusters will be included
within the central circle, because the actual measurements for
parallax have excluded this possibility.   But the various clusters
of the N.G.C. may be plotted within the outer circles, or beyond
them all, according to the results given by Herschel's rule of brightness.

2.   It is required therefore to locate the clusters, and to indicate their apparent angular diameters by dots of appropriate size.
Some allowance must of course be made for the varying stages of
development of the different clusters, but if there is a decreasing
angular diameter with distance it may be held that the method of
estimating distance devised by Herschel is essentially valid, and
in fact our only method of fathoming these immense distances,
and thus determining the depth or profundity of the Milky Way.

3.   A careful attempt has been made to apply this method
using the data of the N.G.C., and the results of the Crossley photographs recently obtained at Lick Observatory.   The results of
this investigation are shown to confirm the present theory.

§9.   FINAL TEST OF THE INDEFINITE EXTENSION OF THE MILKY
WAY DESIRABLE.

This should be made by the graphical method just outlined,
but by means of more powerful instruments than any yet systematically employed in this work.   To feel satisfied that the universe
extends on indefinitely, we must have proof of additional clusters
of stars of smaller magnitude, and more compressed constitution,
as from the narrowing effect of perspective, at great distances.
Probably we shall not know what the sidereal heavens contain in
the way of *vanishing clusters* till the Milky Way is systematically
photographed for just such objects, and this very likely will require
a long campaign of photographic research with a large instrument.

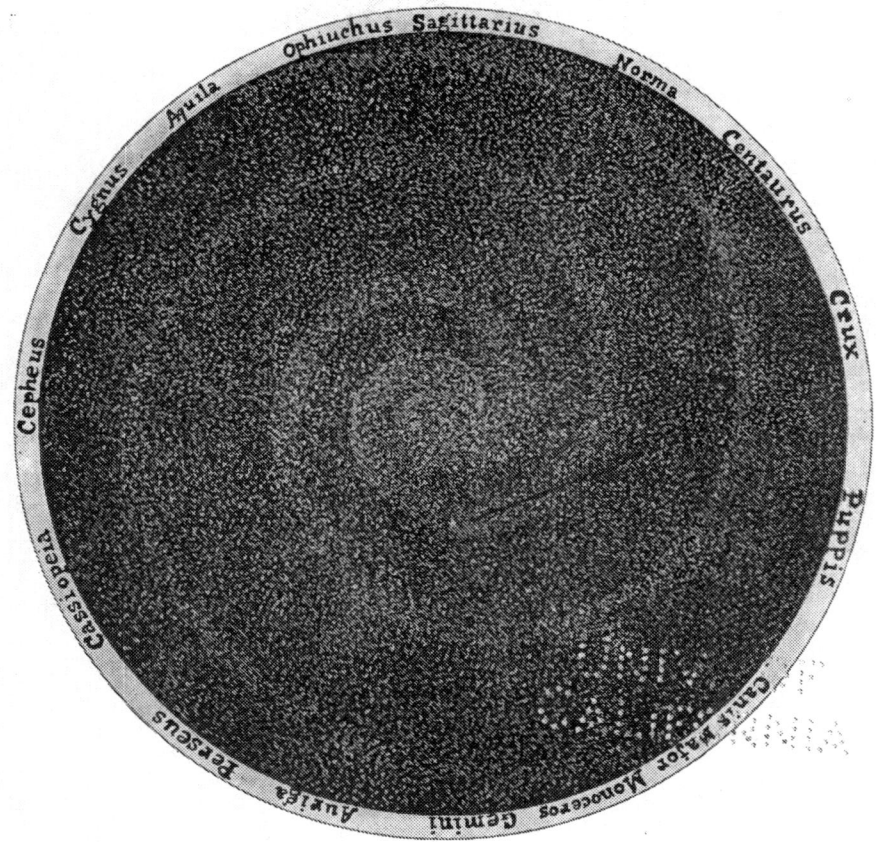

THE HERSCHEL-SEE THEORY OF THE GALAXY.

The Sun and all the Stars visible to the naked eye are included within the small white speck, below the center. The vacant lane extending to the right from this speck may produce the dark areas of the Coal Sacks near the Southern Cross. When we look outward from our eccentric situation the Milky Way appears brightest and broadest towards Sagittarius, and faintest and narrowest towards Monoceros. The diameter of the whole Sidereal Universe as here shown is so great that light could not traverse it in less than five million years. This Herschel-See Theory of the Galaxy gives the reader a good idea of the real nature of the magnificent collection of millions of stars which appears to us as the clustering stream of the Milky Way.

But as many large reflectors are now coming into use, we may hope for it before many years elapse. This would be completing on a modern scale the sidereal soundings left somewhat incomplete by the systematic explorations of the Herschels.

In a private letter, written in response to my recent inquiry regarding the power of the 60-inch reflector of the Solar Observatory at Mt. Wilson, Professor W. S. Adams, the acting director, informs me that this fine instrument probably will show visually stars as faint as 18th magnitude. He points out, however, that the magnitude scale is not well defined for such faint objects, and that very few astronomers have enough experience to fix it at the present time.

Adams also informs me that from a photograph of the region of the northern celestial pole of four hours' duration, Professor E. C. Pickering has derived a value of 21.0 magnitude for the faintest stars, by the system of photographic magnitudes in use at the Harvard College Observatory. Obviously there is some uncertainity in this value, but it probably is not extreme.

In answer to an inquiry as to the possibility of getting still fainter stars by prolonging the exposure, Professor Adams assures me that it can be easily done, the only limit being the brightness of the background of the sky; but that with the clear air of Mt. Wilson this would not be reached till the exposure had extended over many hours. He adds that it takes about three times the exposure to obtain a star one magnitude fainter. From the data here supplied it seems certain that stars as faint as 21.0 magnitude may be photographed at Mt. Wilson, with the 60-inch reflector, and that by prolonging the exposure several additional hours or through whole nights, stars of 22.0 magnitude probably could be obtained.

It is therefore well established that stars 17 magnitudes fainter than the 225 helium stars, with average magnitude of 4.14, recently investigated at Lick Observatory, may now be photographed with more than one instrument; and the value of $\triangle = 2,512$ used in our calculations is amply justified. In fact it seems probable that instead of 2,512 as our distance multiplier for stars 17 magnitudes fainter, we might have used the larger value 3,981, corresponding to stars 18 magnitudes fainter than our 225 helium stars with average magnitude of 4.14. This would almost have doubled the calculated depths of the Milky Way throughout the foregoing discussion, and given us over two million light-years, exceeding the profundity originally concluded by Herschel in 1802. In the *Phil. Trans.* for 1800, pp. 83–4, Herschel finds by a different process that a cluster of 5,000 stars visible in his 40-foot telescope is distant 11,765,475,948,678,678,769 miles, "a number which exceeds the distance of the nearest fixed star at least three hundred thousand times." With modern data this proves to be 460,355 times the distance of Alpha Centauri, or 2,001,120 light-years.

§10. SUMMARY OF THE CHIEF RESULTS OF THE DETERMINATION OF THE DEPTH OF THE MILKY WAY.

From the several independent and mutually confirmatory arguments here adduced it follows that the depth of the Milky Way decidedly exceeds a million light-years, and substantially accords with the profundity concluded by the illustrious Herschel one hundred and ten years ago.

1. Herschel concluded that with his forty-foot reflector he perceived stars whose light had occupied two million years in reaching the earth; and he justly remarked that he had seen further into space than any human being before him. The visual power or light grasp of Herschel's telescope is somewhat surpassed by modern instruments; and much additional power is given to the modern instrument by the use of photography.

2. But if, on the one hand, the modern instruments surpass Herschel's in power, there is on the other some increased need for this in that we now attempt to take account of the extinction of light by cosmical dust in space. Neglecting this loss of light, Herschel may have slightly overestimated the distances to which his telescope could penetrate, but the error was scarcely of sensible importance.

3. With our greatest modern instruments and the use of photography it is certain that we can observe stars* at a distance of over two million light-years, and it is very probable that we can penetrate to a depth of about five million light-years. A modern silver-on-glass reflector of twelve feet aperture would give about six times as much light as the 60-inch reflector at Pasadena, and with this gain of two magnitudes in light power it is probable that we could penetrate into space at least twice this distance (theoretically 2.512 is the factor) or *to a depth from which the light would take ten million years to reach the earth.*

At the present time a 12-foot reflector is possible, and the depth to which we can penetrate is simply a question of telescopic power, which can be vastly but not indefinitely increased. And this is true in spite of the extinction of light by cosmical dust in space. There is a limit to the distance to which any given telescope can penetrate, but it increases steadily with the aperture, since the only question involved is one of enormous light grasp.

It is to be hoped that a telescope of not less than 12 feet aperture may be built for use on the Milky Way. With such a giant instrument discoveries of the highest order might confidently be anticipated. A modern expansion of our views of the sidereal universe analogous to that which marked the great epoch of Herschel would follow, with the most beneficial effects upon every branch of astronomical science. Recent developments in many lines show that the epoch of great discoveries has not passed, but is in fact just beginning: and the estimates here laid down, as to the depth and magnificent extent of the Milky Way, convey to us but a dim outline of the discoveries which await the builders of the giant telescopes of the future. In this great advance America may naturally be expected to take the leading part.

Starlight on Loutre,
    Montgomery City, Missouri, November 4, 1911.

---

* In *Astron. Nachr.*, No. 4,536 Nov. 13 1911, Professor F. W. Very concludes that the *White Nebulæ* may be galaxies at a distance of a million light-years. The view adopted in my "Researches," Vol. II., 1910, however, is much more probable, since it gives continuity to the various types of bodies observed to constitute the sidereal universe. Note added Dec. 16, 1911.

CHAPTER XV.

1912.

THE HERSCHEL-SEE RESEARCHES ON THE ORIGIN OF CLUSTERS AND ON THE BREAKING UP OF THE MILKY WAY, UNDER THE CLUSTERING POWER OF UNIVERSAL GRAVITATION.*

By T. J. J. SEE.

IN entering upon a popular address, in commemoration of the 174th anniversary of the birth of the illustrious Sir William Herschel, on the general subject of the origin of clusters and the breaking up of the Milky Way, I must offer a slight apology for the coupling of my name with that of Herschel. It has arisen not so much from any preference of my own, as from a faithful effort to discriminate between the original somewhat undeveloped views of that unrivaled astronomer, and the extension and verification of his theories recently made by me, upon the basis of modern observational data, and the use of mathematical methods unknown in Herschel's time. According to modern standards, Herschel's views were not developed to a highly finished state; and yet they contain the germs of some of the most remarkable advances recently made in Astronomy.

Immediately after recovery from a very critical illness early in 1909, I was fortunate enough to become intimately acquainted with Herschel's neglected but priceless researches on the construction of the heavens and on the development of the various types of celestial bodies. And somewhat later, in co-operation with the late Sir William Huggins, ex-President of the Royal Society, I was able to start the successful movement for the republication of Herschel's *Collected Scientific Papers* by the Royal Society and Royal Astronomical Society of London, 1912. Moreover, I have been enabled very recently to verify the wonderful

---

* Address delivered at Mare Island, California, Nov. 15, 1912, in commemoration of the 174th anniversary of the birth of Sir William Herschel.

SIR WILLIAM HERSCHEL (1738–1822).

(From a pastel by J. Russell, R. A., 1794 *Herschel's Collected Works*; Vol. I, 1912.)

conclusions of Herschel regarding the depth of the Galaxy, and the origin of the Globular Clusters, as well as the breaking up of the Milky Way, under the clustering power of universal gravitation. Under these circumstances probably it was natural that astronomers should unite my name with that of Herschel, in describing these modern developments, to distinguish them from the original views of a century ago, which have now been established on a firm basis of observation and mathematical demonstration. One can scarcely depart from this discriminating usage without introducing into Science a confusion which would be quite inadmissible.

The researches on the depth of the Milky Way were finished in 1911, and published in the *Proceedings* of the American Philosophical Society at Philadelphia; and the same illustrious society has also done me the honor to include in its *Proceedings* for April and June, 1912, the "Dynamical Theory of the Globular Clusters and of the Clustering Power inferred by Herschel from the Observed Figures of Sidereal Systems of High Order," which was read on April 19, 1912.

In entering upon the topic of the depth of the Milky Way and the observed distribution of clusters it may naturally be asked why the distribution of clusters is associated with the depth of the Milky Way. To this question we reply that it was found by Sir William Herschel that the clusters congregate along the path of the Milky Way, which thus appears to traverse the heavens as a *clustering stream*. Moreover, it was found by Herschel that the sidereal universe is enormously extended in the direction of the plane of this starry stratum, and is relatively of but very small thickness.

In the *Philosophical Transactions* for 1800, pp. 83-4, Herschel calculates that a cluster of 50,000 stars visible in his 40-foot telescope is distant 11,765,475,948,678,678,679 miles, "a number which exceeds the distance of the nearest fixed star at least three hundred thousand times." With modern data this proves to be 460,355 times the distance of Alpha Centauri, or 2,001,120 light-years. In the *Philosophical Transactions* for 1802, p. 498, Herschel again resumes the problem of the distance of the most remote objects visible in his 40-foot telescope, and concludes that certain clusters having a nebulous aspect from the effect of distance alone are so remote that their rays of light have been on their way "almost two millions of years."   He adds that his great telescope has enabled him to penetrate not only into the profound depths of space, but also has the power of penetrating into time past; so that Humboldt remarks in his *Cosmos*, Vol. I, p. 145, Bohn Translation, "the light of remote heavenly bodies present us with the most ancient perceptible evidence of the existence of matter."

Now the point of this whole matter of the great depth of the Milky Way is that the clusters, being scattered somewhat at random in this starry stratum, are by the effects of the perspective, incident to the vast depth of the stratum, made to appear to lie in or near the Milky Way.   Hence the Milky Way appears to traverse the heavens as a *clustering stream*, as was long ago remarked by Herschel.   Accordingly, on the one hand, it is the vast distances of the clusters — more than usually condensed masses of stars — which causes such swarms of stars to appear drawn to small dimensions in the face of the sky; and, on the other, it is the great depth of the Milky Way, in contrast with the small thickness of this starry stratum, which causes the clusters, by the effect of perspective, to be projected along the path of the Milky Way, which thus assumes the aspect of a *clustering stream*.

If we did not know the great depth of the Milky Way, we might underrate the absolute magnitude of the clusters observed along its path; and moreover the projection of these masses in that direction would be unaccountable.   Herein lies the great significance of Herschel's researches a century ago; for that unrivaled man solved this problem with such amazing accuracy that we are just now enabled for the first time to appreciate the sublime truths at which he arrived, by the sure instinct of genius, when there was little positive data to guide the judgment of an early explorer of the heavens.

Having thus obtained some insight into the reasons why the clusters appear to follow the course of the Milky Way, owing to

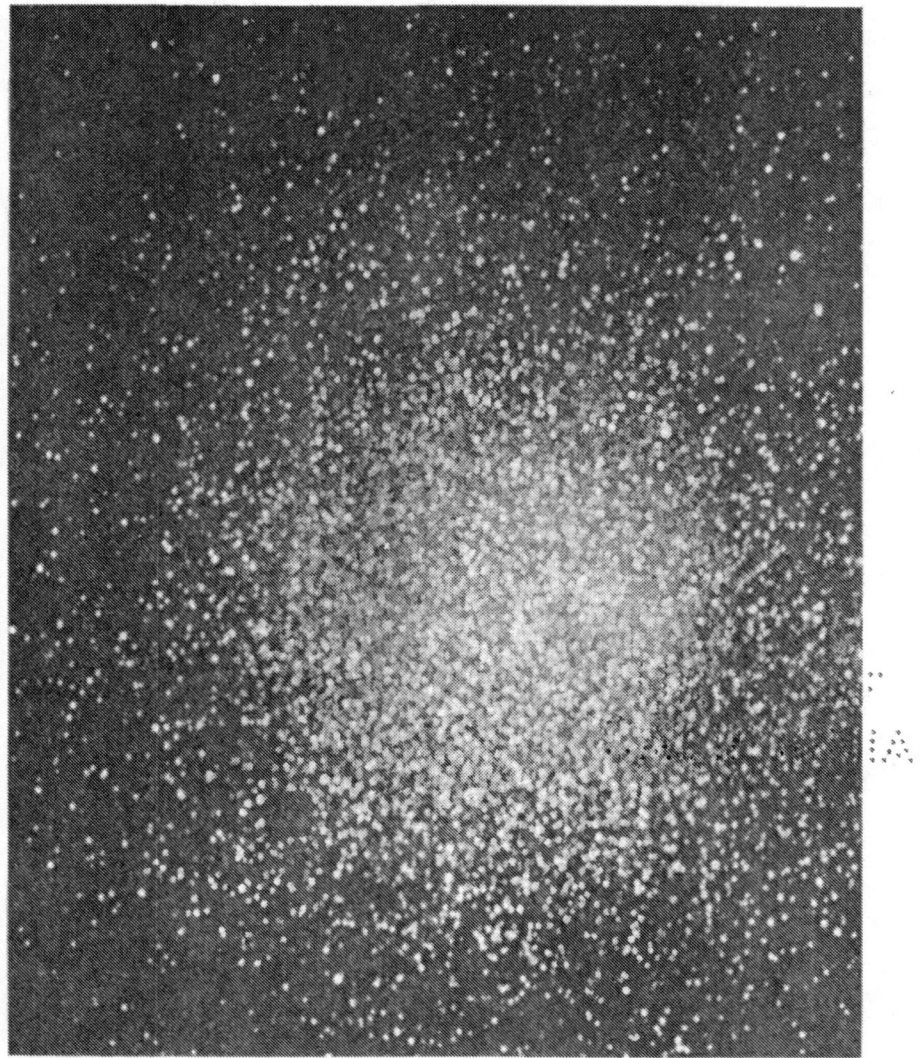

Plate 1

PHOTOGRAPH OF THE GREAT STAR CLUSTER OMEGA CENTAURI,

TAKEN AT THE D. O. MILLS BRANCH OF LICK OBSERVATORY, SANTIAGO DE CHILE,

BY H. D. CURTIS, EXPOSURE $2^h 30^m$.

(From See's *Researches*, Vol. II, 1910).

THE NORTH AMERICA NEBULA, NEAR ALPHA CYGNI.

From a photograph by Barnard, 1905, Sept. 4. Exposure 4 hours. This photograph shows the veil of cosmical dust diffused over the dark regions of Celestial Space.

the depth of that starry stratum, the profundity in places being not less than two million light-years, it remains to consider the origin of the globular clusters of stars, which are justly considered among the most wonderful objects of the sidereal universe.

When Sir William Herschel surveyed the starry heavens with his mighty telescopes he found great numbers of clusters each tending to the globular figure, like a drop of dew, or a planet of the solar system; and he inferred that by their mutual gravitation the stars were being collected into swarms and globular masses. Herschel's conjecture, however, was not tested by rigorous mathematical research, and it was only in January of the present year that a method of attacking the problem occurred to me. The paper developed in February and recently published in the *Proceedings* of the American Philosophical Society deals with the mathematical theory of the origin and development of clusters, by the capture and condensation of stars gradually collecting in a given region of space. It confirms and establishes forever the Capture Theory of Cosmical Evolution as the general Law of Nature, because it is easy to show that the clusters can have originated in no other way whatsoever.

By a fortunate train of thought it occurred to me to make use of what is known to geometers as Green's theorem, involving sextuple and even nonuple integrals — the very highest order of mathematics. By an ingenious use of the principles of the Calculus as applied to the expressions for the mutual potential energy of the system, which must decrease with the time, owing to inevitable exhaustion, it was possible to prove how a cluster slowly captures the stars entering the region of its development, and at the same time condenses into a smaller space and becomes more and more compressed, until it finally passes into a perfect blaze of starlight at the center. The unrivaled Sir William Herschel declared that the globular clusters, with this growth of central accumulation, are the most magnificent objects in the heavens, and they never ceased to fill him with wonder. Well may their formation engage our attention now!

It is needless to say that the successful treatment of this great question requires that the highest order of mathematical knowledge and intuition, be combined with the deepest physical insight into the order of Nature, such as few have possessed since Herschel. And it is not probable that anyone among living philosophers could have solved this titanic problem, which, it has been said, calls for the united intuition of Herschel and Newton in one individual, had it not been for the notable outline of a method of attack sketched by Herschel himself.

But with the guidance of Herschel's thought and modern mathematical methods, based on the transformations of Green's theorem, I somehow obtained results which must be rated among the notable achievements of Modern Astronomy. For it was proved that these masses of stars arise from the clustering power of universal gravitation.

This clustering power was imagined by Herschel to operate like gravitation in rounding up the figure of a planet. He also compared it to the action of the molecular forces which give a drop of dew such globular aspect. We see the same influence at work in producing spherical globules of mercury, and in fact of all liquids which do not wet the support on which they rest. The effect of surface tension in decreasing the volume and rounding up the figure of a soap bubble is almost exactly analogous to the clustering power of universal gravitation as it operates to mould the figures of clusters of stars. With these several illustrations before us, we shall be able to understand the Clustering Power noticed by Herschel to be at work throughout the sidereal universe.

Accordingly when the astronomer of the future surveys the clusters along the starry path of the Galaxy, he will indeed behold traces of the Clustering Power surmised by Herschel, but first established by modern mathematical methods at Mare Island, in 1912. Mathematicians may be excused for holding that such sublime researches on the origin of clusters, as the most wonderful systems in the universe, are among the noblest achievements of the human intellect,— for until very recently we would scarcely have believed such developments possible; and yet it appears that the mathematical proof of the general theory outlined by Herschel has been heartily welcomed by the scientific world. Thus Dr. J. L. E. Dreyer, the learned editor of *Herschel's Collected Scientific Papers*, recently wrote as follows:

OBSERVATORY, ARMAGH, 12 July, 1912.

MY DEAR PROFESSOR SEE:

I have read your remarkable paper on globular clusters with great pleasure, and it seems to me that your theory of their origin and progress accounts perfectly for all the phenomena which have hitherto been so obscure, particularly for the strange fact of nearly all the stars being of the same brightness. You have of course gone very much further than William Herschel did, but all the same, he was wonderfully clear-sighted, and it is a pleasure to an admirer of him to see his views so well corroborated and developed. "Back to Herschel," must indeed be the guiding principle in most researches in sidereal astronomy.

Thanking you again for the pleasure your paper has given me, I am with kind regards,

Yours sincerely,

J. L. E. DREYER.

Now it seems to me that if we have learned to go back to Herschel in most researches in sidereal astronomy, and this principle came to be introduced through my studies of Herschel, and the extraordinary good fortune in securing the republication of his *Collected Scientific Papers* through the generous and disinterested efforts of my revered friend, Sir William Huggins, it may not be altogether inappropriate for me to celebrate the anniversary of the birth of Herschel. Indeed, the revival of Herschel's ideas in astronomy is the celebration most needed in the scientific world; and as this has taken place already, we may rejoice that we have lived to witness this notable promotion of truth, in work which has been generally lost sight of for ninety years, since Herschel's death in the year 1822.

Even during his lifetime Herschel worked alone on the great problems which engaged his attention. He was the only astronomer of his age with a penetrating vision into the spacial depths of immensity, and into the millions of ages of time required in the building of the universe. Proctor likewise has noticed this isolation of the great Herschel; for in *Our Place Among Infinities*, p. 258, he says:

"It may be that the difficulty and complexity of the problem he had taken in hand, or perchance the quiet and unobtrusive manner in which he presented it as it then appeared to him, or some other cause may have been in operation, but certain it is that very little notice was taken of Herschel's special work then, or during the remainder of his life. None helped him, though his researches were manifestly far beyond the strength of a single worker. No comments on his stellar observations, so far as they related to the great problem he was attacking, were made by contemporary astronomers."

The contrast between the manly independence of the great Herschel in pursuing single-handed really important researches, and the feeble policy of dependency adopted by many weak astronomers of our time, under the euphonious name of co-operation, is striking and worthy of attention. One policy represents real power of leadership. strength and capacity for achievement; the other, such weakness and incapacity that it requires to be propped up.

To consider Herschel's impressions of the origin of clusters and nebulæ, we need only recall his argument for a Clustering Power drawing the stars together into clusters; and in the case of nebulæ the corresponding argument on central powers, based on the increase of brightness towards their centers. Herschel noticed that all the globular clusters have a central accumulation of brightness rapidly increasing towards the center; and in the thousands of nebulæ he found that a similar central accumulation of brightness was observable. He reasoned that the clusters were formed by stars being drawn together from the surrounding space, under the clustering power of universal gravitation. The central accumulation of brightness in the nebulæ was to his mind an equally clear indication of the operation of central powers arranging the nebulosity in concentric shells of uniform brightness, but with the brightness rapidly increasing towards the center, so that the nuclei of the nebulæ frequently are occupied by stars.

One must admit that the force of Herschel's argument is unanswerable. Anyone who studies it will be convinced that it rests on a firm foundation. And as gravitation draws bodies together, it was natural that Herschel should explain this clustering tendency by the continued operation of this central power throughout millions of ages. For in 1802 Herschel was able to adduce proof that some of the double stars he had observed twenty years before were in orbital motion; and the force causing this orbital motion could be nothing else than universal gravitation. If therefore double and multiple stars are governed by Newtonian gravitation, the same force must be assumed to operate in clusters and nebulæ throughout the sidereal universe.

This argument of Herschel is very fine, and cannot be improved upon to-day; but we had to subject it to an observational test, to see if gravitation really governs the motions of double and multiple stars, and will account for the law of star-distribution in clusters. This test I was able to make for the double and multiple stars some seventeen years ago; and during the present year I was so fortunate as to develop a mathematical proof that the clustering power operating in globular clusters is nothing else than Newtonian gravitation.

This proof is not only one of great generality, from the mathematical point of view, but also accords with the theory of the mutual potential energy of a cluster of stars, and its inevitable exhaustion under the mutual approach of these bodies. Thus as the stars by mutual gravitation tend to be drawn together, the cluster is gradually more and more compressed, with density accumulating towards the center according to certain laws admitting of accurate mathematical expression.

Moreover, I was able to show that a star falling into such a cluster will have a tendency to be entrapped, so that it cannot again escape, but works down towards the interior of the mass. This explains the central accumulation of density in both clusters and nebulæ; for the nebulæ are now known to be discontinuous masses of solid particles, with luminous elements interspersed, not really fluid masses with figures of equilibrium sustained by hydrostatic pressure, as was long believed by Laplace and his successors.

The law of gathering in, which is applicable to the globular clusters, is therefore applicable also to the nebulæ, and the central condensation observed in all these bodies may be directly referred to the clustering power of universal gravitation, and to no other force whatsoever. It is a great satisfaction to have proof that there is only one central power in the universe — namely Newtonian gravitation, which is shown to govern the motions of the bodies of the solar system with such wonderful accuracy.

The Herschel-See researches on clusters and nebulæ thus clearly established their mode of formation. And the same argument applies to the breaking up of the Milky Way. The grandeur of the latter conception is worthy of the genius of Herschel, who studied the effects of forces now at work as they will accumulate in the course of millions of ages.

My own proof that dust is expelled from the stars to form nebulæ in the desert regions of starless space, and thus tend to preserve the Milky Way from the indefinite effects of the ravages of time, completes the argument outlined by Herschel on the breaking up of the Milky Way, and shows that there is a Cyclical Process at work in Nature for the preservation of the entire sidereal system.

This question, as well as that of the depth of the Milky Way, was discussed by Herschel, Laplace, and Napoleon at Paris, Aug. 8, 1802, as we learn by the account of this interview noted down by Herschel at the time and recently brought to light by the publications of Herschel's *Collected Scientific Papers*.

On page LXII of Dr. J. L. E. Dreyer's introduction to Herschel's works we read from the notes made by Herschel at the time:

"The First Consul then asked a few questions relating to astronomy and the construction of the heavens, to which I made such answers as seemed to give him great satisfaction. He also addressed himself to M. LaPlace on the same subject and held a considerable argument with him, in which he differed from that eminent mathematician. The difference was occasioned by an exclamation of the First Consul's, who asked in a tone of exclamation or admiration (when we were speaking of the extent of the sidereal heavens) 'and who is the author of all this?' M. de La Place wished to show that a chain of natural causes would account for the construction and preservation of the wonderful system; this the First Consul rather opposed. Much may be said on the subject; by joining the arguments of both we shall be led to 'Nature and Nature's God.' . . . . . . "As M. La Place and I went and returned in a carriage by ourselves, I led the conversation upon the subject of my last papers, of which I gave him some of the outlines. I mentioned the various possible combinations of revolving stars united in double or triple systems. When I mentioned three stars at an equal distance revolving round a center, he remarked that he had shown in, I believe, his *Mécanique Céleste*, that six stars could turn round in a ring about their common center of gravity."

It is now evident that the great questions considered most wonderful by Herschel, Laplace and Napoleon have recently been revived and their solutions verified mathematically. Accordingly it only remains to illustrate by means of the lantern the wonders of the starry heavens, and to point out the visible breaking up of the Milky Way so clearly foreseen by the great Herschel a century ago. He was so far in advance of his age that we are just now beginning to appreciate his genius, after an unaccountable neglect of ninety years. It is one of the proudest recollecttions of my life that I was able to start, and, with the co-operation of the late Sir William Huggins, make effective the movement for the republication of the Collected Works of Herschel, — by which this great man may again speak to the world and teach us some of the sublime truths he discovered in the course of his profound explorations of the sidereal universe.

Mare Island, California.
November 15, 1912.

CHAPTER XVI.

1912

CONCLUSIONS DRAWN FROM THE NEW SCIENCE OF COSMOGONY.*

By T. J. J. SEE.

IT may be found convenient, as an aid to the memory, in making a rapid review of the problems of Celestial Evolution, to collect in one place a summary of the principal conclusions at which we have arrived as a result of the development of the New Science of Cosmogony. The following paragraphs are based chiefly on those given in the "Dynamical Theory of the Globular Clusters"† and in a longer article entitled "Outlines of a New Science of the Stars,"‡ and thus very complete; but we leave it essentially unaltered, as it seems better to suffer the inconvenience of slight repetition than to fail to give the general reader a sufficiently succinct and impressive view of this vast subject of sidereal evolution.

1. The most remarkable result of the New Science of Cosmogony is the intimate and necessary connection shown to exist between the most diverse celestial phenomena; so that they are woven into an unbroken and continuous whole, thus assuring the perfect order and harmony to be expected from the discovery of true Laws of Nature.

2. The time-honored theories of Kant and Laplace and their followers are permanently abandoned, as being definitely overthrown, and therefore of no validity in the present state of science. In the future the interest in these theories will be purely

---

* A work on "*Popular Cosmogony*" embodying the substance of these conclusions is shortly to be published by Doubleday, Page & Co., New York.

† *Proceedings* American Philosophical Society, Philadelphia, April–June, 1912.

‡ Communicated to *Crelle's Journal for Pure and Applied Mathematics,* Berlin, November, 1912

historic, like that, for example, in the abandoned Ptolemaic system of Astronomy.

3. In the place of these abandoned hypotheses there is developed the Capture Theory of Cosmical Evolution, based on the general principle of the independent formation of the nuclei of all bodies at a great distance and their gradual aggregation into systems, under the clustering power of universal gravitation, by which the attendant bodies are added to the central masses about which they now revolve as satellites, planets, components of double and multiple stars and clusters.

4. This New Foundation for Cosmogony is proved to be a Fundamental Law of Nature, operating uniformly throughout the sidereal universe. Under repulsive forces cosmical dust is expelled from the stars and diffused throughout space for the formation of new nebulæ, as it gradually collects into clouds under the influence of universal gravitation; and the condensation of the nebulæ produces sidereal systems of every description, from the very lowest to the very highest order. This dual process of repulsion and attraction, involving the mutual interaction of Nature's chief forces, makes possible the development of a New Science of the Stars.

5. From the tabular data* calculated by Babinet's criterion it is clear that no such phenomena as the detachment of Laplacean rings or zones of vapor in the solar nebula ever took place; but on the contrary, the planets were added on to the sun and the satellites added on to their several planets, the nuclei in every case having originated in the distance, and subsequently approached the centers about which they now revolve.

6. And when it was discovered that the roundness of the planetary orbits had arisen from the secular action of a nebular resisting medium, a new ground became available for concluding that the nuclei of the planets were formed by accretion at a great distance from the sun; and as they neared that center, by the growth of the sun's mass and by the tangential resistance to their

* The table is given on p. 168.

orbital motion, their orbits were made rounder and rounder, till they so much resembled circles as to lead the Greek philosophers to infer that the Deity had chosen this supposed perfect geometrical figure for the paths of the heavenly bodies.

7. Now the drawing in of the planets from a great distance towards the sun requires the building up of the central mass, to accomplish this narrowing up of the system; and such growth of the sun's mass would naturally follow from the destruction of millions of myriads of comets passing very near the sun in perihelion and by their disintegration giving a resisting medium of cosmical dust for building up the planets, and decreasing the major axes and eccentricities of their orbits.

8. What therefore can the comets be but survivals of the ancient nebula out of which the solar system has been built up? Fortunately this logical inference is confirmed by Strömgren's celebrated investigations showing that all the cometary orbits are elliptical; and thus they come to us from a distant "home", which was also the birthplace of the nuclei of the planets.

9. It will be observed that the process of development here outlined is always from the outside towards the center — diametrically opposite to the abandoned doctrine of the throwing off of rings and zones of vapor, which has in fact no existence in Nature.

10. And this principle of formation in the distance and building up towards the center by the transfer of matter from the periphery towards the interior regions is fully verified in all types of systems, from the satellites and planets, to the double and multiple stars and clusters and star-clouds of the Milky Way.

11. Upon this secure basis of observation and known centripetal tendency of universal gravitation, the Capture Theory is seen to be a logical development of the Clustering Power of gravitation noticed by Herschel to be moulding the figures of nebulæ and clusters throughout the sidereal universe.

12. As intimated in the first section of the paper on the "Dynamical Theory of the Globular Clusters," the problem of n bodies, under ideal dynamical conditions, remains forever beyond

the power of the most general methods of analysis; but the dynamical theory of clusters gives us the one secular solution of this problem found under actual conditions in nature. For when n is of the order of 1,000, so as to give rise to a cluster, the Clustering Power observed by Herschel operates to exhaust the mutual potential energy of the system, and bring about increasing accumulation in the center, so that the cluster finally unites into a single mass of enormous magnitude. Probably the giant stars of the type of Canopus and Arcturus have arisen in this way.

13. And since attendant bodies of every class — as satellites, planets, comets, double and multiple stars — tend everywhere to approach the centers about which they revolve, as an inevitable effect of the growth of the central masses and of the action of the resisting medium over long ages, it follows that the secular solution of the problem of clusters is more or less valid for all cosmical systems. They finally end by the absorption of the attendant bodies in the central masses which now govern their motions.

14. The dynamical theory of globular clusters shows that the Clustering Power inferred by Herschel is nothing else than the action of universal gravitation; and that it operates on all sidereal systems, but does not produce the cumulative effect which Herschel ascribed to the ravages of time inside of millions of ages.

15. The globular clusters are formed by the gathering together of stars and elements of nebulosity from all directions in space; and this points to the expulsion of dust from the stars of the Milky Way, and its collection about the region of the formation in such manner as to give essential symmetry in the final arrangement of the cluster, which doubtless has some motion of rotation, and originally a tendency to spiral movement.

16. The stars and smaller masses are captured by the mutual action of the other members of the cluster, and worked down towards the center of the mass. This gives a central density in excess of that appropriate to a sphere of monatomic gas in convective equilibrium (A.N., 4053, and A.N., 4104).

17.   The density of the clusters is greater on the outer border than in a globe of monatomic gas, which shows that stars are still collecting from the surrounding regions of space.   The starless aspect of the remoter regions about clusters is an effect of the ravages of time, as correctly inferred by Herschel in the course of his penetrating sweeps of the starry heavens.

18.   And just as clusters under the mutual gravitation of the component stars contract their dimensions, with time, chiefly owing to the growth of the central masses, so also do other systems, whether the mass-distribution be *single*, giving a system made up of a sun and planets, or *double, triple* and *multiple*, giving binary, triple or multiple stars, or sidereal systems of still higher order. The tendency everywhere is from a wider to a narrower distribution of the large bodies; while the only throwing off that ever occurs is of particles driven away from the stars by the action of repulsive forces.

19.   The orbits of the stellar and planetary systems are decreased by the growth of the central masses and rounded up by the action of the nebular resisting medium.   And in like manner all clusters tend to assume spherical or globular figures, so as to justify the expression of Plato, that the Deity always geometrizes; or Newton's remark that the agency operating in the construction of the solar system was "very skilled in mechanics and geometry."

20.   Newton required the intervention of the Deity to give the planets revolving motion in their orbits, because in the absence of repulsive forces he could not account for the dispersion of the matter, so as to produce the tangential motions actually observed. By means of the theory of repulsive forces, however, it is now possible to explain these projectile motions, which Herschel likewise pointed to as the chief agency for the preservation of sidereal systems.   The only assumption necessary is an unsymmetrical figure of the primordial nebula, giving a whirling motion about the center as the system develops; and since the dust gathers from all directions it is certain that this lack of perfect sym-

métry will nearly always develop, as we see also by the spiral nebulæ.

21. It is this unsymmetrical form of the spiral nebulæ produced by the gathering of the dust from the stars, or the slight relative tangential motion of stars formed separately but finally made to revolve together as a binary system, that gives the binary stars the projectile forces, with which they are set revolving in their orbits. In no case have they resulted from the rupture of a rotating mass of fluid under conditions of hydrostatic pressure, as formerly believed by Darwin, Poincaré and See.

22. Even if the rotation could become rapid enough to produce a separation, under conditions of hydrostatic pressure, by rupture of a figure of equilibrium, there would still be the equal or greater difficulty of explaining the origin of the primitive rapid rotation. This last difficulty escaped our notice till we came to assign the cause of rotations, and found that mechanical throwing off was impossible under actual conditions in nature. It is therefore recognized, from the definite proof furnished by Babinet's criterion in the solar system, that such a thing as a throwing off never takes place; but that all planetary and stellar bodies are formed in the distance, and afterwards near the centers about which they subsequently revolve.

23. *This gives us a Fundamental Law of the Firmament—the planets being added on the sun, the satellites added on to their planets, the moon added on to the earth, and the companions added on to the double and multiple stars — which is now found to be beautifully confirmed by the dynamical theory of the globular clusters. It is not often that such a great Law of Nature can be brought to light, and it is worthy of the more consideration from the circumstance that it explains all classes of stellar systems by a single general principle.*

24. And just as the clustering power of gravitation follows from the Newtonian law of attraction, so on the other hand are repulsive forces required throughout Nature to produce the primordial dispersion of dust for the subsequent condensation of this nebulosity into stars and systems.

25. Returning now to the solar system, and noticing this building up of the central masses from without, we find that of the many small bodies crossing the orbits of the planets, some have been captured and made satellites, most of them revolving direct, but a few revolving retrograde.

26. By the preponderance of direct revolving satellites, and the collision of such masses with the planets, their globes are given direct rotations on their axes; and their obliquities thus tend to disappear, as in the typical case of Jupiter, with an obliquity of only three degrees.

27. The satellites therefore were originally independent planets revolving in regular elliptical orbits about the sun; and what is true of the satellites generally is true necessarily of the satellite of our earth. The moon therefore is a captured planet.

28. All these satellites are now much nearer their centers of motion than when first captured; for the planetary masses have grown as their satellites revolved in the nebular resisting medium which so beautifully rounded up their orbits.

29. The resisting medium implies collisions of the larger bodies with smaller ones, and thus the craters and maria on the moon bear witness to the terrible impacts involved in the creative processes by which the present beautiful order of the solar system was developed.

30. Similar impacts once indented the terrestrial globe, and the depressions now occupied by our oceans arose from the larger of these catastrophes. But since the atmosphere and oceans developed, geological changes have modified the earth by destroying the original craters and building up mountains formed by the sea and therefore running as great walls along the margin of the oceans, as in the typical case of the Andes in South America.

31. The mass of the sun still is growing, and thus there is a small secular acceleration of the sun, as first inferred by Euler in 1749, which was recently confirmed by Dr. Cowell's researches on the records of ancient eclipses, handed down by the Greeks and Babylonians.

32. In the same way the ancient eclipses show an outstanding secular acceleration of the mean motion of the moon amounting to $2''.0$ per century. This is observational proof that the moon still is nearing the earth, and it points directly to the capture of our satellite at an epoch some 400 million years ago.

33. The mass of the excessively brilliant helium stars may be decreasing, because more matter is carried away by repulsive forces than is gathered in by universal gravitation; but eventually a balance will be attained, and when the solar stage is reached, and the mass increases, the attendant planets will have their mean motions accelerated as in the solar system.

34. The increase of the central mass alone may draw the planets nearer, but nothing can decrease the eccentricities of their orbits except motion in a resisting medium, as has been shown by the researches of Lehmann-Filhés and Strömgren, (A.N., 3,479-80; A.N., 3,897).

35. The resisting medium is proved to pervade all space by the nebulosity shown on the background of Barnard's magnificent photographs of the Milky Way, and by the phenomena of variable stars, which are thus fully explained. In the related phenomena of temporary stars the collisions are intense enough to produce violent conflagrations, and therefore are with attendant bodies of the order of planets or very large Comets.

36. As the moon is a captured planet, it is evident that the earth never did rotate much, if any, faster than at present; and the theories ascribing to the moon a terrestrial origin advanced by Lord Kelvin and Sir George Darwin in 1879 must therefore be unconditionally given up. Their reasoning was justifiable at the time, but is now recognized to be vitiated by a false premise, and thus is one of the most singular deceptions in the history of Science.

37. When the great Euler in 1749 inferred that the planets had originated far from the sun, he anticipated to some slight extent the theory held today. But the appearance of the rings of Saturn, and the roundness of the orbits of the planets and satel-

lites caused Laplace to develop the theory of detachment by rotation, from very oblate figures of equilibrium as first calculated by Newton. This unjustifiable inference long proved deceptive, and made it impossible to develop a Science of Cosmogony based on the actual processes of Nature.

38. From the original extent of the solar system it is now evident that other planets exist beyond Neptune; and that the present planetary system is of vast extent, otherwise Neptune's orbit would not be so perfectly round as it is observed to be.

39. And just as the light of our moon is variable, owing to the craters and maria by which the surface is covered, so also the variability of the satellites of Jupiter and Saturn must be ascribed to the same cause. The roundness of the orbits of the satellites shows that they have suffered innumerable collisions with smaller masses; and naturally they too are covered with craters and maria which produce the variability in their light established by the photometric researches of Guthnick.

40. The observed smaller eccentricity for spectroscopic than for visual binary stars is in accord with the modern Capture Theory; for as the bodies near the center so as to become spectroscopic binaries their orbits are more and more rounded up, and thus in contracting they acquire small eccentricity.

41. The arrangement observed in triple stars, with the close companion well within the orbit of the remote companion, is the outgrowth of stable movements surviving, while unstable ones have been destroyed, as in the solar system, and generally throughout the sidereal universe.

42. The central accumulation of stars in clusters is the outgrowth of the Capture Process, slowly gathering in masses from without, just as Jupiter gathers the passing comets within his own orbit.

43. As sidereal systems of lower order are conserved by projectile forces, it is probable that the clusters likewise have a spiral motion of rotation, with similar projectile forces tending to counteract simple progressive collapse. The period of the orbital

revolution of the stars of a cluster is found to be common to all, without regard to the dimensions of the elliptical orbits described, and thus the whole system may have a common period of oscillation, after which the initial condition is perfectly restored. This possibility in the dynamics of a cluster is exceedingly wonderful, and results from the central attraction depending directly on the distance.

44. The equality of brightness in star clusters shows that some process of compensation between the attractive and repulsive forces has produced stars of wonderful uniformity of luster. Thus the present investigation confirms the previous researches on the evolution of the stellar systems, which have laid the foundations for a new science of the starry heavens.

45. Accordingly, the Capture Theory of Cosmical Evolution being now firmly established for the clusters, where the nature of the process is entirely clear, it becomes at once a guide to us in dealing with systems of lower order; and we see that the Law of Nature is uniform and everywhere the same—the large bodies working in towards the centers of attraction, while the only throwing off that ever takes place is of small particles driven out of the stars by the action of repulsive forces. All planetary bodies are formed in the distance, and have their orbits reduced in size by increase of the central masses, and rounded up by moving in a resisting medium. *This is a perfectly general law of the sidereal universe. It verifies the early conjectures of Plato and Newton as to the stability of the order of the world, and shows that these illustrious philosophers were quite justified in concluding that the Deity always geometrizes.*

The spiral nebulæ tend to develop systems with rounder and rounder orbits, and the clusters made up of thousands of stars assume globular figures with minimal surfaces and internal density so arranged as to give maximum exhaustion of the potential energy.

46. This is geometry of the most marvelous kind, as we find it impressed on the systems of the sidereal universe; and the perfection of this most beautiful science of celestial geometry may be considered the ultimate object of the labors of the astronomer.

The philosophic observer is not and never can be content with mere observations of details which do not disclose the living, all-pervading spirit of Nature.

47. If, then, the mystery of the gathering of stars into clusters is now penetrated and traced to the clustering power of universal gravitation, so also is the mystery of the *converse problem of starless space*, which was a subject of such profound meditation by the great Herschel.

48. This incomparable astronomer likewise correctly concluded that the breaking up of the Milky Way into a *clustering stream* is an inevitable effect of the ravages of time; but we are now enabled to foresee the restorative process, under the repulsive forces of Nature, by which new nebulæ, clusters and sidereal systems of high order eventually will develop in the present depopulated regions of starless space.

49. If there be an incessant expulsion of dust from the stars to form nebulæ, with the condensation of the nebulæ into stars and stellar systems, while the gathering of stars drawn together by a clustering power operating over millions of ages gives at length a globular mass of thousands of stars accumulating to a perfect blaze of starlight in the center, but surrounded externally by a desert of starless space resulting from the ravages of time, certainly the building of these magnificient sidereal systems may well engage the attention of the natural philosopher.

50. As remarked by Newton in his second letter to Bentley (Horsely's edition of Newton's *Opera Omnia*, Vol. IV, p. 436), it was pointed out by Blondel in his work on *Bombs*, (Paris, 1685, p. 199) that Plato affirms that the motions of the planets is such as if they had all been created by the Deity in some region very remote from our system, and let fall from thence towards the sun, and so soon as they arrived at their several orbs, their motion of falling turned aside into a transverse one.

51. Newton adds that "this is true, supposing the gravitating power of the sun was double, at that moment of time in which they arrive at their several orbs; but then the Divine power

is here required in a double respect, namely, to turn the descending motions of the falling planets to a side motion, and at the same time to double the attractive power of the sun. So then gravity may put the planets into motion, but without the Divine power it could never put them into such a circulating motion, as they have about the sun; and therefore for this, as well as other reasons, I am compelled to ascribe the frame of this system to an intelligent agent."

52. This great historical problem of how the planets acquired their transverse motions has now been solved in a satisfactory manner; and it is remarkable that Plato's idea of formation in the distance, with subsequent approach to the sun, is verified by the most rigorous researches of modern science.

53. The transverse motion is now shown to have developed from the unsymmetrical figure of our primordial nebula, which finally gave the system a whirling motion about an axis, with most of the bodies near the plane of maximum areas, and thus the orbits are but little inclined to the Invariable Plane discovered by Laplace in 1784.

54. The turning of the planets from descending motions in very elongated orbits, to orbits of small eccentricity, thus giving the lateral motions discussed by Newton, is now satisfactorily explained by the secular action of the nebular resisting medium; but while the mystery is solved, we must admire the perfection of this wonderful process established by the Deity for rendering the planets habitable for living beings requiring uniform conditions of temperature. And this process exists for developing habitable planets wherever a star twinkles.

55. Having established how the planets were formed about our sun, we are enabled to affirm that as all stars developed from nebulæ, they also have developed about them corresponding planetary systems, or become spectroscopic or visual binary stars. At least one-fifth of the stars are spectroscopically double and the other four-fifths have attendant bodies too minute to be detected by our most delicate instruments. All the stars therefore are

centers of systems of some kind, but most of them forever beyond our powers of observation.

56. The orbits of these remote planets in other systems are rounded up like our own, by motion in the nebular resisting medium; and their moons are covered by craters due to collision, as in the case of our moon. These planets thus acquire small obliquities, and axial rotation giving day and night, as in the solar system.

57. As these distant planets have the same chemical elements which we are familiar with, and in many cases are habitable, it follows that they also are inhabited by intelligent beings; otherwise it is necessary to hold that life upon the planet Earth in the solar system is contrary to the general order of the universe and therefore an accident and a mistake, existing in violation of the Laws of Nature. No philosopher could admit this latter possibility, for it leads to a *reductio ad absurdum* as convincing as any in geometry.

58. As the Earth always rotated about as at present, and never had a day of a few hours length, as formerly concluded by Kelvin and Darwin, it follows also that her twin sister planet Venus rotates about as the earth does, and has a day of about the same length, or slightly shorter, $23^h\ 21^m$. With its abundance of air and water vapor, as shown by the brilliant surface of clouds, the planet Venus therefore is habitable, and inhabited like the Earth.

59. When we behold the Milky Way in the region of Sagittarius, the naked eye easily perceives the star-clouds into which the millions of stars have become collected by the clustering power of universal gravitation. This is a convenient witness to the effects produced by the ravages of time under the operation of the central powers observed by Herschel to be gradually breaking up the Milky Way.

60. And just as the majestic arch of the Milky Way visibly exhibits the effects of the clustering power of universal gravitation, so also the reversal of these centripetal tendencies leads at

once to a more primordial state of wide diffusion under repulsive forces in nature, which made possible the observed clustering stream of the Galaxy. The operation of repulsive forces is thus as evident to the mind as the clustering which is visibly breaking up the Milky Way.

61. With the flight of immeasurable ages the clustering now observed may become more pronounced, but the restorative process, under repulsive forces, for developing sidereal systems in the vacant regions of starless space is also at work.

62. The depths of the Milky May into which our telescopes can penetrate is shown to be several million light-years, as held by Herschel in 1802, and thus about a thousand times greater than astronomers have recently believed.

63. The Milky Way being of very great profundity, and the clusters being aggregations of stars in this starry stratum, they are by the effects of perspective made to appear projected along the path of the Galaxy.

64. The same process of capture which is gathering the stars into clusters operates on a larger scale in the star-clouds of the Milky Way, and thus the process is everywhere uniform from the very lowest to the very highest order of sidereal systems.

65. If there is any truth in Herschel's theory that a clustering power has moulded the figures and internal arrangement of density in clusters and nebulæ — of which we are assured by the central accumulations noticed in many thousands of these objects throughout the sidereal universe — then it necessarily follows that the Capture Theory corresponds to the true Law of Nature.

66. For it is essentially a theory of the Clustering Power of universal gravitation, supplemented by the theory of repulsive forces, and of the modifications produced by such agencies as the resisting medium.

67. It should be remarked that in the time of Herschel, Newtonian gravitation was not yet established as the central force governing the motions of double and multiple stars; but subse-

quent investigations, especially those included in the first volume of the writer's *Researches*, have established this fact beyond doubt, and thus enabled us to affirm, without further observations, that gravitation holds also for the nebulæ, clusters and star-clouds of the Galaxy.

68.   It is upon the basis of the Great Cyclic Law of Nature involving the mutual interaction of attractive and repulsive forces operating throughout the sidereal universe and illustrated by the grandest of celestial phenomena, that Cosmogony now takes rank as a New Science of the Stars.

69.   It is justly remarked that an astronomer of the philosophic intuition of Herschel, but with modern mathematical insight into the exhaustion of the potential energy of a cloud of stars, under the central power of gravitation, by merely directing his vision along the clustering stream of the Galaxy, over the region of the bifurcation, from the Southern Cross through Centaurus, Sagittarius and Cygnus to Cepheus, would be able to deduce not only the breaking up of the Milky Way, but also the origin of our planets at a great distance from the sun, and thus the principal laws of the formation of the solar and sidereal system.   As an obvious deduction from the accumulative effects of universal gravitation visible in the sky, surely this is no small gain.   For it places the new science of Cosmogony easily within the grasp of the mathematician and the natural philosopher, who contemplate the starry heavens with no instruments or applicances beyond the simple naked eye.

70.   The fundamental cosmogonic law of the firmament, that all bodies are formed in the distance and subsequently drawn to the centers about which they now revolve, is confirmed by the Herschel-See theory of the depth of the Galaxy and of the Clustering Power found to be gathering the stars into groups, swarms and immense star-clouds, and thus breaking up the Milky Way. Accordingly it is now obvious why this stupendous arch of light appears to span the heavens as a *clustering stream* exhibiting to the naked eye the most unmistakable effects of the ravages of time.

71. Among all the sublime discoveries which have crowned the labors of philosophers throughout the centuries, wonders are many, but none is more wonderful than this amazing triumph of human ingenuity, by which mysteries are fathomed that the entire life of our race would scarcely enable us to deduce from changes such as might be observed in the star-clouds of the Milky Way; and yet from established laws of Nature may be concluded with even more certainty than if they rested on the evidence of actual observations authentically transmitted from the remotest ages.

72. The foremost geometers of the eighteenth century, including Lagrange, Laplace and Poisson, were greatly occupied with the problem of the stability of the solar system; and in his historical eulogy on Laplace the penetrating Fourier justly remarks that the researches of geometers prove that the law of gravitation itself operates as a preservative power, and renders all disorder impossible, so that no object is more worthy of the meditation of philosophers than the problem of the stability of these great celestial phenomena.

73. *But if the question of the stability of our single planetary system may so largely absorb the talents of the most illustrious geometers of the age of Herschel, how much more justly may the problem of the stability of clusters, involving many thousands of such systems, claim the attention of the modern geometer, who has witnessed the perfect unfolding of the grand phenomena first discovered by that unrivaled explorer of the heavens?*

74. The grandeur of the study of the origin of the greatest of sidereal systems is worthy of the philosophic penetration of a Herschel!   The solution of the dynamical problem presented surpasses the powers of the most titanic geometers, and would demand the inventive genius of a Newton or an Archimedes!

75. Yet notwithstanding the transcendent character of the problem, and the hopelessness of a rigorous solution in our time, even an imperfect outline of Nature's laws may aid the thoughtful astronomer, in penetrating the underlying workings of the sidereal

universe, and thus enable him to perceive the great end subserved by the development of the Cosmos. If so, he may well rejoice, and exclaim with Ptolemy:

> "Though but the being of a day,
> When I the planet-paths survey,
>   My feet the dust despise;
> Up to the throne of God I mount
> And quaff from an immortal fount
>   The nectar of the skies."

(Translated by Professor W. B. SMITH.)

Starlight on Loutre,
  Montgomery City, Missouri, December 10, 1912.

CHAPTER XVII.

THE REVOLUTIONARY CHARACTER OF THE RECENT DISCOVERIES IN COSMOGONY AND THEIR TRIUMPHANT VERIFICATION BY EMINENT ASTRONOMERS.

FROM what has now been shown it is apparent that See's work in Astronomy and Cosmogony can only be described as *revolutionary*. That is to say, he has torn down mental processes and structures long used by men of science and grown venerable and hoary with age. Yet not content with being a mere iconoclast, he has substituted new structures for the rubbish and cobwebs which have been swept away. Evidently such a revolutionary movement is of great importance to the scientific world.

When the Nebular Hypothesis of Laplace was proposed in 1796, it did not pretend to be more than a *plausible hypothesis*. Laplace considered it *highly probable*, but not demonstrated. It came into use little by little, and has now found a place in every important work on Astronomy, most books on Geology, and nearly all treatises on Philosophy. It has therefore become deeply intrenched, from mere usage, and in default of a better explanation. But it is now recognized that See's discoveries have shaken it to the very foundations, and all who keep abreast of progress realize that Laplace's hypothesis involving the detachment of planets and satellites is permanently overthrown. The use of that antiquated and abandoned theory hereafter will be nothing less than a sign of fossilization and of mental incapacity.

See's proof that the planets have been formed in the distance and have since neared the sun, as their orbits were reduced in size by growth of the central mass and rounded up into almost perfect circles by the action of a resisting medium, is of a mathematical character, and admits of no dispute. The theory that the planets have been added on to the sun from without and the satellites likewise added on to the planets therefore is generally accepted by progressive investigators throughout the scientific world. For example, in his *Lectures on Cosmogony* at the University of Paris, 1911, the late celebrated mathematician Poincaré devotes two chapters to See's work, in spite of the fact that the *Lectures* were nearly finished when the *Researches*, Vol. II, reached Paris, and thus Poincaré could not treat adequately of See's discoveries. In the same way the interest in this great advance has been profound in every civilized country.

At the Monist Congress in Hamburg, September, 1911, the celebrated Professor Suante Arrhenius of Stockholm delivered the principal address. Naturally it related to progress in the physical sciences, and was largely about the discoveries of Professor See, as the most significant recent development in physical philosophy.

In October, 1911, these discoveries were the subject of lively discussion at the meetings of the Paris Academy of Sciences. Professor Charles André, late director of the observatory of Lyons, tried to reply to See's argument overthrowing the Cosmogony of Laplace. It seemed to be a matter of national pride for the French. They were shocked at the sacrilegious thought of giving up the venerable views of the great French geometer of the days of Napoleon, which they had accepted from childhood. André's argument, however, is no match for that of See, and the latter has therefore paid no attention to the late director of the observatory of Lyons.

The late M. Poincaré, the greatest and most sagacious of the French men of science, was too wise and just to attempt to defend the indefensible; and promptly abandoned Laplace's theory and adopted the new theory of the American astronomer. Naturally France will recognize the views of Poincaré and See as correct, and the only ones entitled to serious consideration in the future.

In England a curious movement occurred, but there, too, most men of science were disinclined to contest the ground with the American astronomer. It happened that Professor See's work overthrew the thirty-years-old theory of Lord Kelvin and Sir George Darwin that the moon was thrown off from the earth, and thus had a terrestrial origin. There are no greater names in British Science than those of Kelvin and Darwin; and naturally British pride was somwehat hurt by this outcome. The modern successors of Newton at Cambridge were accustomed to think that in Science their authority was supreme, and found it a little hard to realize that they would have to learn from an American.

It is a matter of deep regret to record the somewhat unexpected death of Sir George Darwin, Dec. 7, 1912, in the 68th year of his age.

In announcing the death of this eminent mathematician to the Royal Astronomical Society, Dec. 13, 1912, Professor F. W. Dyson, Astronomer Royal for Great Britain, remarked that it had been a cherished thought with Sir George Darwin that as his father, the celebrated Charles Darwin, had outlined the laws of terrestrial evolution, so too, he in turn had added to our knowledge of celestial evolution. Darwin's last paper to the Royal Astronomical Society, read in June, 1912, was submitted with the remark by Sir George himself that he had labored for the development of Cosmogony.

There can be no difference of opinion on this point. Professor See recognized Darwin as master in all his earlier work, and departed from his teachings in later years only when he found the Darwinian premises insecure.

Perhaps the occasion of a memorial resolution, such as was passed at the meeting of the Royal Astronomical Society, Dec. 13, 1912, would not have permitted anything to be said in behalf of another still living; but it has been remarked that the Astronomer Royal might with strict regard for truth better have said that one of Sir George Darwin's greatest services to Science had consisted in his early support of Professor See, who finally established correct premises and laid the Foundations of Cosmogony, by reviving and greatly extending the theories of Sir William Herschel.

SIR GEORGE H. DARWIN, F.R.S. (1845-1912). AT THE AGE OF 47.

One of the most eminent of recent British mathematicians, and the author of many profound investigations in Dynamical Astronomy and on the Figures of Equilibrium of Rotating Masses of Fluid. Unfortunately the premises underlying his work in Cosmogony were insecure, and the results are therefore largely inapplicable to the actual universe. One of Professor See's earliest British friends.

Competent men of science are now agreed on the truth of Herschel's theory that throughout the sidereal universe Newtonian gravitation acts as a clustering power; and on the truth of See's supplementary but equally important theory of the restorative process going on under repulsive forces in nature. These two fundamental conceptions form the Foundations of Cosmogony; but the subject could hardly be called a Science till it had a mathematical basis like that outlined in See's *Researches on the Evolution of the Stellar Systems*, Vol. II, 1910, and in the *Dynamical Theory of the Globular Clusters*, 1912.

Darwin's last public utterance, in his address as president of the International Congress of Mathematicians at Cambridge, August 22, 1912, contained a distinct note of despair in regard to the applications of mathematics to the physical universe. He cited the correctness of the mathematics in Lord Kelvin's researches on the secular cooling of the earth, but added that his reasoning was invalidated by conditions not taken account of, such as the effects of radio-activity. In other words, Lord Kelvin reasoned from false or unsatisfactory premises.

Sir George Darwin obviously could not be expected to allude to the failure of much of his own work in Cosmogony, but it is impossible to doubt that it was the similar flaws found by See in the premises underlying these investigations that so deeply impressed on Darwin's mind the difficulty of applying mathematics to the physical universe. His last public expression is thus a tacit admission of the truth of See's discoveries, and a concession to his triumphant overthrow of the old ideas in Cosmogony. For on the appearance of the *Researches*, Vol. II, 1910, Darwin had written Professor See to the effect that it would not be right to leave the impression that he had "as yet adopted the theory;" but that he would study it attentively, and no doubt he did so. Moreover, Darwin had received the "Determination of the Depth of the Milky Way" in May, and the "Dynamical Theory of the Globular Clusters" early in July, 1912; and he was thus aware of the complete verification of the results first outlined in See's *Researches*, Volume II, 1910.

The following extracts from a circular issued by the Thos. P. Nichols & Son Co., of Lynn, Mass., publishers of See's famous *Researches*, will more fully explain some points relating to the triumph of the Capture Theory:

1. Professor W. S. Adams, Solar Observatory, Mt. Wilson, California: "A beautiful book which will prove of the greatest service in connection with my future work."

2. Professor Suante Arrhenius, Stockholm: "A great and splendid treatise to which I shall give months of study."

3. Professor Benjamin Baillaud, Director of the Paris Observatory: "A magnificent and important work."

4. Professor E. E. Barnard, of Yerkes Observatory: "A great work of deep interest, with every subject splendidly treated."

5. Professor A. Belopolski, of Poulkowa Observatory: "This book contains much food for human thought."

6. Professor K. Bohlin, Director of Observatory, Stockholm: "A very beautiful and splendid work."

7. Professor E. W. Brown, Yale University: "The beautiful printing and magnificent illustrations are a very unusual feature, and make the book a welcome addition to any library, quite apart from the contents."

8. Professor Chas. Burkhalter, Chabot Observatory, Oakland, California: "It is a superb volume, a monumental work and its effect on astronomy will be profound."

9. Professor S. W. Burnham, Yerkes Observatory: "It is a great work in every sense, and will constitute a most enduring monument."

10. Professor H. S. Carslaw, University of Sydney: "It is a most important work."

11. Professor R. T. Crawford, University of California : "Admirably prepared and full of most interesting and important matter."

12. Professor Sir G. H. Darwin, University of Cambridge, England: "In passing final proof of 'Tides' for Encyclopedia

Britannica yesterday, I gave a reference to this work by erasing several sentences in existing type, but was unable to enter into any discussion."

13. Professor H. Delandres, Director of Observatory, Meudon, France: "A work of vast extent and profound interest."

14. Professor F. W. Dyson, Astronomer Royal for Great Britain: "A magnificent work, which will be greatly appreciated by astronomers."

15. Sir David Gill, President Royal Astronomical Society: "A wonderful and beautiful book of Researches, and I look forward with great interest to the study of its pages."

16. Professor R. T. A. Innes, Director of Transvaal Observatory: "It is indeed a remarkable production for one man."

17. Dr. Otto Klotz, Dominion Observatory, Ottawa, Canada: "It will give food for thought for many a moon."

18. Professor H. Ludendorff, Astrophysical Observatory, Potsdam: "It will mark an epoch in Cosmogony."

19. Professor H. Poincaré, University of Paris: "I have made use of your book (Researches, Vol. II) in my course this year, although I had not expected to do so, since I did not receive the volume till near the close of the last lesson: I then insisted, with profit, on the capture of planets by a resisting medium."

20. Professor C. L. Poor, Columbia University, New York: "A very valuable work in which the problems are ably presented."

21. Professor H. von Seeliger, Director of Observatory, Munich: "A work of vast extent and deep interest."

22. Professor W. B. Smith, Tulane University: "A majestic, magnificent volume, a monument more lasting than brass, more lofty than the kingly form of pyramids."

23. Professor Elis Strömgren, Director of Observatory, Copenhagen: "It revolutionizes our thought in many lines."

24. Dr. Alexander Roberts, Lovedale, South Africa: "A monumental work which will be the standard for all issues in astronomy for many and many a year."

25. Professor Max Wolf, Director of Observatory, Heidelberg; "A splendid work of deepest interest."

26. Professor A. Wolfer, Director of Observatory, Zurich, Switzerland: "A beautiful work treating of discoveries of transcendent importance."

Considering the extremely revolutionary character of See's discoveries, it must be held that they have had a very favorable reception from the scientific world. Those whose work is overthrown by the new advance naturally have been unable to take a calm and disinterested view of recent progress. But as more time has elapsed it is noticed that acceptance of the results is general, and that acquiescence in See's conclusions becomes more and more universal.

It is a deplorable fact that as the newer processes of Astronomy have developed, such as the various branches of spectroscopic and photographic research, the number of astronomers who can understand difficult mathematical arguments like those built up by See, has decreased rather than increased. This is the unfortunate outcome of the narrow specialization of our age. It makes solid progress in the deeper problems of Astronomy very slow, and dependent on the few rather than on the many. Yet the final results, as given in a work such as the *Researches*, may be followed by any fairly well trained student at college, who has a clear grasp of the elements of mathematics. *The need of such a comprehensive work was very great.* Prior to its appearance it looked as if progress on a large scale had been disintegrated by specialization, and that the threads of the argument could never again be woven into a substantial and durable fabric. But for the unusual grasp of See's mind it is doubtful if it could have been done; for no one else had even made a beginning in the development of the New Science of Cosmogony.

If we look back at the great revolutions of thought in the past, we find that most of them involved severe struggles, which extended over considerable periods of time. This was true, for example, of the heliocentric theory of the solar system which was published by Copernicus in 1543, but not generally accepted till after Galileo's invention of the telescope in 1610. It was much the same way with the discoveries of the laws of planetary motion by Kepler (1619). They were not fully adopted and universally recognized till the age of Newton (1686). And in the case of Newton himself, the law of gravitation was not universally adopted till the next generation, when Clairault and Euler greatly extended the theory. So also for physical discoveries, like that made by Roemer of the velocity of light (1675), which was at once accepted by a few eminent men like Huyghens and Newton, but not generally adopted by physicists till after Bradley's discovery of the Aberration of light in 1727. For long after Roemer's discovery, Fontenelle, perpetual secretary of the Paris Academy of Sciences, went so far as to publicly congratulate himself that he had not believed in so great a heresy as the gradual propagation of light.

In our time the progress of the world is much more rapid than in former centuries; and consequently it is probable that See's discoveries will find more immediate adoption than could be expected of similar theories in the past. This is in fact indicated by the progress already made towards a general adoption of these discoveries in different countries. New theories, however, not only have to triumph over the old, by virtue of inherent superiority, but also have to displace them from current thought, by the gradual teaching of the correct principles, before the new discoveries can be said to be fully effective. As the modern world is organized, this ought to be possible within ten years, possibly in less time. But this clarification of the public mind and its acceptance of new truth is always a somewhat gradual process.

As for the final effects of progress, much improvement is possible but not perfection. There are persons who still believe in the flat theory of the earth, even at the present time; just as there are some individuals of obscure mind who believe in astrology. But these aberrations will always exist, in spite of the great modern development of the sciences. As the Roman historian Tacitus remarks of astrologers: "It is a class of men which, in our city, will always be prohibited (by decrees of the senate) and will always exist." The wisdom of this penetrating observation is as apparent now as it was 2,000 years ago. Yet when we speak of progress, we mean among those both capable of learning and willing to accept the truth. It is for these that the sciences are developed, in order that some beneficial influence may be extended by the capable over the less fortunate portion of mankind.

It may be thought by some that discoveries in *pure science*, like those made by See, appeal less to the multitude than *inventions* in the useful arts, or discoveries in medicine and surgery. This may be largely, but it is not wholly, true; for it was the original discoveries in pure science by Copernicus, Kepler and Newton which made possible all the later developments in the useful arts and in medicine. And here again history will repeat itself in the future. Pure truth is a perennial spring which flows through all generations, and as the stream descends it nourishes not only all sorts and conditions of men famishing with thirst, but even the dumb cattle in the vale below.

If See has proved, for example, that there are inhabited planets revolving about all the fixed stars, and that life is a general phenomenon of nature, as universal as the stars in space, will it not give us a better and nobler philosophy of life on this earth? As we behold the starry heavens on a cloudless night are we not inspired by his proof that life exists wherever a star twinkles? And are we not comforted by the thought that we are not alone on this dark planet, but a part of the great order established by the Deity from the creation of the world? Will not these discoveries give us a nobler philosophy, more reverent views of our mission in the world? And if so, will it not benefit even the humblest of mortals who may be unable to make discoveries, but can yet understand them when presented by others who have caught this Divine Message from the Stars? See believes that his new philosophy will be eminently useful, and it is this hope of adding something to the nobility of our view of life that has so largely sustained and inspired him in his great labors extending over a quarter of a century.

If See's efforts eventually accomplish this improvement in our philosophy and religious thought, it will bring about a revolution not only in science, but also in philosophy and ethics, and thus ennoble and benefit the life of the humblest citizen. Surely this improvement of mankind must be one of the ultimate objects of all discovery. Professor See is known to be a man of very reverent thoughts, and ever thankful that he has been able to bring this inspiring message to the world, even at the cost of so much labor and sacrifice.

As a philosopher of wide experience he believes that a purely materialistic view of the universe is not and never will be sufficient to explain all known phenomena. There is a world of mind, largely independent of the material universe. In his celebrated *Researches* Vol. II, pp. 712–14, See has treated of the problem of Life in relation to the order of nature. Those pages are justly famous and we quote them here in full:

"§324. Life a General Phenomenon of Nature, and Almost as Universal in Its Distribution as Matter Itself.

"If therefore the laws of nature are such as to form planetary systems of the cosmical dust expelled from the stars, through precipitation, condensation and falling together under the attraction of gravitation; while on the other hand the dust itself in a finer condition is originally expelled from the stars, by the action of the repulsive forces arising from high temperature, intense radiation-pressure and powerful electric charges, it follows that there is a cyclic process by which stars and systems arise from nebulæ, while nebulæ in turn are formed from the stars. On this point there does not seem to be the slightest doubt; and we may regard this cyclic process as perhaps the greatest of all the laws of nature. Indeed, it seems to operate on a stupendous scale throughout the sidereal universe.

"Since therefore the starry heavens are shown to be filled with many millions of planetary systems, and an indefinite number of habitable worlds, is it not obvious that these worlds as a rule are also inhabited* *From the uniformity of the laws of nature, it would seem that this must be so, and, so far as one may now judge, this is the most inspiring message yet delivered to mankind by modern science.*

"Let us see on what foundation this conclusion rests: (1) Gravitation operates according to the same laws in other parts of the sidereal universe as upon the earth; (2) The velocity of light, and electricity, and no doubt of other physical agencies, is the same in all parts of space; (3) The chemical elements are the same everywhere, whether the light involved comes from a flame in our laboratory or from one of the stars; (4) Mechanical laws are the same in the solar system, and among the nebulæ and fixed stars, and this makes possible the development of cosmical systems of the same general type throughout nature; (5) Electronic, atomic, molecular, gravitational and electric and other repulsive forces are the same everywhere; (6) Life depends in some way for its physical basis on electronic, atomic and molecular forces, and as these forces and elements on which they act are the same everywhere, and the universe is shown to be full of habitable worlds made up of the same elements subjected to the same forces as in the case of our own planets revolving around the sun, it follows incontestably that life is a general phenomenon of the physical universe, and almost as universal as matter itself.

"It is true that the psychical and spiritual element of life is not yet fully understood, but whatever be its character, it can flourish elsewhere in nature quite as well as on the planet called

---

* In his thoughtful address at the dedication of the Flower Observatory, Philadelphia, Mar. 12, 1897, Professor Newcomb discusses the plurality of worlds as follows:

"There is one question connected with these studies on which I have not touched, and which is, nevertheless, of transcendent interest. What sort of life, spiritual and intellectual, exists in distant worlds? We cannot for a moment suppose that our own little planet is the only one throughout the whole universe on which may be found the fruits of civilization, warm firesides, friendship, the desire to penetrate the mysteries of creation." Again, in the article "Stars," *Encyclopedia Americana*, he remarks that the stars in clusters may have planets revolving around them.

the Earth in the solar system. Our sun is simply a fixed star of very ordinary magnitude, and the Milky Way includes hundreds of millions of such centers of planetary systems. Accordingly, in view of the established uniformity of nature's processes throughout the immensity of space, who can doubt that life is a general phenomenon ordained by the Deity from the creation of the world, and destined to develop wherever planets are forming and the stars are shining? Whatever be the nature of life, it has as much right to develop as planetary systems or combinations of atoms; it is indeed the bloom of nature, the culmination of the highest creative forces. *To hold any other views than those here announced would be to violate the doctrine of uniformity, which lies at the basis of natural philosophy as formulated by Newton in the Principia (Lib. III); and moreover lead to the conclusion that life upon the earth was an accident and a mistake in violation of the usual order of Nature,* which is infinitely improbable and, in fact, impossible for a philosopher to admit.*

"If therefore life is as universal as the stars in space, it is evident that when we behold the starry heavens and contemplate the glorious arch of the Milky Way on a cloudless night, we receive from distant suns and worlds ethereal vibrations which tell us at the same time of living beings throughout immensity. Let us, therefore, quietly rejoice, when we survey the starry heavens in

---

* If life on the earth exists by a mere accident and in violation of natural laws, is it likely that it would have shown such power of propagation and of resistance to adverse conditions as it is known to have possessed throughout geological history? It seems to have been a veritable spark which simply could not be extinguished, and must therefore have been burning on and flourishing, not in violation of, but in accordance with, natural laws. Those who believe that life is an accident and a mistake, a noxious development flourishing in violation of the laws of nature, may with consistency deny the existence of life throughout the universe. But having shown that habitable planets revolve everywhere about the fixed stars, in orbits which are nearly circular, and rotate so as to give alternation of day and night, as on the earth, it seems to me more philosophical to follow the example of Sir William Huggins, in regard to the chemical elements, and declare that life exists wherever there is a sun to warm and light its attendant planets, and therefore wherever a star twinkles in the depths of space. The other view, that life is an accident, leads to a *reductio ad absurdum* as conclusive as those employed in geometry.

all their splendor, and remember this sublime message telling us that we are not mere dust confined to this dark planet, but a part of the flower of the visible creation, which blooms everywhere with the cosmic order, and is as universal as the stars which illuminate the depths of immensity.

"Without the sublime researches of *Sir William Herschel*, we should have a very inadequate conception of the profundity to which our telescopes can penterate into the blackness of unilluminated space, and thus could poorly interpret the message of the universe. But this great astronomer showed that the stars extend principally in the direction of the Milky Way, and light up that region so brilliantly that we can extend our explorations to a distance which it would take the light millions of years to traverse. Thus the Milky Way is like a great but somewhat narrow corridor lighted up by the stars to the remotest regions to which our telescopes can penetrate, with no indication of an end to the starry stratum. To realize on good, substantial and indisputable scientific grounds that life accompanies the stars to the remotest depths of space, and that we can look out upon such countless worlds from our tiny abode near the sun, and thus connect the feeble life of our globe with the universal life in the endless order of inhabited spheres, is not the least inspiring message in the Epic Poem of Science. It is indeed a Message from the Stars. And it seems to me that if astronomy had achieved no other result than this, it would more than justifly all the labors which have been bestowed upon it from the earliest ages.

"This Message from the Stars passeth not away, but endureth unto all generations. As ageless as the heavens from which it comes, it will continue to travel downward with the starlight,* and thus awaken new life and hope in the hearts of mankind. For it is absolutely impossible for this order of mind, life and intelli-

---

* "Were a star quenched on high
    For ages would its light.
  Still traveling downward from the sky,
    Shine on our mortal sight."—*Longfellow.*

gence as widespread as the stars in space, to have been established throughout Nature without design and abiding great and good purpose; and therein lies the proof of the existence of the Deity. The teachings of true science are therefore among the most sacred which have ever been delivered, and they deserve the veneration which is always due to Ultimate Truth."

AN INSPIRATION FROM ARISTOTLE, AND ITS MODERN EXTENSION.*

In concluding this interesting subject it seems well to quote the following remarkable passage from Aristotle, which is lost in the Greek original, but has been preserved to us in Cicero's book on the Nature of the Gods:

"If there were men whose habitations had been always under ground, in great and commodious houses, adorned with statues and pictures, furnished with everything which they who are reputed happy abound with; and if, without stirring from thence, they should be informed of a certain divine power and majesty, and after some time the earth should open and they should quit their dark abode to come to us, where they should immediately behold the earth, the seas, the heavens; should consider the vast extent of the clouds and force of the winds; should see the sun and observe his grandeur and beauty, and perceive that day is occasioned by the diffusion of his light through the sky; and when night has obscured the earth they should contemplate the heavens, bespangled and adorned with stars, the surprising variety of the moon in her increase and wane, the rising and setting of all the stars and the inviolable regularity of their courses, — when, says he, 'they should see these things, they would undoubtedly conclude that there are gods, and that these are their mighty works.'"

The fascination of this marvelous train of thought is such that we add another based on our knowledge in the twentieth century, which may be said to afford a sublime vision of the progress of science in the twenty-two centuries since the age of Aris-

* The substance of this closing inspiration is drawn by permission, from Professor See's "*Popular Cosmogony*," referred to on page 224.

totle. It naturally fills us with wonder at the triumphs of the human intellect, but the evidence that the soul is divine and independent of what we call time, so as to be immortal, is not less inspiring:

If there be men of miscroscopic minuteness dwelling on the planet earth, as it revolves close to the star of the Milky Way which is the center of the solar system, and while in the narrow limits of this so-called mortal life they are told of the unspeakable glories of the sidereal heavens as made known by the more talented of their race — in the form of natural laws that would enable them to think the thoughts of the Deity after Him, as Kepler said—thus giving us a science of the creation of the stars, revealing both the wonders of the Deity as they now appear in a glorious Galaxy of sidereal systems and nebulæ spread over a space which light itself requires millions of years to traverse, and as they will appear under creative processes, which include the effects of the ravages of time, throughout the millions of ages to come; and they then learn also that systems of worlds habitable and inhabited by living beings revolve in the depths of the firmament wherever a star twinkles, so that life appears to be as general a phenomenon in nature as the very stars and the elements of which they are composed — when one of our so-called mortal race reflects on these marvelous things, and finally realizes likewise that our thoughts triumph over both space and time, so that, as Kant said, neither of these appearances really exist, or the soul exists anywhere and forever, and hence we are now living in the time of Socrates and Plato or with Christ and the Apostles, or as the poet Holmes truly says:

"The souls that voyaged the azure depths before thee
    Watch with thy tireless vigils all unseen—
    Tycho and Kepler bend benignant o'er thee
    And with his toy-like tube the Florentine—"

does he not perceive that this whole arrangement of the universe is beyond mortals wonderful, and the soul divine and imperishable, because it constantly imitates the Deity in penetrating through and contemplating the Creation over which He hath presided since the origin of time?

HONORABLE CHAMP CLARK.

Speaker of the National House of Representatives, and for twenty years Member of Congress from Professor See's home district in Missouri.

CHAPTER XVIII.

'THIS MOST INDEFATIGABLE AND INTREPID OF EXPLORERS' 'THE AMERICAN HERSCHEL' AND 'THE NEWTON OF COSMOGONY.' IN CO-OPERATION WITH SIR WILLIAM HUGGINS SECURES THE REPUBLICATION OF HERSCHEL'S COLLECTED SCIENTIFIC PAPERS, THUS RESTORING SIR WILLIAM HERSCHEL TO HIS RIGHTFUL PLACE IN MODERN ASTRONOMY.

THE *World's Work* for December, 1912, and January, 1913, contains an account of "Exploring Other Worlds" by Mr. William Bayard Hale, the well known author and recent biographer of Woodrow Wilson, now President of the United States. In the first account of these discoveries among the stars Mr. Hale places Professor See "among the foremost leaders in the development of the New Astronomy," and in the second refers to him as "this most indefatigable and intrepid of explorers."

At a much earlier date, in a public address delivered in the West, the Honorable Champ Clark, Speaker of the National House of Representatives, discussed the scientific discoveries of Professor See, as a friend and citizen of his congressional district; and after recalling the great significance of these researches for the advancement of Astronomy in our time, predicted that Professor See would take rank with Sir William Herschel for the unrivaled eminence of his discoveries in the starry heavens. And quite recently Speaker Clark has said that See is "The American Herschel, the greatest astronomer now living."

The suggested parallel between Herschel and See is much more appropriate than might be imagined by a superficial reader who does not yet appreciate the significance of contemporary progress for the future exploration of the sidereal universe. This is already realized by the people of his own State, who have known him from childhood, and watched his triumphant progress for a quarter of a century.   His neighbors know the discoveries he has made and they can find no parallel to them on the part of anyone since the memorable explorations of Sir William Herschel.

It therefore is no wonder that on the occasion of a public address to an immense audience in the Court House at Montgomery City, Mo., in a spontaneous welcome home, May 4, 1911, the people came from all over the surrounding country and literally overflowed the largest auditorium in the county.   Nor is it surprising that after the address (which was subsequently printed in *Scientia*, Milan, Italy, Jan. 1, 1912), as the people gathered around him, some friend recalled Oliver Wendell Holmes' welcome to Dr· Benjamin Apthorp Gould, on the latter's return from South America, May 6, 1885, as even more appropriate to the founder of a new science than to the great cataloguer of the southern stars:

"A WELCOME TO DR. BENJAMIN APTHORP GOULD."

"Once more Orion and the sister Seven
  Look on thee from the skies that hailed thy birth —
How shall we welcome thee, whose home was Heaven,
  From thy celestial wanderings back to earth?

"Science has kept her midnight taper burning
  To greet thy coming with its vestal flame:
Friendship has murmured, 'When art thou returning?'
  'Not yet! Not yet!' the answering message came.

"Thine was unstinted zeal, unchilled devotion,
  While the blue realm had kingdoms to explore —
Patience, like his who ploughed the unfurrowed ocean,
  Till o'er its margin loomed San Salvador.

"Through the long nights I see thee ever waking,
  Thy footstool, earth, thy roof, the hemisphere,
While with thy griefs our weaker hearts are aching,
  Firm as thine equatorial's rock-based pier.

"The souls that voyaged the azure depths before thee
  Watch with thy tireless vigils, all unseen —
Tycho and Kepler bend benignant o'er thee,
  And with his toy-like tube the Florentine —

"He at whose work the orb that bore him shivered
　　To find her central sovereignty disowned,
While the wan lips of priest and pontiff quivered,
　　Their jargon stilled, their Baal disenthroned.

"Flamsteed and Newton look with brows unclouded,
　　Their strife forgotten with its faded scars —
(Titans, who found the world of space too crowded,
　　To walk in peace among its myriad stars).

"All cluster round thee — seers of earliest ages,
　　Persians, Ionians, Mizraim's learned kings,
From the dim days of Shinar's hoary sages
　　To his who weighed the planet's fluid rings.

"And we, for whom the northern heavens are lighted,
　　For whom the storm has passed, the sun has smiled,
Our clouds all scattered, all our stars united,
　　We claim thee, clasp thee, like a long-lost child.

"Fresh from the spangled vault's o'er-arching splendor,
　　Thy lonely pillar, thy revolving dome,
In heart-felt accents, proud, rejoicing, tender,
　　We bid thee welcome to thine earthly home."

When the Kansas City *Star*, shortly after this visit home, nominated Professor See for the hall of fame, it faithfully interpreted the sentiments and opinions of the people of the State of Missouri.

Let us now very briefly examine into the suggested parallel between Herschel and See, and find out how far it is justified. Sir William Herschel was gifted with great enthusiasm, and tireless energy and boundless ambition for the exploration of the heavens. He spent his whole life in these profound researches, and loved his work so dearly that no effort was too great for him to make in the hope of extending our knowledge of the sidereal universe. It is not necessary nor desirable to recall here the long list of his brilliant discoveries. It is more to the point to say that he was most *true and just* in all the relations of life. For after his discoveries proved to be so revolutionary that it was appropriately inscribed on his tomb at Upton that "he broke through the barriers of the heavens" (*coelorum perrupit claustra*), Arago could still pronounce upon him the incomparable eulogy: "Good fortune and glory never altered in him the fund of infantine candour, inexhaustible benevolence, and sweetness of character, with which nature had endowed him." (Biographies of Distinguished Scientific Men, by Francois Arago, translated by Smyth, Powell and Grant, 1859.)

In all his labors Herschel showed true scientific independence, unfaltering devotion to truth, and unfailing sympathy with those less fortunately situated in the world. During his lifetime he had helped his brothers Alexander and Diedrich, and his sister Caroline; and when the latter outlived him he provided generously, by an annuity, for the old age of the one human being who had done most to sustain him in the labors of his great career. Those who have studied the life of Herschel most intimately find him the very prince of philosophers; amid many embarrassments and difficulties he never once failed to reflect in his life the very glory of the heavens.

As See is still living, and a comparatively young man, the time has not come to make any final estimate of his career, but those who know him best recognize unmistakably the same personal and philosophic qualities which so eminently distinguished Sir William Herschel. See is especially noted for being independent, and remaining untrammeled in his freedom of action.* In some cases it is said that offers of financial assistance have been made under conditions which might place him under obligations expressed or implied, but they have always been courteously declined, and the work done at his own expense or left undone. With George Washington, he believes in the cardinal principle of "friendly relations with all, entangling alliances with none;" and practices in his relations with other scientific men the rule laid down for us, a nation, by the Father of his Country. Without this

---

* The reader should compare the similar independent course of Herschel, as described by Proctor in Chapter XV p. 219 above.

wise rule of conduct it is not too much to say that a true philosopher cannot exist; for however advantageous the formation of alliances may be in ordinary commerce, the interests of truth will seldom permit such combinations in science, and never except with individuals of exalted merit.

Funds indeed may aid struggling genius, but they will not produce genius; and even the aid will be in vain unless extended in such a way as not to compromise the independence of the investigator. It is well known that as now managed our most heavily endowed institutions have proved to be almost a total failure. Probably nine-tenths of the vast sums expended ostensibly for science on observatories and other similar institutions have been utterly wasted. Naturally any self-respecting man of science is better off without entanglements with such institutions, but this recognized state of affairs is a grave reflection on the conditions of scientific life in our country.

Those who are connected with these wasteful and inefficient institutions are not really eminent and great philosophers, but small and narrow specialists, quite devoid of real independence and creative power; in fact they have neither the ability nor freedom to attack the greater problems of the age, and thus after all their labors come to little.*

It was the ability to search for Truth, not worldly ends, which so greatly distinguished Newton and Herschel. No amount of questionable patronage would have aided the genius of these great men, though a few grants were allowed Herschel, without condition, and thus aided him in building his great telescopes.

As another point of similarity between the careers of Her-

---

* Routine Astronomy was also cultivated by the majority of workers in the time of Sir John Herschel, and the breadth of mind of that eminent philosopher was appreciated by few. In 1847 Herschel had to be selected as President of the Royal Astronomical Society, to save it from dissolution; but Captain Smyth records that Herschel's *name* was the main thing desired, for in the judgment of the members, "The President must be a man of brass (practical astronomer)— a micrometer-monger, a telescope-twiddler, a star-stringer, a planet-poker, and a nebula-nabber. If we give bail that we won't allow him to do anything if he would we shall be able to have him, I hope."

schel and See, it may be noted that their discoveries have been equally revolutionary. *Many persons could have built great reflectors before Herschel, but nobody actually did it. So also many mathematicians now living could have carried out the work done by See, if they had been guided by his sense for physical truth in nature; but no one really had this deep intuition.* Herschel's opportunity lay in building telescopes and exploring the heavens; See's opportunity, on the other hand, consisted in reducing to law and order the vast mass of observations on clusters, double stars and nebulæ accumulated by Herschel and his successors. See did not duplicate, but rather extended the unfinished labors of Herschel; just as Herschel did not duplicate, but rather extended and verified in the heavens the theoretical conclusions of Newton.

In no age can the work of a great scientific discoverer be exactly repeated. It must rather be extended along a new line. Thus Kepler's discoveries were observational, but Newton's largely mathematical, while Herschel's again were chiefly observational. And when a great mass of data had been thus accumulated by the exploration of the heavens, See's mathematical work became possible in the effort to give us a theory of the development of the clusters, double stars, nebulæ and other types of the heavenly bodies. By establishing the mutual interaction of attractive and repulsive forces, with the resulting cyclical order of cosmical development, where only confusion and chaos had reigned before, See thus gained the highest rank of Creator of a New Science — "The Newton of Cosmogony." This has been recognized by the most eminent contemporary astronomers, but more especially by such sage philosophers as Huggins, Schiaparelli and Poincaré.

As is well known Sir William Herschel was born in Hanover in 1738, and his family of Germanic origin. His earliest known ancestor, Hans Herschel, had two brothers. They were Protestants, and, to escape from religious persecution, fled from Moravia early in the seventeenth century, and settled near Dresden. Here two sons were born to Hans Herschel, the one named Abraham in 1651. One of Abraham Herschel's sons, Isaac Herschel, born in

1707, was the father of Sir William Herschel. After being left an orphan at the age of eleven, he studied music in Berlin and Potsdam and finally settled in Hanover, whence the migration to England, and the rise to fame of the son, Sir William Herschel.

A singular parallel between the ancestry of Herschel and of See is remarkable enough to be worthy of record. It will be recalled that two brothers, Adam See, and Michael Frederick See, were natives of Prussian Silesia, which joins Moravia, from which the Herschel brothers had fled about a century before. The Sees too were Protestants and fled likewise to escape from religious persecution. But instead of stopping in northern Germany, like the Herschels, they came direct to America, with the colony of Schwenkfelders, in 1734, and settled first in Pennsylvania, and afterwards moved to Virginia, and Missouri, where the great astronomer was born and rose to fame as the "American Herschel." Thus it will be seen that there is striking similarity of ancestry in these two great men who have so profoundly revolutionized the Science of Astronomy.

It is needless to say that See is a member of many learned societies throughout the world. The following list is incomplete, but sufficient for our present purposes:

Fellow of the Royal Astronomical Society; Mitglied der Astronomischen Gesellschaft; member of the London Mathematical Society; American Mathematical Society; Deutsche Mathematiker Vereinigung; Société Mathematique de France; Circolo Mathematico di Palermo; Calcutta Mathematical Society; American Philosophical Society held at Philadelphia; Washington Academy of Sciences; Philosophical Society of Washington; Academy of Sciences of St. Louis; American Physical Society; Société Francaise de Physique; Fellow of the American and British Associations for the Advancement of Science; member of the British Astronomical Association; Société Astronomique de France; Astronomical Society of the Pacific; California Academy of Sciences; Seismological Society of America; National Geographical Society; Honorary Member of the Sociedad Astronomica de Mexico; etc.

In this connection the question may properly be asked whether the standard of Science is higher in Europe than in America. Perhaps it will be no surprise to learn that some elderly gentlemen who live in the past, and still think as they did a generation ago, hold that it is; and that the great European learned societies are the best judges of contemporary progress and discovery.

The opposite view is taken by Professor See, who has shown that America is now first in purely scientific discovery as well as in inventions. In fact the rapid progress of the past twenty years has given America the first place in every line of human activity. This appears to be realized by the younger workers in Science, who keep pace with recent progress, but it is not yet appreciated by the American public.

A kindred problem to that just considered relates to the nature of genius. In what does genius consist? And how are discoveries made? These questions are not easy to answer, and yet one may say immediately that discoveries are not made by following popular habits of thought. So far from originating discoveries the great majority of people require careful instruction before they can grasp the results reached by individuals of clearer intuition. Besides, the most incompetent often are in authority, and it is difficult for the people to recognize the few grains of truth from among the mass of error set before them by blunderers.

As Napoleon once said: "France possesses clever practical men; the only thing necessary is to find them, and to give them the means of reaching the proper station; such a one is at the plough, who ought to be in the council; and such another is minister, who ought to be at the plough" (Montholon, Vol. III, p. 187).

After recalling the ingenious labors of the celebrated Fourier for discovering the laws of heat, Arago exclaims in his eulogy of that extraordinary man:

"Such is the privilege of genius; it perceives, it seizes relations where vulgar eyes see only isolated facts."

Admirably said! *This seeing of mere isolated facts, without ability to seize relations is the bane of our age, and brings about stagnation in Science.* Such a condition may arise from narrowness of view, when one's knowledge is not sufficiently extensive to bring into the vision a wide range of apparently unrelated facts; or from mental inability to weave the threads of thought into a continuous fabric even when the connection is noticed.

The power to do this higher constructive work in Science is that of genius and given to very few. To judge why this is let us recall the sketch of the *Character of Newton,* given by Whewell in his *History of the Inductive Sciences,* Vol. II, p. 183-5:

"It is not easy to anatomise the constitution and the operations of the mind which makes such an advance in knowledge. Yet we may observe that there must exist in it, in an eminent degree, the elements which compose the mathematical talent. It must possess distinctness of intuition, tenacity and facility in tracing logical connexion, fertility of invention, and a strong tendency to generalisation. It is easy to discover indications of these characteristics in Newton. The distinctness of his intuitions of space, and we may add of force also, was seen in the amusements of his youth; in his constructing clocks and mills, carts and dials, as well as the facility with which he mastered geometry. This fondness for handicraft employments, and for making models and machines, appears to be a common prelude of excellence in physical science;* probably on this very account, that it arises from the distinctness of intuitive power with which the child conceives the shapes and the working of such material combinations. Newton's inventive power appears in the number and variety of the mathematical artifices and combinations which he devised, and of which his books are full. If we conceive the operation of the inventive faculty in the only way in which it appears possible to conceive it;—that while some hidden source supplies a rapid stream of possible suggestions, the mind is on watch to seize and detain any one of these which will suit the case in hand, allowing the rest to pass by and be forgotten;—we shall see what extraordinary fertility

---

*As in Galileo, Hooke, Huyghens, and others.

of mind is implied by so many successful efforts; what an innumerable host of thoughts must have been produced, to supply so many that deserved to be selected. And since the selection is performed by tracing the consequences of each suggestion, so as to compare them with the requisite conditions, we see also what rapidity and certainty in drawing conclusions the mind must possess as a talent, and what watchfulness and patience as a habit.

"The hidden fountain of our unbidden thoughts is for us a mystery; and we have, in our consciousness, no standard by which we can measure our own talents; but our acts and habits are something of which we are conscious; and we can understand, therefore, how it was that Newton could not admit that there was any difference between himself and other men, except in his possession of such habits as we have mentioned, perseverance and vigilance. When he was asked how he made his discoveries, he answered, 'by always thinking about them;' and at another time, he declared that if he had done anything, it was due to nothing but industry and patient thought: 'I keep the subject of my inquiry constantly before me, and wait till the first dawning opens gradually, by little and little, into a full and clear light.' No better account can be given of the nature of the mental *effort* which gives to the philosopher the full benefit of his powers; but the natural *powers* of men's minds are not on that account the less different. There are many who might wait through ages of darkness without being visited by any dawn."

These sagacious remarks on Newton apply of course equally well to a modern philosopher. Like the illustrious Poincaré, See is a student not of *single, isolated facts*, but of the *principles* which connect the most intricate of things into one continuous whole. In the introduction to the *Researches*, Vol. II, he justly exclaims: "One true principle gives unity and mental connection to millions of isolated facts, and it is only by means of such principles that the observed facts can be interpreted. Why not therefore give a little more attention to the discovery of principles? All the important epochs in the past history of science have been made in this way; yet this very tendency, to the development of new conceptions and the introduction of new physical laws, is the one which to-day is least encouraged. Few are supported or upheld in breaking away from the leading strings of tradition. Journals and Learned Societies are nearly all ultra conservative, and very timid about entertaining new thought. It is only daring individuals, not aggregations of men, who have the courage to lead the way. Under the circumstances can any one be surprised that years, decades, and even centuries pass by without giving birth to one grand principle, one new physical law?"

See's powers of mathematical and physical intuition have thus enabled him to establish two new physical sciences — *Cosmogony*, treating of the *Origin of the Heavens;* and *Geogony*, dealing with the *Origin of the Earth*. The sublime *Vision of the Creation*, according to Nature's Laws, thus unfolded to the imagination, never before dawned on the human mind; and as Halley said of the discoveries in Newton's *Principia*, such revelations are "almost Divine."

It is by reason of men of See's type that early in the 20th century the center of gravity of discovery was finally transferred from Europe to America, where it is likely to remain for a long time to come. It is well known that European science has gone to seed in narrow specialization. Besides, the old countries of Europe can no longer compete with the lusty vigor of this mighty Republic, with its uniformly high type of citizenship.

It is needless to say that the discoveries of See alone have given America the first place in the sciences of Astronomy and Cosmogony, and the Physics of the Earth, which embraces the sciences of Geology, Seismology and Geodesy. The opening sentence of the address reprinted in Chapter XIII: "We are assembled to consider the great Law of Nature which governs the Evolution of Worlds, and to celebrate the Founding of a New Science of the Starry Heavens," grand and comprehensive as it is, recalls but a part of his most significant discoveries.

The general Law of Nature established by See to the effect that all planetary bodies are formed in the distance and afterwards near the centers about which they revolve is indeed magnificient. This Capture Theory, or theory of addition from without, in contrast to Laplace's abandoned theory of throwing off, is shown to apply to the entire sidereal universe. It is illustrated by phenomena observed in the spiral nebulæ, the planetary system, the double and multiple stars and clusters and the star-clouds of the Milky Way. Beyond a doubt this theory of cosmical evolution, under the mutual interaction of both attractive and repulsive forces, and the resisting medium resulting from the dispersion of dust from the stars, is the most comprehensive scientific generalization since the establishment of the law of universal gravitation by Newton in 1687.

Accordingly, the daring young American astronomer who had the mathematical ability and the physical and philosophic intuition to reduce to law and order the hopeless chaos of the nebulæ, and thus found a new science of the starry heavens which won him the title of the Newton of cosmogony (1910), by his latest feat in fathoming the depth of the Milky Way and developing mathematically the Herschel-See theory of the globular clusters, and thus restoring the grand ideas, after securing the republication of the Collected Works of Sir William Herschel, has amply fulfilled the earlier prophesy that he would become the Herschel of America.

After an unaccountable neglect of ninety years the works of Sir William Herschel have just been reprinted under the auspices of the Royal Society and Royal Astronomical Society of London. The movement was started by Professor See and ably seconded by the illustrious Sir William Huggins, ex-president of the Royal Society and founder of *Astrophysics.* As many persons may not know that this whole matter of republishing Herschel's Scientific Papers was planned by Professor See in his quiet study at Mare Island, California, we give an account of this important movement. Soon after his recovery from the critical illness early in 1909, Professor See sought access to Herschel's papers in the *Philo-*

SIR WILLIAM HUGGINS, (1824–1910).

Ex-President of the Royal Society, Founder of the New Science of Astrophysics, and one of the greatest philosophers of all time. He was a steadfast friend of Professor See, and among the first to adopt his discoveries in Cosmogony and Geogony.

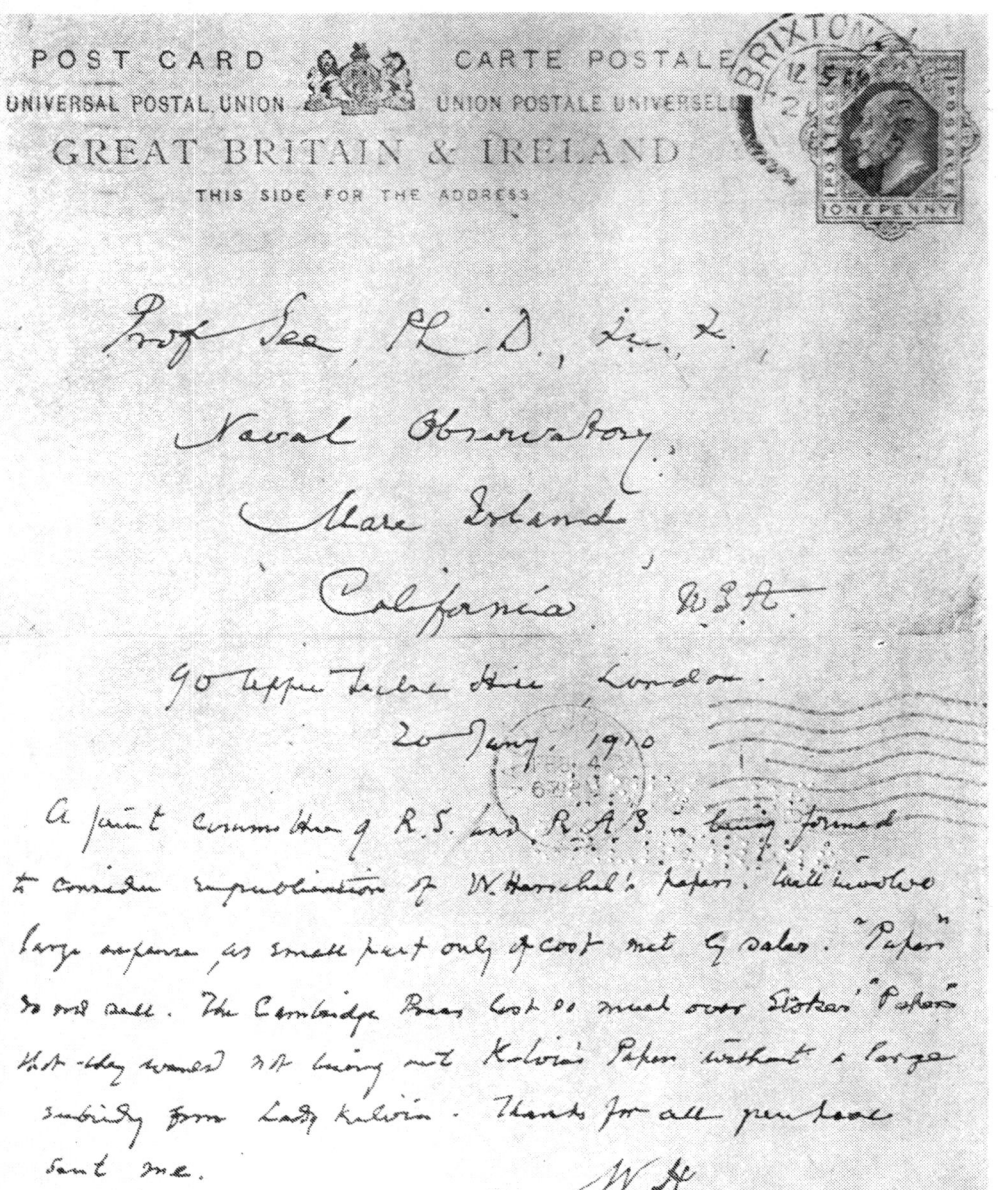

AUTOGRAPH POSTAL CARD FROM SIR WILLIAM HUGGINS.

It notifies Professor See that his request had been granted, and action taken by the Royal Society and Royal Astronomical Society looking to the republication of the Collected Scientific Papers of Sir William Herschel.

sophical Transactions, at the library of the University of California. By courtesy of Mr. J. C. Rowell, librarian, he was enabled to carry home with him such arm-loads of these rare volumes as his bodily strength then permitted, and abstract the parts that would serve immediate needs. Upon application to other prominent astronomers, who would presumably have these papers, he found that no one had a copy, or had ever studied Herschel's works with care and attention. Professor See was much surprised at this neglect of Herschel's priceless papers, and it set him thinking about a method of restoring the great Herschel to his rightful place in modern astronomy.

Accordingly it occurred to him to write letters to the *Observatory*, *Nature*, and the British Astronomical Association, urging a movement for the republication of Herschel's Collected Works. In a formal letter to the council of the Royal Astronomical Society he not only urged the republication of Herschel's Collected Works, but himself started the movement by formally offering a subscription of $100 as the first step.

A little later it occurred to him to appeal directly to Sir William Huggins, ex-president of the Royal Society, to move for the appointment of the needed joint committee of the Royal Society and Royal Astronomical Society, to consider this great undertaking, which would bring such high honor to these illustrious societies. Professor See concluded his appeal to Sir William Huggins by saying that if he could see his way to take the initiative in this movement, it would be one more noble service to Science, and a long delayed tribute to the memory of so great and good a man as Herschel.

The appeal had the desired effect — since Herschel's memory is justly revered in England — and on January 20, 1910, Sir William Huggins wrote to notify Professor See that the step he recommended had been taken, as shown by the accompanying autograph of Sir William Huggins. This was the last communication addressed to Professor See by Sir William before his lamented death, in the eighty-seventh year of his age, May 12, 1910.

This remarkable chain of events, causes one to reflect on what small matters, at the right time, great events depend; and if they are not done then the opportunity passes by, and the enterprise may be defeated forever. The recovery of Professor See early in 1909, after his life had been despaired of, was considered by his physicians almost miraculous. The completion of his *Researches*, Vol. II, was the immediate incentive to an examination of the neglected and forgotten works of Herschel. This led to the movement for republishing Herschel's Collected Works, which took shape just in time to be well started under the revered leadership of Sir William Huggins, who was able to attend but two meetings of the Joint Committee before he was himself called to join Herschel of blessed and everlasting memory.

Every student of scientific truth may well be grateful that the chain of events was fortunate enough to make possible the re-issue of the priceless papers of Herschel. This movement could not well have been inaugurated by anyone except the illustrious Sir William Huggins, whose whole life was unselfishly devoted to the advancement of truth. It is fitting that such a noble monument to Herschel will always be associated in the minds of men with the justly revered memory of Sir William Huggins, "the Herschel of the spectroscope."

In concluding now the work of this biography it remains to note that eminent philosophers agree that four of See's most brilliant achievements constitute a series of discoveries without a parallel since the age of Newton:

1. The Establishment of the Cause of Earthquakes, Mountain Formation and kindred phenomena connected with the physics of the earth, and thus a Science of Geogony, May 21, 1906.

2. The Founding of Cosmogony as a New Science of the Starry Heavens,—thus giving us the laws of the formation of the solar system and of cosmical systems generally. July 14, 1908.

3. The fathoming of the Milky Way to the depth of several million light-years — thereby proving that the extent of the

sidereal universe is about a thousand times greater than astronomers have recently believed.   November 4, 1911.

4.   The development of the dynamical theory of clusters and of the clustering power inferred by Herschel from the observed figures of sidereal systems of high order.   February 19, 1912.   This establishes forever that the Capture Theory is the great Law of Nature, and is the latest and mathematically the profoundest of the researches on sidereal evolution.

It is not too much to say that these unrivaled results of the Herschel of America have shed imperishable luster upon his country and upon his age!   Posterity may well marvel over the wonders of Nature which he alone was able to explain.   This was the attitude taken by the illustrious Poincaré, himself the greatest mathematician since Archimedes.

Our successors will witness the extension of the grand phenomena whose laws he discovered, yet they will recognize in the circularity of the paths of the planets and satellites the operation of the nebular resisting medium which he first brought to light. Throughout the long course of centuries the secular acceleration of the moon will continue to bear witness to the capture of our satellite by the earth, and astronomers of future time will look back to this great triumph of human ingenuity.   The system of the comets will be more fully revealed to us by discoveries to be made hereafter, but the elongated forms of their elliptic orbits have already made it clear that these mysterious bodies are mere survivals still coming to us from the outer shell of the ancient nebula which formed the solar system.

Even in the remotest ages astronomers will still be gazing at the starry heavens, and natural philosophers marveling at the mysteries of the spiral nebulæ, but their labors will be simplified by the new theory of repulsive forces, and the sublime proof that the Deity always geometrizes, and thus develops out of chaos the exquisite order of the system of the world, that it may become a fit abode for the children of men.   These are a few of the recollections which always will be associated with the early life of the Herschel of America, who was the first to interpret the lesson of the geometry of the heavens.

In the unfolding of this majestic panorama of the creation, the spectacle of the stars will change, and improved methods of analysis will come for the treatment of the problems which he proposed; but the wonders of the starry heavens, growing and decaying under the mutual interaction of attractive and repulsive forces, will always bear witness to the philosophic penetration of the illustrious geometer, who alone was able to establish the laws of their evolution.

Yet as the poet Thomson sang of Sir Isaac Newton:

"But who can number up his labors? Who
His high discov'ries sing? When but a few
Of the deep-studying race can stretch their minds
To what he knew: in Fancy's lighter thought,
How shall the Muse, then, grasp the mighty theme?"

* * * * * * * *   "Ye mouldering stones,
That build the tow'ring pyramid, the proud
Triumphal arch, the monument, effac'd
By ruthless ruin, and what'er supports
The worshipp'd name of hoar Antiquity,
Down to the dust! What grandeur can ye boast,
While Newton lifts his column to the skies,
Beyond the waste of Time?"

*   *   *   *   *   *   *   *   *   *   *

O'er thy dejected country chief preside,
And be her Genius call'd! her studies raise,
Correct her manners, and inspire her youth.
For, though deprav'd and sunk, she brought thee forth,
And glories in thy name; she points thee out
To all her sons, and bids them eye thy Star."

Owing to the intimate friendship of twenty years existing between Sir William Huggins, the illustrious founder of *Astro-*

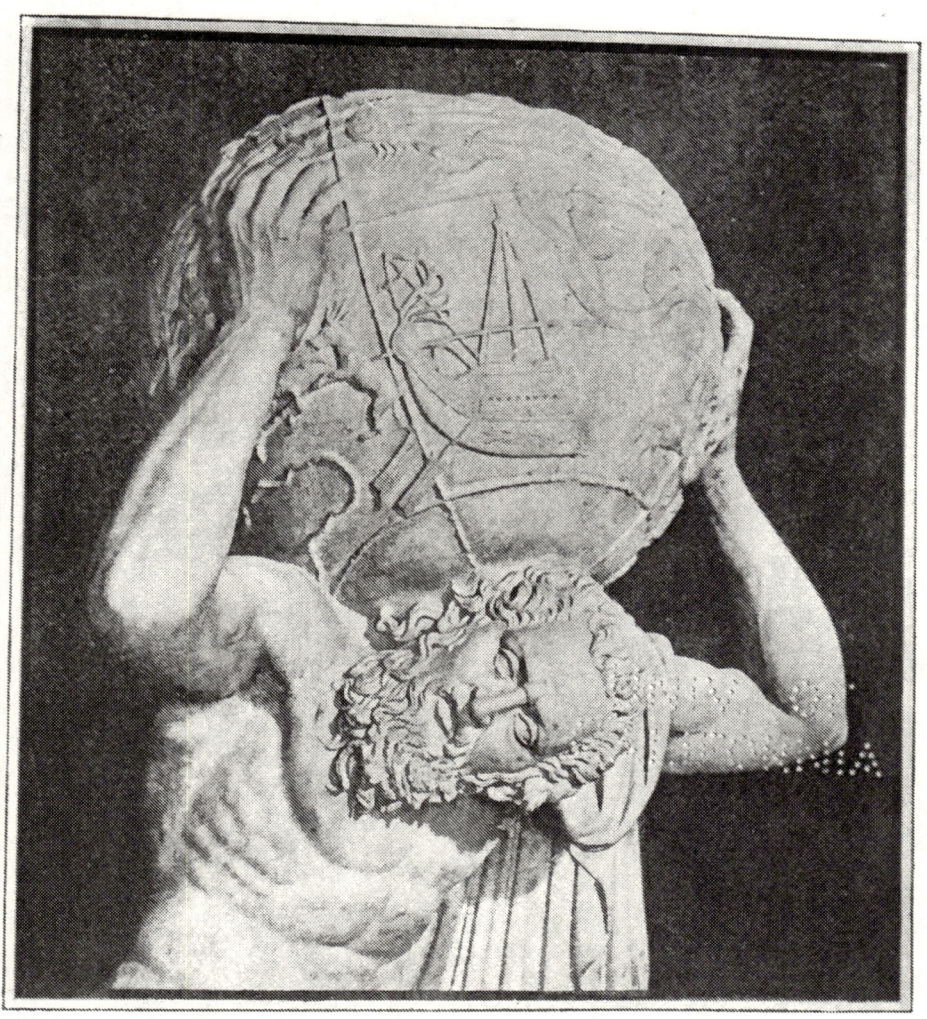

From a Photograph of the Farnesi Globe in the Museum, Naples

A Greek marble globe of great beauty; ca. A.D. 300

J. C. Houseau, *Bib. Gén. de l'Astron.*, T. I., P. I., Int. Chap. IV., p. 138

physics, and Professor See, the Founder of Cosmogony—the only two new sciences of the stars established within the memory of living investigators — it will be appropriate to close this biography with the beautiful and impressive *L'envoy* employed by Sir William and Lady Huggins to conclude their *Atlas of Representative Stellar Spectra:*

"We conclude filled with a sense of wonder at the greatness of the human intellect, which from the impact of waves of ether upon one sense-organ, can learn so much of the universe outside our earth; but the wonder passes into awe before the unimaginable magnitudes of Time, of Space, and of Matter of this Universe, as if a Voice were heard saying to man, "Thou art no Atlas for so great a weight."

APPENDIX.

NOTES ON SOME EARLY PROPHECIES AND ON THE PUBLIC BANQUET TENDERED DR. SEE BY THE SCIENCE ASSOCIATION OF THE UNIVERSITY OF MISSOURI, JANUARY 20, 1898.

It has been noticed by many sagacious observers that from his earliest years young Mr. See was so fortunate as to inspire, by his superior talents and steadfastness of purpose, the utmost confidence in a career of the highest eminence in Science. At the University he always lived up to high principles, and was frank and open in his stand on all questions, without the least thought of *mere popularity*, which he regarded as beneath contempt. He was thus recognized as a rugged character, as steadfast as a mountain peak towering calmly in the light of the Sun, high above the clouds and tumult of the elements below. Though sometimes misunderstood among his associates, his influence was well-nigh all-powerful, and far exceeded that of any former student of the University.

As illustrating this situation it is interesting to recall the fact that when Mr. See graduated with such high honors, in June, 1889, the *Columbia Statesman*, one of the oldest and most influential newspapers in Missouri, dwelt editorially at some length on the *extraordinary power for breaking through the crust* which young Mr. See had shown by his University career — a prophecy since fulfilled also in the larger affairs of the world of Science. This appraisement by the *Statesman* was for Mr. See's entire college career of five years.

As intimated above, there were times when he had been somewhat misunderstood, or misrepresented by envious individuals of inferior genius; but these efforts at injuring him never were successful with discerning persons. Thus, during a college controversy of 1887, which had been incited by jealousy, the thoughtful student, Mr. S. H. VanTrump, now of Gervais, Oregon, made the well-known prophecy that "See had the scientific genius of a Darwin, and that the day would come when the University would be famous as his Alma Mater."

Likewise, near his home in Montgomery County, his name was always a synonym for eminence and high achievement. Thus in September, 1893, Hon. Emil Rosenberger, now President of the Historical Society of Montgomery County, published an article in the *Montgomery Standard*, describing the giant Yerkes Telescope, then on exhibition at the *Columbian World's Fair* in Chicago, and predicting that Dr. See would become the future Alexander von Humboldt of America.

When Dr. See had been a year and a half with Lowell surveying the Southern double stars in Arizona and at the City of Mexico, and was in the East to publish his results, it occurred to the University of Missouri Science Association to invite him to a Public Banquet and celebration in honor of his discoveries. His admirers at the University were very numerous and influential, and the plans were made without acquainting Dr. See with the details. It was the largest banquet of the kind ever held at the University of Missouri, and included various toasts to Science and to the honored guest.

Dr. See was so surprised at the enthusiasm of the celebration as to be visibly embarrassed; and gently indicated to his friends that he would have felt obliged to decline had he known that such high encomiums were to be pronounced upon him. His classmate, Professor C. F. Marbut, for example, in response to the toast to the Class of 1889, concluded by remarking that Dr. See's leadership in Science was such that he could only say:

"It is superfluous to praise the gods."

REMARKS ON THE SIGNIFICANCE OF DR. SEE'S RESEARCHES AND DISCOVERIES.

(Embodied in a letter from his former teacher, Professor W. B. Smith, of Tulane University, New Orleans, to Professor Milton Updegraff, for the University Science Association, on the occasion of a banquet and celebration in honor of Dr. See, held at the University of Missouri, January 20, 1898.)

Tulane University of Louisiana,
College of Arts and Sciences,
New Orleans, La., Jan. 17, 1898.

DEAR PROFESSOR:

Please accept the assurance of my sincere thanks for the invitation to hear the address of Dr. See on the twentieth and to attend the banquet to be given in his honor, along with my unfeigned regret at not being able to accept. No one could sympathize more heartily than I in any recognition of the distinguished merits and achievements of Dr. See in the domain of exact astronomy. He has borne the name of Missouri in honor into eternal regions where the fame of her extent, her industries, her commerce, her products, her cities, her railroads, her newspapers, yea, even of her statesmen and her warriors must remain forever silent. It would be the merest commonplace to enlarge upon the fact that researches like his in the most inaccessible provinces of the sublimest of applied sciences have enduring virtue, outlasting marble, brass, or strength of steel, but it may be allowed to stress in a few words their important bearing on the deeper problems and higher hopes of our common humanity. For, unless I widely err, the determinations of pure science are the stable elements of our present civilization, they are the pillared trust of the generations yet to come. It is an age of cynicism, realism, indifferentism, moneyism. Unrest and unfaith in the true, beautiful and good are widespread and daily becoming more insolent. No clear-eyed patriot can look around upon our whole civil polity without grave and just alarm. On all sides our high ideals are falling and the walls of distinction are crumbling away. In art the contrast of the beautiful and the ugly is openly rejected; in literature the clean and the unclean walk side by side; in politics the cry waxes louder that "Fair is Foul and Foul is Fair;" "Black spirits and white, red spirits and gray" mingle and hobnob in the world's congress of religions; in medicine the most advanced methods contend with degrading superstitions, and splendid temples are dedicated to the worship of humbug; right and wrong are confounded in morals, while worth and unworth are rated precisely alike on the rolls of reward. Science alone, exact science, still proclaims uncompromisingly the immutable antithesis of true and false, still sinks deeper and deeper the foundations, raises higher and higher the pinnacles of knowledge, a house not made with hands, eternal as the heavens.

But while it is the glorious mission of all exact science thus to establish and defend the objective verity of the universe against prevalent skepticism, it is an especial virtue of the science of the stars to quicken the saving sense of the *dignity of man*, a sense dulled and endangered daily by the gigantic developments and consolidations of modern industrialism. The ennobling worth of such sublime studies has been felt and celebrated in every age. It was Ptolemy that said:

> "Though but the being of a day,
>   When I the planet-paths survey,
>   My feet the dust despise;
>   Up to the throne of God I mount
>   And quaff from an immortal fount
>   The nectar of the skies."

Both the State and the University, therefore, honor themselves in honoring their eminent son, and they do well to point their youth to such examples. With heartiest greetings to yourself and family,   Very sincerely yours,

                                        W. B. SMITH.

To Prof. Milton Updegraff.

(Reprinted from the University *Independent*, of May 28, 1898.)

INDEX OF NAMES

INDEX OF NAMES

sentative of Montgomery County, Mo., 7; raiser of fine stock, and of celebrated ox "Stonewall Jackson," weighing 4,300 pounds, 7

See, John, captured by the Indians at age of 5, 3; ransomed by his uncle Adam See, 3; grew up with his cousin George See, 3; both fought in the Revolution, John badly wounded at Brandywine, pensioned, 3; gives account of early history of family to his grandson, Rev. Michael See, 3; died at Peoria, Ill., at age of 90, 3

See, John, a brother of Noah See, his wife a first cousin of Jacob Stewart, who was the tried friend of Noah See's family during the war, 22

See, Lucy Elizabeth, talented child, little sister of Professor See, died at age of 2½ years, 6

See, Mrs. Margaret (Stewart), wife of John See; the brother of Noah See, and a first cousin of Jacob Stewart, 22

See, Mrs. Mary A., mother of Professor See, born Jan. 14, 1832, 12; her ancestry, 5; noted for force of character, 5; greatly beloved by whole community, 5; universally regarded as a noble and good woman, 10; managed farm as well as household during the war, 9-10; refuses to allow ox to be killed and orders the soldiers off the place, 10; depredations of the soldiers, 10; her education at Loutre school house, 12; very fond of trees, 24

See, Rev. Michael, grandson of John See, 3; obtains early history of family from John See in his old age, 3; appointed by President Lincoln on the Sanitary Commission, 3

See, Michael, son of George See, and father of Noah See, served in War of 1812, 4; married Catherine Baker, and raised a family of nine children, record of their names, 4; moved to Randolph County, Va., about 1795, 4; follows his son, Noah See, to Missouri in 1838, 4; dies in 1857 very highly respected, 4

See, Michael Frederick, came to America, 1734, 2, 263; his wife named Catherine, 2; first settled in Bucks Co., Pa., but moved to Va., 1745, 3; killed in Greenbrier Massacre, July 17, 1763, 3; his wife and family captured by the Indians and carried to Chillicothe, Ohio, 3

See, Millard Filmore, eldest brother of Professor See, great reader of scientific literature, 6; well read in law and public administration, 6; father of Russell See, civil engineer in U. S. Reclamation Service, 6

See, Noah, father of Professor See, obtains authentic data on early history of family from Hon. Charles Michael See, 3; born Sept. 19, 1815, in Randolph Co., Va., 4; youngest of nine children and the most talented, 4; visits Missouri on horseback in 1837 and settles in Montgomery County, 4; educated at Beverly, Va., and trained as a cabinet-maker, surveyor, civil engineer and architect, 4; serves faithfully as bridge commissioner for 30 years, 4; by natural abilities and legitimate industry becomes a wealthy and influential citizen, 5; marries Miss Mary A. Sailor, Oct. 18, 1853, and raises a family of nine children, record of their names, 5-6; owned two or three slaves before the war, 8; Southern sympathizer and persecuted during the war, losing property worth $1,600, 8-9; worked as carpenter on block house when military prisoner in Danville, 9; when in hiding, like Daniel Boone in his conflicts with the Indians, meditates on the Deity, 9; one of the largest land holders in northeast Mo., 14; journeyed to Palmyra, by the stars at night, 15; settles on the prairie, in 1852, 14; purchases land on Loutre from Philip Cobb, in 1837, 15; names sons after presidents, but dislikes politics, 15; twice elected County Surveyor, 15; bridge inspections, surveying, political meetings, 16; a great admirer of Henry Clay, 16; absent from home on business, 16; only country schools for his children, 16; T. J. J. See goes to University, 16; "good in figures" and teaches T. J. J. See arithmetic, 17; his description of the great meteor of Jan. 1, 1877, 20; observed without alarm star shower of Nov. 12, 1833, 20; falls and injures foot, moves to large place of 920 acres on Elkhorn, his friend Jacob Stewart of war times on visit, 22; his poor opinion of the legal profession, 25; buys land in Southwestern Missouri, his family well provided for, 25; gratified at scholastic record of his son, T. J. J. See, 44-45; failing health and death, Feb. 9, 1890, 44-45;

Medal, 36; stands first in University, but of positive character, and others occasionally more popular with the multitude, because See belonged to Greek Fraternity, 37; takes leading part in reform of university in 1889, 37-38; graduates at head of class, with highest honors, 39-42; returns home, and finds father in failing health, 44; proceeds to Berlin, via Washington, Baltimore, Princeton, New York, London, Paris, 45-46; loneliness on his arrival at Berlin, his residence established, 46; interviews his future teachers, Weierstrass, Fuchs, Foerster, Helmholtz, 47; in charge of 9-inch telescope of Royal Observatory, observing till daylight, 47-48; spread of his fame in the university and to other countries, 48; his examination for Doctor's degree, 49; inspiration afforded by Zeller, and visits to Humboldt's country place, 49-50; classic spirit of Berlin, visits to museums to study art, 50; journeys to Italy, Egypt, Greece, 50-52; experiences earthquake at Pyrgos on the visit to Olympia, 51; visits England, friendships with eminent men of Science, 52; obtains Doctor's degree, and speaks German fluently in *Inaugural Discourse*, 52; immediately returns to America, how he came to locate at Chicago, 53-54; plans high-class work in Astronomy at the new University, 55; starts building of Yerkes Observatory by cutting down inflated budget, 56; the starting of the Yerkes Observatory beneficial to various persons, 57; Dr. See not rewarded at Chicago, but by President McKinley at Washington, 57; his work stood high at Chicago, but he had only the rank of instructor, declined offer of assistant professorship, 58; works in co-operation with Burnham on double stars for three years, establishing method of testing Newtonian Law, 1895, 58-59; observes double stars at McCormick and Washburn Observatories in 1895, and finishes Volume I of the *Researches* early in 1896, 59; University of Chicago defaults on agreement to print the *Researches*, Vol. I, and Dr. See issues it himself, 59; Lord Kelvin's estimate of the *Researches*, Vol. I, 60; Schiaparelli's prediction that Dr. See's *Researches* would constitute the third great epoch since those of W. Herschel and W. Struve, 61; joins

Lowell Observatory to observe Southern double stars, 62; influenced in his plans by example of the two Herschels, 62; suffers mild attack of typhoid fever, June, 1896, 63; loses valuable library and other property by fire, Sept. 14, 1897, but saves records and Bowditch's translation of Laplace, 64; his method of sweeping for double stars, 65; the work extended throughout the night and difficult, 65-66; some of the new stars discovered, and the types of double stars, 66; earlier work of Sir John Herschel, 1834-1838, 67; works in cordial relations with Mr. Innes at the Cape of Good Hope, 67; his plans interrupted by illness of Lowell, becomes Professor at the Naval Observatory, Washintgon, 67; stimulating effects of Dr. See's work, 67; Sir David Gill's appraisement of it, 67-68; aids in rebuilding Lowell Observatory at Mexico City, 69; ascends Popocatepetl, 69; lectures on sidereal astronomy at Lowell Institute, Boston, 1899, 69; propounds doctrine of expulsion of dust from stars under repulsive forces, 70; considered for and appointed to professorship of mathematics in the navy by President McKinley, 70-71; surprised by Secretary Long's announcement of his appointment, 70; assigned duty at Naval Observatory, Washington, and occupied with meridian work, 71; recommends removal of piers of 6-inch transit circle, 72; observes satellite of Neptune and discovers belts on planet, 1899, 72; in charge of 26-inch equatorial telescope of Naval Observatory, 72; systematic measurement of many satellites, 73, 74; investigates constants of irradiation by new methods, 73; results generally accepted by astronomers, 74; inquiry into the method by Lord Kelvin, 1902, 74; his satellite measures used by Dyson, Bergstrand and Struve, 74; his work commended by Callandreau, Schiaparelli, Burnham, Barnard and Struve, 75; aids in improving *personnel* of Naval Observatory, 75; works very hard and finally becomes ill, 75; his double star observations and micrometer researches, 76; observations of Eros for parallax of Sun leads to good result, 76; eminent success of his work at Washington, 77; his illness at the naval academy, 78; sympa-

WORKS OF DR. T. J. J. SEE

Researches on the Evolution of the Stellar Systems. Vol. I.

By T. J. J. SEE, A.M., Ph. D.

This work is the first volume of an extensive investigation which Dr. SEE has undertaken on the evolution of our stellar systems. The introduction begins with a sketch of the nebular hypothesis of our solar system. In Chapter I the author gives the common proof of the Newtonian law of force for our solar system, and then proceeds to consider the proof for the orbits of binary stars. Chapter II contains the orbits of forty binary stars deducted from the best observations. Chapter III presents a discussion of the results. Price, full cloth, **$5.00.** Postage prepaid, **$5.35.**

Researches on the Evolution of the Stellar Systems. Vol. II.

By T. J. J. SEE, A.M., Ph. D.

This splendid work is indispensable to the astronomer, mathematician, physicist and geologist; it will prove of decided interest also to the chemist, biologist, engineer, and in fact to every progressive student, thinker, investigator, library, college, university, observatory, society, or other institution of science or education.

In this magnificent work, illustrated throughout by views and photographs of the highest beauty, Prof. SEE deals with the conclusions he has arrived at as to the origin of our own and other systems generally from his researches during the last twenty years; and gives in a connected form the matter of numerous papers contributed by him to the *Astronomische Nachrichten, Popular Astronomy*, and other magazines.

Bound full cloth, 736 pp. with about 250 illustrations, including many plates of wonderful photographs of the heavens. Price, **$10.00** per copy, express prepaid.

ADDRESS

THOS. P. NICHOLS & SON CO.

PUBLISHERS

Lynn, Massachusetts

Printed in the United States
139831LV00003B/109/A